The History, Topography and Antiquities of the County and City of Waterford; With an Account of the Present State of the Peasantry of That Part of the South of Ireland

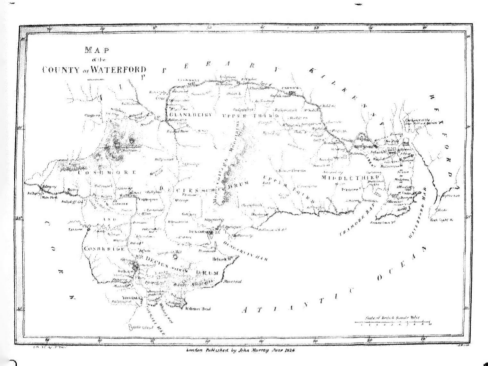

MAP
of the
COUNTY of WATERFORD

London Published by John Murray June 1824

Page 198 — George Lewis Fleury —
daughter Isabella Julia Fleury

THE

HISTORY,

TOPOGRAPHY AND ANTIQUITIES

OF THE

COUNTY AND CITY

OF

WATERFORD;

WITH AN

ACCOUNT OF THE PRESENT STATE OF THE PEASANTRY
OF THAT PART OF THE SOUTH OF IRELAND

Book first published

BY THE REV. R. H. RYLAND.

Rev Richard Hopkins Ryland   Mar 7 . – Dec 30   1788 – 1866

> God of his goodnes praysed that he be
> For the daylie increase of thy good fame
> O pleasant Waterford !—thow loyall cytie
> That five hundred yeres receavest thy name
> Er the later conquest unto thee came,
> In Ireland deservest to be peerelesse,
> Quia tu semper intacta manes   ANCIENT MS

LONDON

JOHN MURRAY, ALBEMARLE STREET.

MDCCCXXIV

The Ryland family settled in Dungarvan in the 16th century. The first Ryland in Dungarvan was Charles Ryland (B 1649 - D. 1718)

Richard. Hopkins Ryland. was the son of Rev. Richard Ryland D.D. (Trinity College Dublin) Born 170? and d.1800 Buried in Dungarvan. and (mother) (Mary Burton b 1764 - d 1798)

Chaplain to William III

Rylands of England

Charles Ryland. — John, Ryland.
B. 1649 - D 1718

Rev George Lous Fleury Arch Deacon of Waterford

Rev Richard Ryland mr Mary Burton

Richard Hopkins. m. Isabella Julia Fleury

Six sons { 2 daughters

Richard   George Fleury   Henry.   William — John - India   Theodore Ireland

John   Minnie   Elizabeth   Henry   Isabel   George
m
Clara Ford

Ronald   Janet Marie   Shirley Noreen   Norma June D. Age 3   Ivan Wray   Sheila Isabel

Theodore   m   m   Ann McLelland   David Hill
Ernest   Bart Willson   7 children
McQueen   Nancy Norma   Elsie Kathy   Kathleen   Sharon

George Ernest

Louise Happer

Scott   Michael

Kirstie   Sarah

TO

HIS GRACE

THE DUKE OF DEVONSHIRE,

THIS VOLUME

IS,

BY PERMISSION,

MOST RESPECTFULLY

DEDICATED.

PREFACE.

———

It was something of a feeling of impatience which first suggested the following work, in which an attempt is made to describe, from personal observation, the striking features in the moral and physical condition of an interesting portion of Ireland. To those who are intimately acquainted with this country, the remarks of strangers have something in them eminently provoking. It is a sad thing to be perpetually harassed with the incorrect ideas and false representations of flying travellers and tourists, who, from a few hasty and undigested observations, draw universal and sweeping conclusions, generalizing from insulated facts, and deducing rules from mere exceptions. It is not presumed to call in question the talents and acquirements of modern writers on Irish affairs; the objection is to their means of information, the general correctness of which may be estimated by a

review of a few of the mis-statements which
have been advanced respecting one particular
district. The most accurate as well as the
most able of those Englishmen who may be
called modern writers on Ireland, are, unquestionably, Young and Wakefield : of the
latter I shall have occasion to speak hereafter. Young has collected a great body of
information respecting the condition of the
peasantry, which, allowing for some slight
modifications, is strictly true at the present
day; but in some important particulars, and
which he should not have taken from report,
he is guilty of the most glaring errors. Speaking of the river Suir, he describes it as " nearly
a mile across;" an error which has been literally copied by all succeeding writers, and
even by Wakefield, who expresses no surprise that a bridge of 832 feet should cross
a river nearly a mile in breadth.

" The scientific tourist" is equally accurate in this point; but when we find the same
writer gravely asserting, that the county of
Waterford rests on a bed of granite, not one
particle of which is visible within its limits,
we should perhaps be grateful to him that
he has not described us as incumbent on a

mass of fire,—an assertion which, according to the opinion of some, is as true as that granite exists beneath the soil of the county.

The author of a tour in Ireland, who travelled over a great part of the country, and wrote two bulky octavos within a period of two months, might well be supposed a personage of extraordinary diligence and labour, were it not known that his personal knowledge of one county, that of Waterford, was collected in about twenty minutes, which, previous to his entering into the city, he devoted to a conversation with a Quaker gentleman. A fair estimate may hence be made of the credit for accuracy and research, to which tourists are generally entitled.

Wakefield has heaped together a vast mass of information, but unfortunately in the point, and perhaps in the only point in which he is flagrantly incorrect, he has been constantly quoted, and considered as the best authority. In his statements and calculations respecting church property and the incomes of the bishops, he is totally mistaken; and were it not that the heads of the establishment have suffered his assertions to pass uncontradicted, the pretended facts and the reasoning found-

ed upon them would have long since melted
into air.   It would require a distinct examination of the revenues of. all the dioceses to
overturn his general statements; but as the
absolute and palpable incorrectness of one of
his assertions has come within my knowledge,
the mention of it may serve to shew the degree of credit to which his other statements
are entitled.

The lands belonging to the see of Waterford are estimated at £70,000 per annum.
This has been stated over and over again,
till to doubt it would be considered the ut-
most stretch of incredulity.   It is a fact, nevertheless, that the see lands of Waterford,
if let to-morrow to the highest bidder, would
not produce one-sixth of the estimated
amount!   To descend to particulars :   supposing the lands of the see of Waterford to
amount to 9,000 acres, (and this exceeds the
true estimate by at least 500,) and supposing
the average value at the present moment to
be twenty-five shillings per acre, (which is
also considerably above the truth,) the entire rental of these lands would not exceed
£11,500 per annum.

Having offered these few observations, it

only remains to say something of the work itself.

In the execution of the present publication, no labour or expense has been spared in rendering it as perfect as the nature of it would admit. The original idea was to reprint, with additions and corrections, the " History of Waterford," published by Dr. Smith in 1746, and which, according to booksellers' phraseology, is now " out of print:" but it being so replete with extraneous matter which the taste and learning of the period at which he wrote required him to introduce, it was judged more advisable to write a new work, taking freely from all the publications which could add interest or information to the subject.

I cannot conclude without offering my acknowledgments *generally* for the assistance which has been afforded on the present occasion; and in particular, I must return my most sincere thanks to his Grace the Duke of Devonshire for the liberty he has given me to peruse the MSS. at Lismore; and to Colonel Currey for the facilities he afforded me on that occasion.

To the Right Honourable Robert Peel, to

whom I am indebted for permission to examine the many valuable records relative to Ireland which are preserved in the State Paper Office, I beg leave, respectfully, to express my obligations.

To W. Hughes, Esq. for the paper, On inclosing the back strand at Tramore; and to Robert Jacob, Esq. for the paper relative to the Waterford coins, my acknowledgments are due.

In addition to the Manuscripts and other documents in this country to which I have had free access, I am indebted to some friends in London for some curious and valuable information collected from the records in that capital. To this general statement, I cannot refuse myself the satisfaction of adding, how much I am obliged and assisted by the zeal and talent of the author of Researches in the South of Ireland, T. Crofton Croker, Esq. With all these advantages, however, it is feared that the present work will be found very imperfect; but such as it is, it is offered to the public with one circumstance, at least, to recommend it, *it is not published before it was called for.*

INTRODUCTION.

A FAITHFUL and accurate description of the
past and present state of Ireland, of its natural
and acquired advantages, of its prospects and
its actual enjoyments, can alone enable us to
ascertain the correctness of the often quoted
observation, that Providence has done much
for this country and man but little:—a remark
frequently recurring to the mind, when we
contrast what Ireland might be with what she
is.

A consideration of the advantages which
might be derived from the maritime situation
of the county of Waterford, from its proximity
to England, its noble harbours, its navigable
rivers, which flow through its entire extent,
from its fertility, internal treasures, and numerous population, will be amply sufficient to
justify the expectation that this portion of the
empire may yet be raised to a high degree of
wealth and improvement.

The county of Waterford is situated between
the latitude of 51° 50′ and 52° 15′ north, and

between the longitude of 7° 10′ and 8° 24′ west.
The latitude of the city of Waterford is 52° 8′.
the exact longitude, deduced from a number of
observations made on the immersions of Jupi-
ter's satellites, and corrected by an observation of the great solar eclipse in 1820, is 7°
19′ west. The variation of the magnetic needle
at Hook Tower, at the eastern entrance of the
harbour of Waterford, as taken at different periods, was as follows. In 1736, it was found
by Mr. Doyle to be 14° 15′ westerly: by Mr.
Mackenzie, in 1763, it was determined at 21°
30′ westerly. In 1808, it had increased to
28°. In 1824, it was 27° 30′.

This county is bounded on the north by the
river Suir, which separates it from the counties
of Tipperary and Kilkenny; on the east, by the
harbour of Waterford, which divides it from
the county of Wexford; on the south, by the
sea; and on the west, by the counties of Cork
and Tipperary.

The river of Waterford unites its water with
those of the Barrow and the Nore. From its
navigable part at Clonmel to that of the river
Blackwater at Cappoquin, the distance is only
17 miles; from Carrick to the river Nore at
Kilkenny, the distance is not more than 22
miles; and from within three miles of Cashel,

where the Suir is still a respectable river, to the Shannon, near Limerick, the distance is only 25 miles. Hence it will be seen that few places possess greater advantages of communication than the city of Waterford.

The extreme length of the county is about forty miles; the greatest breadth, twenty.

Independent of the city and liberties of Waterford, which are a county in themselves, the county of Waterford is divided into seven baronies:— Gaultier, Middlethird, Upperthird, Decies without Drum, Decies within Drum, Coshmore and Coshbride, and Glanaheiry.

The total superficial contents of the county are estimated at 290,944 acres, or in English acres, 471,281.

The several divisions contain as follow:

	Acres
County of the city of Waterford .	5,978
Gaultier, including Woodstown Strand, which contains 651 acres	17,524
Middlethird, including Tramore Strand, which contains 1438 acres	27,080
Upperthird	54,655
Decies without Drum, including Dungarvan Strand, 2153 acres . . .	77,624
Decies within Drum . .	36,311
Coshmore and Coshbride .	55,241
Glanaheiry, including commons of Clonmell, 4995 acres . . .	16,531
	290,944

The fiscal divisions of the county, which were originally arranged according to the value of the lands, are now singularly incorrect. In 1635, the county was divided into $521\frac{1}{4}$ plough-lands. The present division is as follows:

Gaultier	56
Middlethird	$64\frac{1}{2}$
Upperthird	66
Decies without	122
Decies within	75
Coshmore and Coshbride	92
Glanaheny	14
Total ploughlands	$489\frac{1}{2}$

In some places, the grand-jury taxes have been as high as two-and-sixpence an acre.

The early returns of population are likewise extremely defective. By the parliamentary returns it would appear that, in 1777, the County of Waterford had only 9,577 houses; in the year 1788, the number had increased to 16,085 houses. The census of 1813 gives to the

	Houses	Inhabitants
County	19,312	119,457
City	3,581	25,467
	22,923	144,924

According to the last census (1821), which is supposed to have been very accurately taken as far as regards the county and city generally, the entire population amounts to 154,466.

Abstracts of the returns of the several divisions of the county and city follow.

COUNTY OF WATERFORD.

Baronies.	Parishes.	Towns.	Villages.	Townlands	Houses.	Inhabitants.
Gaultier	11	1	3	88	1689	10,314
Middlethird	10	1	2	113	1991	11,750
Upperthird	13	2	3	138	3779	23,308
Decies without Drum . . .	16	1	2	292	5650	32,237
Decies within Drum . . .	8		4	118	3233	20,382
Coshmore and Coshbride . .	6	3	1	94	4451	25,012
Glanaheiry	2			37	700	4,676
County of Waterford contained, in 1821	66	8	15	880	21,493	127,679

CITY OF WATERFORD.

Parishes.	Houses.	Inhabitants.
Trinity Without	1,840	12,715
Trinity Within	320	1,842
St. John's Without	387	2,115
St. John's Within	338	2,930
St. Peter's	81	793
St. Michael's	154	128
St. Olave's	83	697
Killoteran	75	494
Kilculleheen	176	1,087
Kilbarry	86	589
East Passage	73	440
St. Patrick's	270	2,412
St. Stephen's	169	545
City of Waterford contained, in 1821	4,052	26,787

It should be added, that the last enumeration was made in the summer of 1821, at a time when many of the inhabitants of the city of Waterford were residing in the country. A deduction should therefore be made from the number in the county, which should be added to the population of the city.

HISTORICAL SKETCH.

SECTION I.

———◆———

———◆———

WE have historical documents of a very remote
date concerning the ancient condition of the
county and city of Waterford. If the object of
the present sketch were to prove the antiquity of
the inhabitants of this portion of Ireland, it would
be easy to make out a connected and plausible
theory from the works of those Irish historians
who carry their researches to the most distant
periods, with moderate antiquarians, we might
be contented with the testimony of Strabo, or,
with the ultras of romance, commence our history
with Cæsara, a niece of the patriarch Noah.

The history of Ireland has ever been a subject
of dispute. Between those who trace back her
records to the age immediately succeeding the
flood, and those who refuse to Ireland any ancient

B

history, there can be no compromise or agreement; the one party is said to be romantic, the
other is accused of incredulity. To obviate the
difficulty, let us commence this sketch at the æra
of Henry II.'s. invasion of Ireland. This will
enable us to glean something of the traditional
antiquity of the county, without involving us in
doubtful or ill-founded surmises.

[margin handwritten: 1169—1172 1171 to Strongbow as ruler independent of England.]

The Irish, at this period, are represented as
singularly barbarous, devoid of intellectual acquirements, and uncouth in manners and in dress.
But it must be recollected, that at the same time,
England was, also, far removed from that refinement which she has since acquired, and which
now inclines her to estimate unfairly the civilization of former ages. The temper of the times, the
wars and insurrections in which the people were
continually engaged, served to encourage the
fierce demeanour and warlike aspect, for which the
Irish were originally remarkable. The unshorn
beards and whiskers, and the matted and bushy
hair, called glibbs, overspreading the face and
neck, were esteemed necessary qualifications of
a warrior, and served to intimidate their opponents, as well as in some degree to resist the violence of hostile weapons.

The city of Waterford was inhabited by Danes,
Ostmen, or Easterlings, as they were usually called,
who had been long settled in the country, but
still preserved their ancient manners and customs,

and had little intercourse or friendship with the Irish people.

Henry II. with an army consisting of 500 knights, and about 4000 soldiers, landed at Waterford on the 18th of October, 1171. The city had been previously subdued by Richard De Clare, Earl of Pembroke, usually called Strongbow, and offered little resistance to the royal invader. It is said, that an Ostman Lord endeavoured to impede the disembarkation, and for this purpose drew chains across the harbour, but the obstacle was speedily overcome, and Henry entered Waterford, not as a conqueror, but as the rightful sovereign of the country.

Strongbow had been united in marriage to Eva, daughter of the King of Leinster; their marriage was celebrated here in the preceding year, and served to confirm the acquisitions, which this warlike nobleman had previously made. But these conquests could be retained no longer; they had already excited the jealousy of the monarch, and it was now necessary to surrender them into his hands. Upon the arrival of the sovereign within the walls of his newly acquired city, Waterford was formally surrendered to him by the Earl of Pembroke, who was contented to retain his other possessions, as a vassal and subject.

The city of Waterford, Henry's first acquisition in Ireland, was considered, at the period of his

landing, to be a place of great antiquity, and for
trade and riches was esteemed only inferior to
Dublin.   Waterford is situated on the south side
of the river Suir, it was originally surrounded by
a ditch and walls enclosing a triangular space,
with fortified towers at each of the angles.   From
one of these, called Reginald's tower, now the
Ring tower, the city wall ran in a westerly direction, and was terminated by Turgesius's tower,
which formerly stood at the corner of Baron-strand-
street.   From this tower, the wall forming the
second side of the triangle, proceeded in a south-
wardly direction, enclosing the Black Friary,
skirting, but not including, what was formerly the
boys Blue School, from thence it crossed Peter's-
street and ran to the castle, then called St. Martin's Castle, situated at the rear of the girls Blue
School; the third side of the triangle united St.
Martin's Castle with Reginald's Tower.

   Such were the boundaries of the city of Waterford, when it first received Henry II. and his
knights.   While he remained here, he was acknowledged as sovereign by the people of Cork
and Wexford, and as an instance of his royal
authority, committed to Reginald's Tower, a
traitor who had presumed to invade Ireland, without the usual preliminary qualification, a commission from the Pope.

   Having made the necessary arrangements and
appointed governors over the fortified towns,

Henry proceeded to Lismore, where he was waited on by the nobles and chief men of Munster. The archbishops, bishops, and abbots of Ireland, also acknowledged their allegiance to him, and gave him charters, confirming the kingdom of Ireland to him and his heirs for ever. In return for this obsequiousness, the monarch conferred upon them the benefits of the laws of England; a boon which, historians assure us, was gratefully accepted and established by the sanction of an oath. The dominion acquired by conquest, and by compact with the original adventurers, Henry endeavoured to consolidate, by imparting to his new subjects advantages which the people of other places did not enjoy. To the Ostmen of Waterford he granted many rights and privileges, which were afterwards confirmed to them by succeeding monarchs; they were considered as free subjects of England, and entitled to the benefits and protection of her laws. After a sojourn of about six months, Henry prepared to return to England; intelligence of the greatest importance required his immediate presence, and compelled him to relinquish the measures which he had adopted, for the tranquillization of his newly acquired dominion. Previous to his departure, Waterford was entrusted to the care of three of his chosen supporters, lands in its neighbourhood were assigned for the maintenance of knights and soldiers, and every precaution was taken, which might be supposed necessary to strengthen and consolidate his interests. Yet, notwithstanding all the exertions of this brave and enlightened monarch, there are strong grounds for believing the remark of the historian, that at his departure, he left not one true subject behind him, more than he found on coming over.

At this time, a very considerable addition was made to the city of Waterford; new walls were erected, the fortifications were repaired, and gates and towers were superadded to the former defences. The new part comprehended the church, abbey, and street of St. John, New Street, St. Stephen's Street, St. Patrick's Street, and the churches of St. Stephen, St. Michael, and St. Patrick. On the west side of the city there were two gates, St. Patrick's and Newgate, to the south, Bowling-green gate, called also Closegate, and St. John's gate; to the south east, St. Catherine's or Colbeck gate; and to the north, there were several gates communicating with the quay and the river.

Henry II.'s successful invasion of Ireland is to be attributed primarily to the authority and influence of the Pope; his attempt was further assisted by the warlike spirit of his nobles, as well as by the internal divisions of the Irish themselves; still the conquest was neither easy nor secure: he had to contend with a people who hated peace, because they did not appreciate its

blessings, and who detested the yoke of a foreigner, even though in some degree invited by
themselves.—The history of Ireland at this period
is a mere journal of murders and conspiracies;
the proud spirit of the natives rising in opposition to the tyranny of their conquerors, and the
conquerors using every effort to effect the complete subjugation of the people.

It was the wish of King Henry to commit the
superintendence of the affairs of Ireland to his
favourite son John; but the difficulties which attended the government of an imperfectly subdued
country, as well as the incapacity of the Prince
himself, opposed powerful obstacles to this arrangement.

John landed at Waterford, for the first time, on
the 1st April, 1185, attended by many of the
principal nobility of England, and a considerable
force of knights and archers. In order to check
the frequency of insurrections, by establishing
English garrisons throughout the disturbed districts, he erected fortified castles in various
places. One of these, at Lismore, was on the
site of the present noble building, now the occasional residence of the Duke of Devonshire.

Many of the Irish chiefs waited upon John to
congratulate him on his arrival; they were disposed to receive him favourably, and to submit
themselves to his authority; they were satisfied
to consider the King of England as their sovereign,

but so little were their spirits subdued, they could not brook even the appearance of insult from their conquerors, and actually engaged in rebellion, because the young English nobles laughed at their beards and uncombed hair. John soon exhibited proofs of his incapacity for government; he despoiled some of the Irish of their lands, and parcelled them among his followers; the revenues appropriated to the defence of the country he bestowed upon his courtiers, who wasted them in riot and extravagance: he thus disgusted his friends, and weakened his own resources, and the example of indolence and debauchery being followed by the army, every thing seemed to portend the ruin of the English interests. John was only nineteen years of age at this time, and though assisted by many learned men, among whom was Giraldus Cambrensis, his indiscretions cannot excite in us much surprize.—The King, informed of these disorders, recalled his son and his dissolute attendants, and committed the government to John de Courcy, an active and experienced soldier.* When John was seated on the throne of England, his attention was again directed to the affairs of this country. In the seventh year of his reign (1206) he granted a charter of incorporation to Waterford, by which the city and also various privileges and immu-

---

* John returned to England in December, 1185.

nities are conferred upon the citizens; among others, that no itinerant justices, nor justices of assize in the county of Waterford, should for the future vex or disturb the citizens, or oblige them to appear without the bounds of the city, either ·at the King's suit, or at the suit of any other complainant. By the whole tenor of this patent it appears, that it was only a recital and confirmation of former liberties and franchises granted to the citizens of Waterford. This charter expressly mentions the county of Waterford as a distinct district from the city. In the year 1211, on the 6th of June, King John landed at Waterford, with the intention of settling the disturbances which had arisen during his absence. While he resided here, his palace was situated where the Widows' Apartments now stand. Some of the vaults and parts of the foundation of the royal residence were discovered when the workmen were preparing the ground for the present building.—The King proceeded with considerable activity to arrange the affairs of Ireland, and personally visited many parts of the country, attended by a large body of knights and soldiers. Near Clashmore, may still be seen the ruins of a large square building, where the royal cavalcade was accustomed to halt when travelling from Waterford to Cork.

King John, during his residence here, made a large addition to the city of Waterford; some of

the walls built by him are still in existence. He
also founded the priory of St. John, and established in it monks of the Benedictine order.

The long reign of Henry III. is singularly
barren of materials for Irish history; yet the interests of this country were not neglected.—
Waterford received a new charter from this monarch, dated 15th June, 1232. When Edward I.
ascended the throne, he found in the intestine divisions of the people the greatest obstacles to the
peace and prosperity of Ireland; it was therefore
the great object of this, as well as of the two succeeding monarchs, to introduce the laws of England into all those places, heretofore governed by
customs of their own, and to abolish the Irish
law, which Edward declared was hateful to God,
and repugnant to all justice. The privileges
granted to the Ostmen of Waterford were confirmed in this reign by a statute, of which the
following is a translation:

" Edward, by the grace of God, King of England, Lord of Ireland, and Duke of Acquitaine,
to his Justice of Ireland, and all other his bailiffs
and faithful subjects in Ireland, to whom the
present letter shall come, Greeting: Inasmuch
as by inspection of the charter of the Lord King
Henry, son of the Empress, formerly Lord of
Ireland, our ancestor, it appears to us, that our
Ostmen of Waterford ought to have the law of
the English in Ireland, and according to that

law be judged and brought to trial—We command you that ye cause Gillechrist Macgillemory, William and John Macgillemory, and the other Ostmen of the city and county of Waterford, who derive their origin from the aforementioned Ostmen of the aforesaid Lord Henry, our ancestor, to have the law of the English in those parts, according to the tenour of the aforesaid charter, and them to be conveyed according to that law, as far as is in your power, until we shall introduce some other to be ordained according to our counsel.—Witness myself at Acton Burnell, 5th day of October, 11th year of our reign."

The city of Waterford was destroyed by fire in the year 1252, and again in about thirty years afterwards: if to these misfortunes we add a long list of murders and insurrections, we shall have all that requires any notice until nearly the close of the fourteenth century. In 1336, James, the first Earl of Ormond, founded the Friary of Little Carig, in the county of Waterford, for Minorites, of which John Clyn, author of the Annals of Ireland, was the first guardian. Two other Friaries were also founded within the walls of the city about this period, namely, the Dominican Friary of St. Saviour, and the Holy Ghost Friary.

In the year 1394, on the 2d of October, Richard II. landed at Waterford, with an army of 4000 men at arms, and 30,000 archers, and attended by the Duke of Gloucester, the Earls of Nottingham and Rutland, and other distinguished noblemen.

We are told that this expedition was undertaken to assuage the grief of the monarch after the death of his beloved wife, Queen Anne: if he had any other object in view, it was not accomplished, for after a stay of nine months, during which he was flattered with acknowledgments and sub-missions, he returned to England without effect-ing any thing really beneficial to his interests.

King Richard again visited Ireland in the year 1399. He embarked at Bristol, and landed at Waterford on the 13th of May. The monarch was welcomed with every demonstration of joy, and spent six days in receiving the deceitful ho-mage of his people. At this time, the citizens were mean and slovenly in their appearance, and exhibited in this respect, as well as in their dwellings, a degree of poverty and wretchedness which we should not have expected to find in so considerable a city.* But Waterford was not singular in this respect. We find even at a later period a remarkable instance of the poverty of larger cities. It was agreed in council, that, as the hall of the Castle of Dublin, and the windows thereof were ruinous, and that there was in the

---

* In " King Richard II.'s last voyage to Ireland," a strong in-stance is given of the wretchedness of the city at that time   " To unland our baggage," the writer remarks (page 50) " they waded up to the waste in ooze "

treasury " a certain ancient silver seal cancelled," which was of no use to the king, the said seal should be broken and sold, and the money laid out in the repair of the said hall and windows. In the reign of Henry VI. John Talbot, Earl of Shrewsbury, obtained a grant of the county and city of Waterford, and the dignity and title of Earl of Waterford, with the castles, honours, lands, and the barony of Dungarvan, because (as the patent states) that country is waste, " et non ad proficuum, sed ad perditum nostrum redundat."

During the reign of Henry V. there were two charters granted to the city. By the first, dated at Westminster the 6th of May, 1412, the citizens were incorporated under the authority of a mayor and bailiffs. By the second, dated at Dublin the 15th day of January, 1415, the customs, called the great new customs, were granted for the support of the city. It does not appear, whether any new privileges or rights accompanied the grants made by succeeding monarchs. The charters of Henry III. and Edward III. were probably intended to confirm the gifts of preceding sovereigns, as the grant of the English law to the Ostmen of Waterford was merely declaratory of a former statute of Henry II.

Amongst the local disturbances of this period, may be noticed the engagement between the citizens of Waterford and the septs of the O-Hedriscolls and Powers. The latter, hereditary enemies of Waterford, having landed at Tramore, the mayor and citizens advanced, in warlike manner, to give them battle. The contending parties met at Ballymacdane, when the invaders were entirely overthrown, 160 of them slain, and many of them taken prisoners. Among the captives were O-Hedriscoll-Oge and six of his sons, who, with three of their gallies, were carried in triumph into Waterford. It is, probably, in memory of this victory, that three gallies are quartered in the arms of the city.

In the statutes of Edward IV. there are many curious enactments, illustrative of the manners and opinions of the times, which assist in filling up the chasms occasioned by the scantiness of our historical records. The ministers and nobles were strictly prohibited leaving the country; it was even doubted whether they might go coastwise from one part of the kingdom to another; and though the latter restriction was abolished by a subsequent statute, yet we may perceive with what anxiety the evils of non-residence were guarded against.

We also learn from the parliamentary records, that in this reign a new coinage was issued from the mint of Waterford. The 3d of Edward IV. which recites a former statute, 38 Henry VI. providing that the grosse (the groat), the denier, the demidenier, and the quadrant, should be struck within the castles of Trim and Dublin, goes on: " Now, as the mayor, bailiffs, and commons of Waterford are daily encumbered for want of small coins for change of greater, it is enacted, at their petition, that the above mentioned small coins be struck at Waterford, in a place called Dondory, alias Reynold's Tower, and that they be made of the same weight, print, and size, as is mentioned in the said act, to be done in the castles of Dublin and Trim, and that they shall have this scripture, Civitas Waterford." The value of these coins was raised one-fourth above their former value and the currency of England—a miserable expedient, intended to relieve the pecuniary difficulties of the kingdom, and to prevent the practice of clipping money.

During this reign (1463), the town of Dungarvan was incorporated by act of parliament, which recites, that " as the seignory of Dungarvan was the most great and ancient honour, belonging to the king in Ireland, which through war was, for the most part, destroyed, it is provided, that the portrieve and commons of the said town, their heirs, &c. may enjoy all manner of free gifts and customs, as the inhabitants of the honourable manor of Clare, in England, have used and enjoyed, and as the mayor and commons of Bristol have done; the profits to go to the reparation of the walls, under the survey of the Earl of Desmond."

In the year 1487, at the time of the plot to
raise Lambert Simnel to the throne, the citizens
of Waterford took a distinguished part, and gave
the greatest proofs of courage and loyalty: they
manfully opposed the schemes of the impostor *Loyal*
and his artful supporters, and, in the almost ge- *to*
neral insurrection which followed, they alone con- *England.*
tinued firm and loyal to the rightful monarch.

When the factious Irish, under the influence of
the Earl of Kildare, had acknowledged the claims
of the impostor, and admitted the evidence of his
birth, their next step was to endeavour to compel
the inhabitants of other towns to unite with them
in the revolt. The citizens of Waterford were
peremptorily required to proclaim the new king,
and, by a letter transmitted to John Butler, then
mayor, were commanded to receive and assist
him with all the forces of the city. The conduct
of the mayor was eminently dignified, and marked
with the most minute attention to the best prece-
dents of civic etiquette: he answered, that he
would send a written reply by a messenger of his *Rebel*
own, and afterwards informed the Earl of Kildare- *Leader*
that the citizens of Waterford considered all those
rebels to the rightful king of England, who pro-
claimed and crowned the impostor Lambert.—
The Earl, not admiring the answer of the mayor,
commanded that his messenger should be hanged;
and not wishing to be outdone in dignity or

splendour, sent a herald, in his coat of arms, to deliver another communication to the citizens. As he was about to land, the mayor forbad him, and desired him to convey his message from the boat. The herald then, in the name of the Earl, commanded the mayor and citizens, under pain of hanging at their doors, to proclaim the king, and to accept him as their rightful prince. The mayor desired the herald to tell those who sent him, that they should not be troubled to come and hang him at his door; but (God willing) he would, with the citizens, encounter the false king and his adherents, thirty miles from Waterford, where he meant to give them an overthrow, to their dishonour and infamy. The valiant mayor, and the few who opposed the insurrection, were prepared for the encounter, their courage " screwed to the sticking-place"; but the affair terminated here. After a few idle threats against the citizens, whose possessions and franchises were declared forfeited, the new king found himself unable to support his army: he was compelled to change the scene of his adventures, and passing over into England, was met by King Henry, by whom he was taken prisoner, and his forces completely overthrown.—In return for the loyalty of the citizens, the king granted them a new charter, and sent them the following gracious letter:—

Letter of Henry VII. to the citizens of Water-
ford, concerning the treasons of the city of
Dublin, relating to the coronation of Lambert
Simnel, in that city.

Henry, by the grace of God, King of England and of France, and Lord of Ireland,
to our trusty and well-beloved the Mayor,
Bailiffs, and Commonalty of our city of
Waterford, in our land of Ireland, greeting:

Whereas it is evidently known, that our rebel,
the Earl of Kildare, not long ago, confederated
with certain others our rebels and traytors, through
the aid and assistance of the inhabitants of the
city of Dublin, in our said land, and others of their
sect, made great rebellion against us, intending,
as much as in them was, the destruction of our
person, and the utter subversion of this our realm,
if they might have attained unto their malitious
purpose; whose malice, through the grace of
God, and the aid of the loving subjects, we with-
stood, to the final destruction and confusion of
many of them.   And forasmuch as the said earl,
with the supportation of the inhabitants of our
said city of Dublin, and others there, to the high
displeasure of Almighty God, and contrary to the
duty of their allegiance, will not yet know their
seditious opinions, but unto this day uphold and

maintain the same presumptuously, as we certainly understand.

We, therefore, for the good obeysance and loving disposition that ye, to our singular comfort and pleasure, have borne always towards us, (whereof we heartily thank you,) and trusting firmly in the same, will and charge you, and by these our letters, give unto you and every of you, full authority and power, to arrest, seize and take, all such and as many of our said rebels, as ye shall now attain unto, by sea or land, with all manner of their ships, goods and merchandizes, as ye shall find to be carried or conveyed from any other place to our said city of Dublin, and to the parts thereabouts, and to employ the same unto the behoof and commonweal of our said city of Waterford: and that ye fail not daily and diligently to endeavour yourselves, for the execution of this commandment, until the said earl and the inhabitants of our said city of Dublin, with the parties thereabouts of the sequel, utterly and clearly leave and forsake the said rebellion and contemptuous demeaning, and shall be of good and due obeysance unto us, and stand in the favour of our grace.

Charging over this all manner of our officers, true liegemen and subjects, that unto you and every of you, in executing the premises, they be aiding, helping and assisting, in every behalf, as it shall appertain; as they and every of them will

be recommended of good and true obeysance unto
us.

> Given under our privy seal at our castle of War-
> wick, the 20th day of October, the third year
> of our reign.   HENRY, REX.

Shortly after this event, Sir Richard Edge-
combe, who was sent with a force of 500 men,
to oblige the people to renew their oaths of allegiance, proceeded from Kinsale, (where he first
landed,) in a coasting voyage to Waterford, to
commend and confirm the loyalty of the citizens.

The following account of his reception may be
worth extracting:

" Sir Richard arrived in the port of Waterford,
on the 30th June, 1488, about 9 o'clock in the
mornyng, and the same day at afternoon, two
boats came from the citty of Waterford, and brought
the seyd Sir Richard to the citty, and ther the
mayor and worshipful men of the same honourably
receaved hym, and the mayor lodgid the seyd Sir
Richard in his own house, and made hym right
herty cheer." On the following day, " The mayor
had the seyd Sir Richard about the citty, and
shewid unto hym the walls and reparations of the
same; and, that done, brought hym into the
Guild-Hall of the seyd citty, and the councill of
the same ther assemblid; the mayor shewid unto
the seyd Sir Richard the state of the seyd citty,
and the disposition of divers gret men, and of the
common people of the londs; among whych he

shewid, that they understood that the seyd Sir Richard had brought wyth hym the king's pardon for the Erl of Kildare, whych haith always bene, and is, an utter enemie to the seyd citty, and especially for their approved loyalty towards the kyng's grace, as they say; and that when he were sworn, and become the kyng's subget, though he were not made deputy of that lond, yet for the atchieving of his purposed malice agenst the seyd citty, they knew well, that he wuld make such means, that he shuld be made justice of that lond, and thereby he shuld have souch authority, that he wuld find the means by hym and his frends utterly to undoe the seyd citty, and desired especially the seyd Sir Richard that he wuld be the means to the kyng's grace to be their good and gracious lord therein, and that they mought be exempt from the jurisdiction, as well of the seyd Erl, if it fortuned hym to have any rule ther herafter, as of all othir Irish lordes, that shuld bear any rule in that lond for evirmore, and to hold immediately of the kyng and his heirs, and of such lordes of Englounde, as shall fortune herafter to have the rule of Irelound, and of none othirs. To the whych, the seyd Sir Richard answerid and said, that the kyng's grace had given to hym in especiale commaundment to doo and see especiale for the seyd citty of Waterford, and therfore, and for their approved troughthes he wuld labour unto the kyng's grace in this behaulf, as mouch as was in him; and undertooke that if it fortuned the seyd Erl heiafter to bear any rule in the seyd lond, as he knew not that evir he shuld, he wuld soe labour and shew the ways unto the kyng's grace, that the citty shuld be exempte from the power and jurisdiction of the Erl. And that done, the seyd Sir Richard broke his fast with the seyd mayor, and went agen to ship, and the same day at night went out of the same haven, and traversed in the sea all that night, and soe likewise he did the secounde day of July towards Dublyn, the wind being right contraryous."

In the year 1497, it was again the good fortune of the citizens of Waterford to manifest their loyalty to the king; for which, among other honours, they received the following motto—" Intacta manet Waterfordia." On this occasion, they communicated to his majesty the intelligence of the arrival of Perkin Warbeck at Cork, and assured him of their loyalty and affection. An opportunity was now afforded them to prove the sincerity of their professions and the extent of their devotion, for immediately on his landing, the whole strength of the rebel force was directed against Waterford. Perkin Warbeck and Maurice Earl of Desmond, with an army of 2400 men, advanced to the city, and on the 23d of July prepared to invest it: this force was intended to assault the western division, while a fleet of eleven ships, which arrived at Passage, was ordered to engage from the river; there was also a body of troops landed from the fleet, who were to proceed in the direction of Lumbard's marsh and co-operate with the land forces.

To prevent the junction of these two divisions, the ponds of Kilbarry were kept full, the besieged having raised a large mound of earth to stop the course of the river, which flows from Kilbarry into the Suir. The necessary preparations being completed, the siege was vigorously commenced and carried on, for eleven days, with great zeal and activity. In the many skirmishes and sorties which took place, the citizens were generally victorious, and routed or captured their opponents. In the field, the citizens covered themselves with glory; but it is to be regretted that after the fight, their valiant hearts had no touch of pity; on one occasion when, after a successful sortie in which they committed great slaughter, they returned to the city with a numerous band of prisoners, they carried them to the market-place, chopped off their heads, and fastened them on stakes, as trophies of their victory. Their valour and the dread of their cruelty could no longer be resisted; the besieged became the assailants; the enemy were repulsed in every direction, and what served to ensure the victory of the citizens, the cannon planted on Reginald's Tower, after many days hard firing, beat in the side of one of the ships, when the entire crew perished. The enemy, disheartened by all these untoward occurrences, and fearing to await the vengeance of the enraged citizens, raised the siege, and on the night of the 3d of August, retreated to Ballycasheen, from thence they proceeded to Passage, where Perkin Warbeck embarked and fled to Cork.

The citizens pursued him with four ships, and, after an eager chase, followed him to Cornwall, where he landed. When this intelligence reached the king, who was then at Exeter, he ordered the pursuit to be continued, and Perkin was at length apprehended.

The loyalty and courage of the citizens of Waterford were duly appreciated by the monarch, who, in addition to other marks of favour, was pleased to honour them with two letters, copies of which are subjoined.

King Henry the Seventh's letter to the mayor and citizens of Waterford, touching Perkin.

HENRY, REX.

Trusty and well beloved, we greet you well, and having received your writing, bearing date the first of this instant month, whereby we conceive, that Perkin Warbeck came unto the haven of Cork, the 26th of July last past, and that he intendeth to make sail thence to our country of Cornwall, for the which, your certificate in this party, and for the true minds that you have always borne towards us, and now specially for the speedy sending of your said writing, which we received the fifth day of the said month in the morning, we give unto you our right hearty thanks, as we have singular cause so to do, praying you of your good perseverance in the same, and also to send unto us, by your writing, such news, from time to time, as shall be occurrent in those parts, wherein you shall minister unto us full good pleasure to your semblable thanks hereafter, and cause us not to forget your said good minds unto us, nor any your reasonable desires, for time to come; given under our signet at our manor of Westminster, the 6th of August.

We pray you to put your effectual diligence for the taking of the said Perkin, and him so taken to send unto us, wherein you shall not only singularly please us, but shall have also for the same, in money content, the sum of 1000 marks sterl. for your reward, whereunto you may verily trust, for so we assure you, by these our present letters; and therefore we think it behoveful, that you send forth ships to the sea for the taking of Perkin aforesaid; for they that take him, and bring or send him surely to us, shall have undoubtedly the said reward.

Another letter from the same King to the mayor and citizens, touching Perkin and others.

HENRY, REX.

Trusty and well-beloved, we greet you well.

And whereas Perkin Warbeck, lately accompanied
with divers and many of our rebels of Cornwall,
advanced themselves to our city of Exeter, which
was denied unto them, and so they came to the
town of Taunton, at which town, as soon as they
had knowledge that our chamberlain, or steward
of our household, Sir John Cheny, and others
our loving subjects with them, were come so far
forth towards the said Perkin, as to our monastery of Glastonbury, the said Perkin took with
him John Heron, Edward Skelton, and Nicholas
Askley, and stole away from his said company
about midnight, and fled with all the haste they
could.   We had well provided beforehand for the
sea coasts, that if he had attempted that way, as
he thought indeed to have done, he should have
been put from his purpose, as it came to pass:
for when they perceived they might not set to
the sea, and that they were had in quick chase
and pursuit, they were compelled to address themselves to our monastery of Beaulieu, to the which,
of chance and fortune, it happened some of our
menial servants did repair, and some were sent
thither purposely. The said Perkin, Heron, Skelton, and Askley, seeing our said servants there,
and remembring that all the country was warned
to make watch, and to give attendance, that they
should not avoid nor escape by sea, made instances
to our said servants to sue unto us for them—the
said Perkin desiring to be sure of his life, and he

would come unto us to shew what he is, and, over
that, do unto us such service as should content
us. And so, by agreement of our said servants
and them, they wished them to depart from Beaulieu, and to put themselves in our grace and pity.
The abbot and convent hearing hereof, demanded
of them why, and for what cause they would depart? whereunto he gave answer, in the presence
of the said abbot and convent, and of many others,
that without any manner of constraint, they would
come unto us of their free wills, in trust of our
grace and pardon aforesaid. And so the said
Perkin came unto us to the town of Taunton, from
whence he fled, and immediately after his first
coming, humbly submitting himself to us, hath of
his free will openly shewed, in the presence of all
the lords here with us, and of all nobles, his name
to be Pierce Osbeck, whence he hath been named
Perkin Warbeck, and to be no Englishman born,
but born of Tournay, and son to John. Some
time while he lived comptroller of the said town,
with many other circumstances too long to write,
declaring by whose means he took upon him this
presumption and folly, and so now the great abuse
which hath long continued is now openly known
by his own confession. We write these news
unto you; for be undoubted that, calling to mind
the great abusion that divers folks have been in
by reason of the said Perkin, and the great business and charges that we and our realm have been

put unto in that behalf, you would be glad to hear
the certainty of the same, which we affirm unto
you for assured truth.   Sithence the writing of
these premises, we be ascertained that Perkin's
wife is in good surety for us, and trust that she
shall shortly come unto us, to this our city of
Exeter, as she is minded.   Over this, we understand, by writing from the Right Rev. Father in
God the Bishop of Duresme, that a truce is taken
between us and Scotland, and that it is concluded
the king of Scots shall send unto us a great and
solemn embassage for a longer peace to be had
during both our lives.   And since our coming to
this our city of Exeter, for the suppression of this
great rebellion, and so to order the parties of
Cornwall as the people may live in their due
obeysance unto us, and in good restfullness for
themselves in time to come.   The commons of
this shire of Devon come dayly before us, in great
multitudes, in their shirts, the foremost of them
having halters about their necks, and full humble,
with lamentable cries for our grace and remission,
submit themselves unto us, whereupon ordering
first, the chief stirrers and doers to be tried out of
them, for to abide their corrections accordingly,
we grant unto the residue generally our said grace
and pardon, and our commissioners the Earl of
Devon, our chamberlain and our steward of household, have done and do dayly, likewise, in our
county of Cornwall.   Given under our signet, at
our said city of Exeter, the 18th day of October.

These gracious and communicative epistles from so great a prince to such unworthy correspondents, should have excited the warmest sentiments of gratitude and esteem; and though the one thousand marks sterling were not immediately forthcoming, yet it must be admitted, that the exertions and expenditure, on the part of the city, were more than sufficiently compensated by the condescensions of the king.

But the citizens, prudent in peace as they were valiant in war, were not contented with the motto and royal correspondence, the only rewards conferred upon them by their sovereign; they sought a more substantial return, and, in a few years afterwards, (1499,) feeling themselves aggrieved, addressed the following petition to the king.

Petition of the mayor, bailiffs, and citizens of Waterford, to King Henry VII. by William White, recorder, and James Lumbard, citizen.

That the king and his progenitors granted to the mayor, bailiffs, and citizens of Waterford, and their successors, that they should not be compelled, in time of war or peace, to go out of the said city in manner of war, but should defend said city for the king, and, in his name, as one of his chamberlains of his land of Ireland. That they be not suffered to enjoy the effect of said grant, but at all times are commanded, by the deputy or other officers, to go to the field unto far countries. That this procedure, in process of time, will be the destruction of the city, in regard the greatest part of them may be slain, and thereby the city be left desolate.— Further, that the revenues of the city, which were granted for supportation of the walls and towers, must, in such case, be laid out in victualling and wages of men for the field, and the city be left defenceless for want of sufficient reparation. That the city hath been ever kept as a garrison for the king, and never deviated from their allegiance since the arrival of Henry II. at Waterford.— That all kings and princes have ever since landed at Waterford, as being the most commodious place. That when all the kingdom was abased by rebels and enemies, they were resisted and put to rebuke at Waterford; and the citizens pursued Perkin Warbeck in four great ships, at their own charges, and was the cause of his falling into the king's hands. Therefore, they pray that the said city be kept whole in itself, and no interest therein be given to the lords of the land, and the citizens may have the effect of their said grant, and that they may enjoy the benefit of their said charter, as amply as is contained therein.

Granted by the king, under the signet, dated 15th of June.

It thus appears that the claims of the citizens

were not forgotten; the prayer of their petition was granted, and the city at that time, as well as during the following reign, was greatly esteemed for its loyalty.

In 1536, Henry VIII. wrote to the mayor and citizens by William Wise, a gentleman of Waterford, then in high favour at court, and conferred upon them a gilt sword, and also a cap of liberty, to be borne before the mayor when he walked in state.

These honourable badges of loyalty were intended as special marks of favour to the citizens of that time, and are still carefully preserved, and highly valued by their descendants.

The grant accompanying the royal gift is as follows:

" By the King.

" Henry, Rex.

" Trusty and well-beloved, we greet you well: And having received your letters with credence to be referred unto this bearer, William Wyse, Esq. for our body, which thoroughly declared your benevolence and loving acquitals to us in all your proceedings there concerning us and our army, according to your natural duty, and the expectation we have always conceived of you, whose credence with the circumstance of your pursuits we have at length heard and well perceived; and for the same your demeanours, we render you our most hearty thanks, letting you to wit, that we have, at this time, by the advice of our council, so concluded and ordered, that at this next parliament within that our land to be holden, that ye shall not be endamaged nor hindered in any of your liberties and grants of our progenitors made unto you, but always containing and persisting in your accustomed service and well approved fidelitie, we shall, as matter and occasion shall require, from time to time, provide for your public weal, and that our cittie.

" And now at this time, as a remembrance and evident token of our favours, we have sent you, by the bearer, *a Cap of Maintenance,* to be borne at times thought fit by you, and necessary, before you our Mayor, being our officer of that our said cittie, and our successors officers of the same.

Cap of Liberty

> " Given under our signett, at our manor of Greenwich, the last day of April, in the 20th year of our reign.

" To our trusty and well-beloved the Maior and Comminalty of our cittie of Waterford, in the land of Ireland."   *city*

It might be allowable in this place to enter into an elaborate discussion touching the origin and meaning of the cap of maintenance, and to hazard a conjecture as to the precise time when this symbol was first adopted ; but, in pity to the reader, such disquisition shall be here dispensed with, merely suggesting, with all the becoming gravity and caution which belong to the character of a narrator of history, that the tenor of the royal grant appears to favour the use of an honourable decoration, altogether different from that in vogue at the present time; and to hint that the receptacle, or seat of the cap of maintenance, should be an embroidered cushion, or perhaps the hand, and not, as it is now, the unhonoured head of the attendant of the mayor.

It is not to be concluded, from the loyalty of Waterford and other sea-port towns, that the interior of Ireland was now rendered peaceable and submissive to the government of England.

The native Irish were, for the most part, either actually in rebellion or prepared to unite with every ferocious disturber of the peace of the country, whilst the influence of the English monarch rarely extended beyond the limits of the pale.

It would be uninteresting to dwell minutely on the insurrections and disturbances which occurred in the county of Waterford at this remote period: there are, however, some curious facts, involving particulars illustrative of the manners of the people, which it may not be amiss to recount briefly.

The family of the Fitzgeralds, or Geraldines as they were usually called, were frequently engaged in the tumults of the Irish, and even when they professed loyalty to the sovereign, were treated

with unkindness and suspicion.   It happened that
five brothers of the name were arrested by order
of Henry VIII. and conveyed on board ship to be
transmitted to England.

During the voyage, as they endeavoured to cheer
and comfort each other, one of the brothers, who
is represented as more learned than the rest, inquired of the owner what was the name of the
ship.   Being told it was called the Cow, he thus
expressed himself—" Now, good brethren, I am in
utter despair of our return to Ireland, for I bear in
mind an old prophecy, that five earl's brethren
should be carried in a cow's belly to England, and
from thence never return." The prophecy was
fulfilled, and the fame of it immediately reported,
not only in England and Ireland, but even in
foreign lands.   Dominick Power, who was sent
by a nephew of these brothers, to the Emperor
Charles V. to crave his aid towards the conquest
of Ireland, presenting the emperor with twelve
great hawks and fourteen fair hobbies, was informed by his majesty that he came too late, for
that his master and his five uncles had been executed at London.

There was a very important act passed at this
time (1539), respecting the lands of absentees,
which is in some degree connected with the
affairs of Waterford.

Gerald Ailmer, who was Chief Baron of the
Exchequer, and afterwards Chief Justice of the

Common Pleas, had occasion to repair to the court of England, where his services were highly valued, and procured for him from the king, through the influence of the Lord Cromwell, the appointment of Chief Justice of the King's Bench in Ireland. The citizens of Waterford, displeased at the advancement of Ailmer, intreated the Earl of Shrewsbury, also Earl of Waterford, to report his incapacity to the king. The earl complied with their request, and ventured to expostulate with his majesty for bestowing so important an office upon an unworthy person, being, as the noble earl called him, " such a simple John at Stile, no wiser than Patch, the late Lord Cardinall his foole."

The king represented this to the Lord Cromwell, who being well acquainted with the gentleman, intreated his majesty to have a conference with him, assuring him that he would find him perfectly competent, notwithstanding the malicious reports of his enemies. The king agreed, and had a long conversation with Ailmer, whom he found perfectly qualified for the office. In this conference, the king inquired what he considered the chief occasion of disorder in Ireland, and how he thought it might be best reformed.

The reply of Ailmer, whether correct or not, was at all events perfectly national: he informed his majesty that the decay of Ireland was principally to be attributed to the absence of the nobi-

D 2

lity, and to their neglect and inattention to the improvement of their lands: the remedy which he proposed was very simple, and no doubt highly pleasing to the monarch, he suggested that the lands of absentee proprietors should revert to the crown, and that none should enjoy estates who were indifferent to the comfort and happiness of their tenantry. *care for the peasants*

In the next parliament the king had a law passed to this effect, which chiefly applied to the Earl of Waterford, who was thereby deprived of his estates in this county. The evils arising from non-residence of proprietors must have been severely felt at that period, when there appeared little hope of civilizing the native Irish, except by encouraging intercourse with the comparatively refined inhabitants of England.

Nothing can exceed the barbarity of the " meer Irish" of that time, or the wild Irish, as they were called; they are described by an ancient author, as possessing many natural advantages of person and disposition; " the men are clean of skin and hew, of stature tall. The women are well favored, cleane coloured, faire handed, big and large, suffered from their infancy to grow at will, nothing curious of their feature and proportion." In manner and disposition they are represented as, " religious, franke, amorous, irefull, sufferable of infinite paines, very glorious, many sorcerers, excellent horsemen, delighted with wars, great almsgivers, passing in hospitalitie."

Describes the Irish

Yet with all these qualities, they were so ignorant, so corrupt and sensual, and so beastly in
their customs and mode of living, we can easily
conceive that centuries of improving intercourse
with other people, would be necessary for their
perfect civilization.   The ancient Irish had one of
the distinctive marks or characteristics of savage
life: a perfect content or satisfaction with every
thing of their own, united to an entire contempt for
all other people.   The English were churls, an
inferior race, and only to be named as second to a
native of Ireland, as I and you, I and my master.
The Irish were proud of their long and bushy
hair, called glibbs, which they nourished with as
much affection, as if it were the source of all that
was valuable; even at the present day, a remnant
of the ancient prejudice may be perceived, in the
undue importance attached to long and luxuriant,
but frequently neglected hair.   It would be
tedious to dwell upon their other peculiarities,
their howling at the graves, their disregard of
personal comforts, their cruelty and love of rapine;
it will be sufficient, in illustration of their manners,
to refer to authentic accounts of their conduct in
the wars, in which the politic King Henry induced
them to serve.

Henry VIII. had concerted a plan with the
emperor, to invade France with a numerous army,
and in order to complete the proportion of troops
which the English monarch undertook to supply,

Henry VIII wants the Irish for his army

an extensive levy of men was ordered to be made
in Ireland, a politic arrangement, as well for the
overthrow of his majesty's foreign enemies, as for
the peace and security of his own distracted
country. The Irish troops were quickly collected,
and sent into England, under the command of
two gentlemen of this county, the Lord Power
and Surlocke or Sherlock, names well known in
the annals of Waterford. Seven hundred wild
Irish, mustered and reviewed in St. James's Park,
must have excited not a little amazement!

But it was in the enemy's country, that their
services were most extraordinary; they carried
on an irregular and predatory warfare, ranging
through the country, plundering and burning the
villages, and in every case refusing quarter to
their prisoners, whom they murdered without
pity. They also acted as purveyors to the army,
and practised the following method to procure a
supply of food. Having taken a bull, they fastened him to a stake and scorched him with
burning faggots; the cries of the enraged animal
attracted the cattle in every direction, which were
then easily taken, and conveyed to the camp.
The French, amazed at this unusual species of
warfare, sent a herald to King Henry, to inquire
whether his followers were men or devils, for that
they could neither be won with rewards or paci-
fied with pity. The king replied in jest, which
so enraged the French, that they treated the Irish

"Burn the Bull"

prisoners most cruelly, and put them to death with every refinement of torture. After a display of so much barbarity on the part of the Irish soldier, it is only right to relate an instance of his personal courage. At the termination of the siege of Boulogne, a body of French soldiers encamped on the west side of the town, beyond the haven; one of them came forward and challenged any of the English army to fight him in single combat. Every circumstance was in favour of the challenger; the place of combat was near his own party, and the haven to be crossed was deep; yet, notwithstanding all these disadvantages, Nicholas Walsh, an Irishman, accepted the challenge, swam across the water, slew his antagonist and returned back to his own party, with the Frenchman's head in his mouth.

It must not be supposed that the description of the native Irish applies to the inhabitants of Waterford and other sea-port towns. The citizens of Waterford differed in nothing from the English, from whom many of them were descended; they were never cordially united to the Irish people, but were compelled, in self-defence, to confine themselves within the bounds of their walls and fortifications. These circumstances will account for the peculiar customs and manners which prevailed amongst the inhabitants of the cities, and which, notwithstanding their long settlement in the country, made them a distinct and separate people.

The city of Waterford was now a place of trade and consequence, enjoying a regular government, and advancing every day in the improvements and decencies of civilized society. We can now look back with complacency upon the manners of those, from whom many of the citizens of the present day are descended, and from whom the general character of the people may be faintly traced : we have an interest in their courage and loyalty, and are proud or humbled as we read of their good fortunes, or dwell upon the reverses, which it was the lot of their city to experience. The following description of the then citizens of Waterford, written about two hundred and fifty years since, may serve to shew whether the present generation have improved upon the manners of those who preceded them:—" The aire of Waterford is not verie subtill, yea nathelesse the sharpnesse of their wittes seemeth to be nothing rebated or duld by reason of the grossenesse of the aire. For in good sooth the townesmen, and namelie students are pregnant in conceiving, quicke in taking, and sure in keeping. The citizens are verie heedie and warie in all their publike affaires, slow in the determining of matters of weight, loving to looke yer they leape. In choosing their magistrate, they respect not onlie his riches, but also they weigh his experience. And therefore they elect for their maior neither a rich man that is yoong, nor an old man that is poore. They are cheerfull in the interteinment of strangers, hartie one to another, nothing given to factions. They loue no idle benchwhistlers nor lurkish faitors: for yoong and old are wholie addicted to thriuing, the men commonlie to traffike, the women to spinning and carding. As they distill the best aqua vitæ, so they spin the choicest rug in Ireland."

It would be presumptuous to institute a comparison between the citizens of the present and of ancient times; it may however be remarked, that if the moderns have degenerated, they are happy in having pure and exalted models to lead them back into the path of honour. The aqua vitæ remains in abundance, but the choice rug is gone; whether its loss should be regretted, we may learn from the following anecdote, related by the same ancient author:—" A fréend of mine being of late demurrant in London, and the weather by reason of a hard hoare frost being somewhat nipping, repaired to Paris garden, clad in one of these Waterford rugs. The mastifs had no sooner espied him, but déeming he had beene a beare, would faine haue baited him. And were it not that the dogs were partlie muzzled, and partlie chained, he doubted not, but that he should haue béene well tugd in this Irish rug; whereupon he solemnlie vowed never to see beare baiting in anie such wéed."

The art of printing is supposed to have been

introduced into Waterford about the period of which we are now writing; but it would be difficult to adduce any decided authority in favour of that supposition.

The following is therefore given merely as a copy of the title of a book, *purporting* to have been printed in Waterford in the year 1555:

" The acquital or purgation of the most catholyke Christen prince Edwarde the VI Kyng of Englande, Fraunce and Irelande, &c. and of the Church of Englande, reformed and gouerned under hym, agaynst al suche as blasphemously and traitorously infame hym, or the sayd Church, of heresie or sedicion.   They are gone to Baal Poer, and runne awaye from the Lorde to that shamefull Idole, and are become as abominable as theyr louers.   Ephraim flyeth lyke a birde, so shall theyr glorye also."   Dedicated—" To the nobilitie and to the reste of the charitable christen laytie of Englande, John Olde wisheth grace and mercy from God the Father, and from Jesus Christ the common and only sauour of the worlde, with the gifte of perfite faithe and earnest repentaunce "

Printed in black letter, with the quotations in Italics, and the following colophon in Roman:

" Emprinted at VVaterford the 7 daye of Nouembre, 1555 "

There can, however, be no doubt that printing was known in Waterford in the early part of the subsequent century.   Cox, in his History of Ireland, mentions, that in 1644 the rebels had a printing press in Waterford, which was under the superintendence of Thomas Bourke, an Irish printer: and Harris, in his Hibernica, alludes to a quarto publication, entitled " An Argument delivered by Patrick Darcy, Esq. by express order of the House of Commons, on the 9th of June, 1641," which is stated, on the title-page, to have been *printed at Waterford, by " Thomas Bourke, printer to the confederate Catholics of Ireland."* 1643.

SECTION II.

In the interval between the reigns of Henry VIII.
and Queen Elizabeth, there is little to interest us
in the annals of the county or city of Waterford.
At this period, and for some years afterwards, the
native Irish were returning rapidly to their original barbarism; even the English colonists, or
the inhabitants of the pale, were assimilating
themselves to the people of their adopted country,
and becoming every day less solicitous to preserve or advance the interests of England. It required years of suffering, and the united wisdom
of the government of Elizabeth, to restore Ireland
to the state in which she was after the death of
Henry II. when, if there was not much actual
amendment, there was at least the promise and
appearance of improvement. We are now to
dwell upon the insurrections, tumults, and disorders of a rude and discontented people; we are
to trace the secret working of unsubdued spirits,
proceeding from the enforced repose of slaves, to
rapine, to insurrection, and at length to open re-

bellion; and so widely diffused and seductive was this revolutionary temper, we shall find no class of the people, not even the inhabitants of the untouched city, entirely exempted from it. The disaffection of Waterford was first manifested in the refusal to assist the Lord Deputy Sidney, who, being encamped near Clonmell, and expecting to be attacked by the insurrectionary forces, applied to the citizens to assist him with a few soldiers. They attempted to justify their conduct by pleading the privileges of the city, and referred him to the charters granted to them by John. The decisive and energetic government of Elizabeth proceeded zealously to promote the peace of the country: favours and punishments were alternately resorted to, and those who were insensible to the boon of privileges and charters, (three of which were bestowed in this reign on the citizens of Waterford,) were forced to feel the displeasure of the angry monarch, who endeavoured to strike terror into the minds of the people by the severity and frequency of executions: when peace was in some degree restored, the next object was to reform the manners of the people. The peculiar costume of the Irish, particularly the glibbs worn by the men, and the Egyptian rolls, the head-dress of the females, were strictly forbidden. We are told that the prohibition was not at first very graciously received by the softer sex, but that at length they yielded, and adopted the use of hats after

the English fashion: it might be that their submission was remotely owing to the love of novelty,
or perhaps to the becomingness of the dress, as
well as to the more obvious reason, the pliant
facility of their tempers.

1575. It may appear unaccountable that at this
time, when the Irish chieftains were threatened by
the overwhelming power of England, they should
have had leisure or inclination to engage in private and domestic quarrels, which, while they
weakened their resources, gave to their common'
enemy a pretext to invade their few remaining
privileges. The disputes which had long harassed the noble families of Ormond and Desmond
were renewed with so much violence, that at
length a general conflict was the result. The contending parties engaged at Affane, in this county,
when Desmond was routed with the loss of 280
men. This was the source of great disorder and
misfortune, and again involved the people in all
the horrors and miseries of war.

Sir Henry Sidney, who was for the third time
appointed Lord Deputy of Ireland, judging that
decisive measures were necessary to quell these
disturbances, undertook to visit in person the
more disaffected districts, and for this purpose
advanced at the head of her majesty's army, which
was then about 600 horsemen and footmen.

At Kilkenny he was informed of the death of
Sir Peter Carew, and at the entreaty of his friends

proceeded to Waterford to be present at his funeral.

When the Lord Deputy, accompanied by the Earl of Ormond, arrived here, he was magnificently entertained by the mayor and aldermen, and a congratulatory oration, in the Latin tongue, addressed to him by a young scholar clad in white attire. The citizens received him with every demonstration of joy, and both on land, and on the river, prepared splendid pageants in honour of their governor. The Lord Deputy expressed much satisfaction at the kind reception he had experienced, yet he could not avoid alluding to the former conduct of the citizens, which so ill agreed with their present professions of attachment.

After a short stay in Waterford, Sir Henry Sidney proceded to Dungarvan, where he was met by the Earl of Desmond, who offered him his services. This nobleman enjoyed great influence in the western parts of the county, and had made himself master of the castle of Dungarvan, from which he was forcibly expelled. It now suited his interest to affect loyalty to the English government, and it was also convenient to the Lord Deputy to appear to accept his services.

It required all the wisdom and energy of the government to check the spirit of rebellion which was extending in every direction. The county of Waterford was continually harassed by the tumults and reprisals of the contending parties, who were now engaged in open war. It was in vain that politic measures and improvements in the administration of justice were introduced; it was now too late, rebellion had proceeded too far to be checked by any thing except the most vigorous and decisive measures.

The city still preserved the appearance of loyalty, and eagerly embraced every opportunity of manifesting its zeal and devotion.

Sir William Drury, who succeeded Sir Henry Sidney in the government of Munster, was compelled to seek repose in Waterford for the recovery of his health. Still mindful of her majesty's service, he endeavoured to encourage others to a zealous discharge of their duties, and for this purpose conferred the honour of knighthood on Patrick Walsh, the mayor of the city, and on several of the principal officers of the garrison. After the performance of the ceremony, he lingered for a few days, and died at Waterford, on the 30th September, 1579.

Sir William Pelham, who was appointed Lord Justice on the death of Sir William Drury, made immediate preparations to visit the cities of Munster, and leaving Dublin, proceeded along the sea-coast. When he arrived at Ballyhack, he was met by the mayor of Waterford, who had several well appointed boats ready to receive him.

Previous to his arrival in Waterford, the officers

and troops of the garrison exhibited a mock fight, and then retired within the walls to receive him with military honours. The towers, walls, and curtains of the city were ornamented with flags and ensigns, and the cannon of the fortifications and of the shipping gave him a salute. At his landing, the mayor and aldermen, dressed in their scarlet robes, approached, and presented to him the keys of the gates, which he immediately returned. The mayor, bearing the sword of state, then conducted his lordship to the cathedral, and on the way, when the procession arrived at certain places, there were two Latin orations addressed to him.

On his return from the church he was favoured with a third speech, which, to diversify the business, was delivered in English, and thus harangued he retired to seek repose at his lodgings. Here, the Earl of Ormond met him, with advice, that the rebels, under the Earl of Desmond, had advanced as far as Dungarvan. A detachment of 400 foot and 100 horse were forthwith dispatched to oppose them; but the force of the insurgents continuing to increase, a special commission was directed to Sir Warham St. Leger, authorizing him to proceed according to the course of martial law against all offenders, as the nature of their crimes might deserve, provided the parties were not worth forty shillings yearly in land or annuity, or ten pounds in goods. He was also empowered to enter into terms with the rebels, and to grant them protections for ten days, to apprehend and execute all idle persons taken by night; to live at free quarters wherever he went; and by way of check upon this monstrous power, he was required, every month, to certify the number and the offences of persons whom he should order to be put to death.

The Lord Justice, after he had rested about three weeks at Waterford, removed to Clonmell, and from thence to Limerick.

It was at this period, and in this part of Ireland, that the afterwards celebrated Sir Walter, then Captain Raleigh, first distinguished himself in active life, and laid the foundation of that character which was soon to procure the favor and friendship of the discerning Elizabeth.

In the account of the sieges and battles which are handed down to us, his bravery and enterprising spirit are eminently conspicuous: it was the possession of these qualities, at a time when the greatest part of Ireland was in actual rebellion, which raised him so much in the estimation of his superiors. He was very early entrusted by the Lord Deputy and Council with an important commission and a company of horse and foot soldiers, and empowered to act according to his own discretion in suppressing the insurrections of the disaffected nobles. This peculiar command gave a free scope to his bold and romantic disposition,

and was the source of the many gallant actions
and hair-breadth escapes, which are so abundantly
recorded of him.   In the summer of 1580, he
acted as a Commissioner of Munster, and resided
principally in the neighbourhood of Lismore,
where he had, shortly before, received from the
crown grants of 42,000 acres of land at a rent of
100 marks sterling a year.

The lands comprized in the warrant were these:
" the barony, castle, and lands of Inchiquin, in
Imokilly; the castle and lands of Strancally,
Ballynatra, Killnatora, and the lands lying on the
rivers Broadwater and Bride, late David Mac
Shean Roche's and others, with the decayed town
of Tallow; and the castle and lands of Lisfinny,
Mogilla, Killacarow and Shean: and if these were
not sufficient, the deficiency was to be made up,
out of the castle and lands of Mocollop, the castle
and lands of Temple Michael, the lands of Patrick
Condon, next adjoining unto the Shean, and of
the lands called Ahavena, alias Whitesland."   It
was directed that these lands should be near to
the town of Youghall, where Raleigh afterwards
fixed his residence: the house in which he lived
still remains, and was for many years preserved
in the same state in which it was left by its illustrious occupant.   There are recorded of this extraordinary man, numberless brave and adven-
turous exploits, bearing a strong resemblance to
the fictions of romance, yet perfectly according
with the ideas which history and the delineation

of the novelist have served to impress upon our minds. The character of the warfare, and the circumstances of the times, required enterprizing and decisive measures, and were exactly suited to the habits and inclinations of a young and gallant warrior.

The miserable and ignorant Irish, the Gallowglasses and Kernes, as two of the principal degrees or classes of soldiers were called, had been so long treated like beasts of prey, they at length became like them in their habits and mode of life. They lived entirely in the woods and morasses, harassed with perpetual anxiety, and continually changing from place to place; when they dressed their food, which was principally horseflesh, they retired to another place to eat it, and from thence they removed somewhere else to sleep. They prowled about at night and slept during the day, and thus, with difficulty, evading the eagerness of their enemies, they protracted a miserable existence.

This savage warfare was at length terminated by the death of the turbulent Lord of Desmond and his brother, who perished under circumstances of cruelty revolting to humanity and disgraceful to the arms and reputation of their conquerors. It is gravely observed by an historian of this period, in relating that a disaffected chieftain had been drawn, hanged and quartered, that such a fate was, perhaps, " too good for such a bloody traitor !"

It may serve to illustrate the manners of the times, (1583,) to give an account of a judicial combat or wager of battle, which took place in the presence and by the authority of the principal members of the government, and which was sanctioned by the approbation of the English and Irish nobles.

The circumstances of the quarrel and the names of the parties are immaterial : the dispute was of a private and personal nature, between two individuals of some consequence, and nearly allied by birth, and there being no other way of trial, it was agreed to decide the question by an appeal to the sword, according to the laws and rules of single combat as practised in England.

All the preliminaries being arranged, at the time appointed the lords justices, the judges, and the counsellors took the seats appropriated to them, every one according to his rank. The court being called over, the appellant was first brought in, without any covering except his shirt, and armed only with a sword and target, and then having done his reverences to the lords justices and the court, he was conducted to a seat at one extremity of the lists. The defendant was next introduced, in the same order and with the same weapons, and when he had made his obeisances, he was seated at the other extremity.—

The several actions and pleadings being openly read, the appellant was asked whether he would aver his demand, to which he answered that he would. The defendant was then required to say, whether he would confess the action, or stand to the trial of the same. He replied, that he would aver it by the sword. The parties were next severally called on, and each of them required to swear that his quarrel was just and true, and that he would justify it both with his sword and blood: and thus sworn or perjured, as the case might be, they were again conducted to their seats.

At the signal given by sound of trumpets, the combatants arose, and met each other in the middle of the lists: they fought for some time with various success, many wounds were given and received, and blood flowed plentifully on all sides, until at length the defendant received a blow, and terminated the contest with his life.

The appellant then cut off the head of his vanquished enemy, and, with much elegance, presented it to the lords justices, upon the point of his sword. It followed, as a matter of course, that the victor was declared to have had a righteous cause.

Since the reign of Henry II. Ireland had been a burden to the crown of England, requiring a vast army to ensure tranquillity, without making any return to the revenues of the state. Eliza-

beth imagined that Ireland might be made a
valuable addition to her kingdom, and sought to
effect this desirable object by colonization and by
the sword. The wars of this period were wars of
extermination: the native Irish were considered
incapable of improvement, and therefore, according to the ideas of the English government, to
ensure the peace of the country, it was necessary
to make it almost a desert.

The condition of the inhabitants of the county
of Waterford, at the close of this reign, is represented in the most dismal language. Those whom
the sword had spared, were reduced to the extreme of misery by famine, they were seen creeping from the woods, in search of the vilest food,
and endeavouring to prolong a miserable existence by eating carrion, and, in some instances,
human flesh. The land itself was become un-
fruitful; deprived of its cultivators, it resembled
a frightful wilderness, and from one extremity of
the county to the other, except in towns and
cities, scarcely any living creature was to be seen,
save wolves and beasts of prey.

If the flattering historians of the reign of Elizabeth, who write of Ireland tranquillized, are to
be believed, their statements should be coupled
with the fact that it was almost depopulated also.
The queen was ignorant of the cruelty of her servants, until it was almost too late to check it.
When these enormities were represented to her

majesty, she expressed great regret, and declared her fear that the same reproach might be made to her which was formerly made to Tiberius,— " It is you that are to blame for these things, who have committed your flock, not to shepherds but to wolves."

It is difficult to reconcile the statements relative to the persecutions of the government and the depopulation of Munster with the admitted fact, that in a few years after, at the accession of James, discontent and disaffection prevailed to a great degree in the same district, and required the most vigorous and decisive measures to repress them. When King James succeeded to the throne of England, the expectations of his Irish subjects were elevated by the remembrance of his warm and flattering expressions of regard: they were induced to expect a more favourable reign, and perhaps displayed their feelings and wishes with too little reserve. The consequence of disappointment was disaffection, and a determination, scarcely concealed, to oppose the just claims of the monarch. The Lord Deputy Mountjoy, judging that the situation of the affairs of the province required his immediate personal attention, proceeded with a numerous army into Munster; and on the 5th of May, 1603, came to Grace-dieu, within the liberties of Waterford, and summoned the mayor to open the gates and receive him and his army into the city. The

spirit of rebellion immediately appeared, the
gates were shut against him, and the citizens
pleaded that, by a charter of King John, they
were exempted from quartering soldiers.   While
the parties were thus engaged, two ecclesiastics,
Dr. White and a young Dominican friar, came
into the camp, they were habited in the dresses
of their order, Dr. White wearing a black gown
and cornered cap, and the friar wearing a white
woollen frock.   When they entered the lord deputy's tent, Dr. White commenced a violent religious controversy, " all of which," we are told,
" his lordship did most learnedly confute." He
then severely reprehended the conduct of the
citizens, threatened to draw King James's sword
and cut the charter of King John to pieces; and
declared his intention, if they persisted in their
obstinacy, to level their city and strew it with
salt.   His menaces were effectual; the citizens
immediately submitted, and received the lord
deputy and his army within the walls. they afterwards took the oath of allegiance, renounced
all foreign jurisdiction, and to prevent any future
disturbance, a garrison was stationed in the city.
Overt acts of disaffection were thus checked, but
the exciting causes still continued, and manifested
themselves on every occasion where they were
not opposed by the fears or hopes of the people.

The discontent, which heretofore shewed itself
in riots and partial insurrections, was now ripen-

ing into a more settled and serious hostility to the government, and was every day producing that decided opposition which shortly afterwards terminated in the great rebellion. The attention of James the First was early directed to the improvement of Ireland: measures of conciliation and of severity were alternately resorted to, and, in some cases, were attended with the results which he anticipated. Waterford was one of the first cities which submitted to the payment of taxes arbitrarily levied by the monarch, and received in return a new charter, with many additional privileges and grants.

In a few years afterwards, (1617,) we find the Earl of Thomond and Sir William Jones, lord chief justice of Ireland, commissioners appointed to seize on the liberties and public revenues of Waterford, in consequence of the refusal of the mayor to take the oath of supremacy.—The magistrates persisting in their opposition, the city had no regular government for many years, the charter was withdrawn, and the city continued in this state during the remainder of the reign. Charles I. restored to the citizens all their former privileges by a new charter, dated the 26th of May, 1626. This charter arrived at Passage on the 25th of July, in the same year, and cost the city £3000. In a few years afterwards, the citizens received from the same monarch a new charter, which chiefly related to the

grant of the admiralty of the harbour. It is
under the charter of Charles I. that the corporation now enjoy their rights and privileges: there
was another grant from James II. which terminated with his abdication.

The Duke of Ormond arrived in Waterford in
September of this year (1633), after a most expeditious journey. His biographer mentions, that he
left London on a Saturday at four in the morning—arrived at Bristol that evening—sailed from
thence on Sunday at nine o'clock, and arrived in
Waterford the same hour the following morning.

No language can sufficiently describe the deplorable situation of the church at this period: several of the bishoprics (among others that of Waterford) were reduced as low as £50 a year; and
the stipends of some of the vicarages were only
sixteen shillings per annum! It was the practice
of the times to revile the clergy, and no exertion
was left untried to render episcopacy odious.

A stronger instance need not be given of this
than the case of Doctor Atherton, then bishop
of Waterford. It was his duty, on the part of
the church, to commence a prosecution against
the Earl of Cork for the recovery of Ardmore,
Lismore, and other lands, formerly and of right
belonging to the church, but then in possession of
that earl. His lordship compounded for the lands
of the see of Waterford by giving back Ardmore to
the church; but Bishop Atherton sueing for the

remainder, and being well qualified by his talents and spirit to go through with the suit, fell (as there is too much reason to think) a sacrifice to that litigation when he suffered for a pretended crime of a secret nature, made felony in that parliament, upon the testimony of a single witness that deserved no credit, and who, in his information, pretended that the crime had some time before been committed upon himself.

The bishop, during all the time of his most exemplary preparation for death, *and even at the moment of his execution*, is stated to have absolutely denied the fact; and the fellow who swore against him, when he came to be executed himself some time after, confessed at the gallows the falsehood of his accusation:—but even this strong evidence was of no avail—the bishop was executed on the 5th of December, 1640.

From this period until the arrival of Cromwell, the great rebellion and the circumstances preceding it, entirely engross the local as well as the general history of Ireland. These important events, the exciting causes of the insurrection, and its unfortunate results, are unsuitable to the present sketch; they demand the serious and dispassionate investigation of the historian, and do not admit of a hasty or superficial notice. Suffice it to observe, that the county and city of Waterford shared in the crimes and miseries of this unfortunate period, and whatever be the cause in

which the evil originated, the native Irish were
uniformly the sufferers or the victims.

It would seem that the native Irish had for a
time recovered the possession of the greater part
of Munster; which, after an obstinate struggle
with the overwhelming power of England, they
were again obliged to relinquish. The city of
Waterford, and the towns of Dungarvan and Lismore, were nominally in the interest of the government of the country, but their loyalty was
merely enforced; there was no reciprocity of
interest, and therefore no common feeling existed
between them—as plainly appeared on the occasion of the cessation of hostilities, (for it does
not deserve the name of peace,) which was agreed
on, in 1646.

This measure was violently opposed by the
citizens of Waterford, who imagined that the interests of their religion would be compromised by
their adoption of the treaty. The heralds sent
from Dublin to proclaim the peace, were treated
with every indignity: they were unable to discover the mayor's house, until they prevailed on
a little boy, by a bribe of sixpence, to shew it to
them, and after a fruitless delay of ten days, they
were obliged to retire from Waterford without
accomplishing their errand.

The violent commotions which at this time agitated England, had produced, or rather called
into action, the extraordinary talents of Oliver

Cromwell, that "great bad man," who afterwards performed such a distinguished part in the history of this country, and whose memory is still held here in deserved detestation: his name even now retains a hateful notoriety among the lower orders, by whom the "curse of Cromwell" is considered the most bitter malediction.

The parliament of England having unanimously resolved to send a powerful force to repress the disturbances of this country, Cromwell thought it not unworthy of his talents to engage in the conduct of the war, and, after considerable preparation, embarked with an army of 8000 foot and 4000 horse, and landed at Dublin on the 15th of August, 1649. The early part of his career was distinguished by vigour and cruelty, qualities which made a deep impression upon his enemies, and gave facility to his subsequent attempts. The terror of his name advanced before him, and so intimidated his opponents, that they were with difficulty persuaded to make preparations for defence. Ormond endeavoured to arouse them to a sense of duty, and offered to send troops to defend the garrison-towns; but Waterford peremptorily refused to receive any assistance, or to obey the orders of the royalist party. The town of Drogheda, the first of Cromwell's conquests, was taken by storm, and the inhabitants massacred in cold blood: Wexford shared the same fate, and from thence a detachment, under General Ireton, was sent to attack the fort of Duncannon, while Cromwell himself proceeded to lay siege to the town of Ross. The town of Carrick was shortly after surprized, and having been taken by a detachment of Cromwell's army, he himself proceeded thither, and from thence crossed over the Suir, and marched to invest Waterford. The citizens, terrified by the approach of a ruthless enemy, began to prepare for their defence, and gladly accepted a reinforcement of 1500 men, under General Ferral, sent by the Marquis of Ormond to their assistance. The troops of Cromwell, since their arrival in Ireland, had been greatly diminished in numbers, as well by the climate, to which they were not accustomed, as by the destructive warfare in which they had been engaged: the army, when it arrived at Waterford, only amounted to 5000 foot, 2000 horse, and 500 dragoons, yet such was the terror of the timid citizens, they were inclined to submit without awaiting the assault, and actually sent to Ormond to consult about the terms which they should require previous to the surrender of the city. The Marquis of Ormond encouraged them to a vigorous resistance, and by flattering assurances and promises of succour, was successful in inspiring them with firmness and resolution.

Waterford was a walled and fortified town, and though badly situated in case of a siege according to the improved practice of modern warfare, yet at the time of Cromwell's approach, it was sufficiently protected by the batteries and works, with which it was almost surrounded. The siege commenced on the 3d of October, 1649; Cromwell, in person, commanded the besieging army.

After crossing the Suir, at Carrick, the enemy marched along the southern bank of the river, and approached the town on the north-west, but were deterred by the fort on Thomas's hill from occupying the heights of Bilberry Rock, a commanding station then at a considerable distance from the city walls.

The strength of the defences and the numerous batteries protected the town from assault, and compelled the parliamentary forces to have recourse to the tedious process of investment. The Marquis of Ormond, though deficient in money and military stores, and having lost many men by desertion, endeavoured to defend Waterford; and for this purpose, kept a body of troops on the opposite side of the river, prepared to co-operate with the citizens, and to take advantage of any favourable circumstances which might occur.— During the progress of the siege, which was carried on with vigour, Cromwell dispatched a detachment of his army, consisting of six troops of dragoons and four of horse, to the town of Passage, six miles to the south of the city, and took possession of the fort which commanded the river at that place, thereby cutting off the communication between Waterford and the entrance of the harbour.

It was at this time, and shortly after the occupation of Passage, that an event occurred which serves to throw some light on the disposition and character of Cromwell, a character which yet had a few redeeming qualities, though only very peculiar circumstances could bring them into action.

A family, named Aylward, whose ancestors had been brought over by King John, was settled in the castle and estate of Fatlock, a beautifully situated place in the neighbourhood of Passage. The proprietor at that time, John Aylward, had been known to Cromwell in London, who now, in remembrance of former friendship, sought to secure him in his property. Cromwell was aware that his friend was a Roman Catholic, and that he was hostile to the parliamentary forces, and he had resolved that such should be dispossessed;—but, in this particular instance, he relaxed from his usual severity, and required, what to him appeared easy of attainment, that Aylward should conceal his faith, and appear to unite in principle with himself. The inducements were almost irresistible—there was some little balancing between religion and property; but, at length, partly by the advice of his wife, the better cause prevailed, and Aylward prepared to defend his property, or to lose it and his life together. Irritated at what he considered the obstinacy of the man, Cromwell resolved to punish his presumption, and sent a part of his forces and some cannon, under the command of Captain Bolton, whom he ordered to take possession of the estate. The ruins of a castle, around which a moat may be faintly traced, still mark the spot where the contest took place: the result may be anticipated; Captain Bolton was successful, and his descendants, until a few years since, continued to enjoy the conquest.

These occasional engagements produced no relaxation in the siege of Waterford, which was conducted with the enterprize and zeal of experienced warriors, on the one hand, and on the other, with the resolution of men who fought for their existence.

The loss of Passage being attended with serious inconvenience, it became necessary to endeavour to retake it; and for this purpose, the governor, Ferral, marched with a body of troops from Waterford, expecting to be assisted by Colonel Wogan, of Duncannon Fort, who was to advance to the attack from the opposite side of the river. Previous to the advance of the Governor's force, the Marquis of Ormond, attended by fifty horse, had crossed the river, with the intention of animating the garrison, and of making arrangements

for their support; and understanding that an
attack on Passage was meditated, he waited to
know the result.   On the governor's troops leaving the city, Cromwell dispatched a strong force
to attack them, and their danger being immediately perceived, Ormond requested permission to
bring over a body of horse to their assistance;
but the citizens refused the offer, and preferred
leaving the soldiers to their fate. Thus repulsed,
the gallant marquis advanced at the head of his
fifty horse and met the governor's foot soldiers
in full retreat, closely followed by Cromwell's
dragoons. He posted himself in an advantageous
position, and by his courage and a judicious arrangement of his force, checked the farther advance of the enemy, and covered the retreat into
the town. The necessity of retaking Passage,
and the importance attached to it by the enemy,
being thus evident, the Marquis of Ormond proposed to transport his troops over the river, and
undertook to quarter them in huts under the
walls, that they might not be burdensome to the
city: this proposal was also rejected, and it was
even in agitation to seize his person and treat his
followers as enemies. Irritated at their obstinacy
and ingratitude, the marquis withdrew his army,
leaving the citizens to protect themselves. Thus
left to their own resources, and vigorously assailed by the impatient Cromwell, the courage of
the citizens was now beginning to yield; they
declared, that unless they received a reinforce-

ment of troops and a supply of provisions, they could make no further resistance; the assault of the besiegers was hourly expected, and the most fatal results anticipated, when, fortunately, the Marquis of Ormond again arrived on the north of the Suir, immediately opposite the city, and by his appearance changed the aspect of affairs. Disheartened by the duration of the siege, in the course of which he had lost many men by sickness as well as by the chances of war, and discouraged by the difficulties of a winter campaign, Cromwell prepared to retire from the contest, and to seek winter quarters for his harassed army, in some more secure situation.

At this critical moment Ormond proposed to pass some of his troops across the river and attack the rear of the retreating enemy, but the obstinacy of the citizens returned with their hopes of safety, and they refused to supply boats or to admit his soldiers into the city, until the favourable opportunity was lost. Being thus obliged to raise the siege of Waterford, Cromwell resolved to direct his course to the towns of Munster which had revolted to the English parliament, and which now offered a secure asylum to his harassed and distempered forces.

His route lay through the extreme length of the county of Waterford, and, as on former occasions, his progress was distinctly marked by confiscation and blood. About the latter end of

November, Cromwell commenced his march, and
led his troops in the direction of Dungarvan.

It was his custom, when he had traced out the
route of the main body of his army, to proceed
himself, attended by a large force of dragoons, in
the most rapid and desultory manner, to the villages and fortified castles which lay within a moderate distance, and there levy contributions,
confiscate the lands, or execute summary punishment upon the proprietors, as his pleasure, the
wants of his soldiers, or the aspect of his affairs
seemed to require. The terror of his name was
generally sufficient to ensure submission to his
orders wherever he appeared: in the few cases
where resistance was to be apprehended, his
main army was called to his aid, and never failed
to execute immediate and exemplary vengeance.
As the army retired from the liberties of Waterford, the castle of Butlerstown, which lay in
their course, is supposed to have been assailed
and partly destroyed by gunpowder, the effects
of which were for a long time visible. Proceeding to Kilmeaden, distant about five miles from
the city, Cromwell met the first serious opposition
to his career.

The castle of Kilmeaden, situated on the banks
of the Suir, and enjoying a commanding and elevated station, was the residence of a branch of
the family of Le Poer, or Power, an ancient and
illustrious race who derived their descent in a

direct line from Robert le Poer, marshal of King
Henry II., and from whom the present Marquis
of Waterford is descended.

There were three branches of this noble family
at that period, settled in the county, each of
them possessing great influence, and enjoying
vast estates. Their principal residences, and
from which they derived their titles, were Curraghmore, DonIsle, and Kilmeaden. The occupier of the last mentioned place experienced all
the fury of the savage Cromwell, at whose command the castle of Kilmeaden was destroyed, the
lands confiscated and parcelled out amongst the
soldiers, and the unfortunate proprietor instantly
suspended from an adjoining tree. It may be
mentioned here, that this property, which extended from Kilmeaden to Tramore, was divided
among some favourite followers, ignorant and il-
literate men, by whom Cromwell's grant was
afterwards conveyed to a gentleman of the name
of Ottrington. The ancient deed of assignment is
still in existence, bearing the marks of the original grantees, who were unable to subscribe their
names. The new proprietor planted here several
families from Ulster, whose descendants may
still be traced amongst the respectable gentry of
the neighbourhood. In the church of Kilmeaden
is the tomb of John Ottrington, Esq. grandfather
of the Right Honourable Elizabeth, Viscountess

of Doneraile, by whom the present Earl of Doneraile inherits this extensive property.

Having totally exterminated one branch of the
family of Le Poer, Cromwell, leaving his main
body to advance by the most easy road, proceeded
with his dragoons to the residences of the other
members, and having arrived at Curraghmore,
prepared to commence the work of blood.   A cir-
cumstantial account is handed down amongst the
followers of the family, of the means employed to
soothe the bad passions of the invader: the courage and beauty, and ingenuity of a daughter of
the noble owner are still enthusiastically re-
counted : it will be sufficient, however, to state,
that the Lord of Curraghmore preserved his property and his life by an allowable, because an enforced, submission to the savage conqueror, who
was under the necessity of retiring without being
able to satisfy his rapacious followers.   Disappointed of his prey, Cromwell hurried across the
country to DonIsle, and perceiving that resistance
was intended, he waited the approach of a reinforcement of foot soldiers, together with a part of
his artillery, and resolutely prepared to besiege
the place.   The magnificent castle of DonIsle,
still distinguished for its peculiar and romantic
situation, seated on an insulated and lofty rock,
seemed to defy the threats of its assailants.   The
noble owner was a female—confident in support of
her rights, and sustained in the midst of danger,

by the courage and spirit of her race. She is represented as Countess of DonIsle: her coronetted
tomb-stone has recently been discovered in the
adjoining burying-ground. The castle, which is
more particularly described in another place, resisted for a long time the combined force of artillery and storm, but was at length compelled to
yield to the overwhelming numbers of the enemy.
It is to be regretted that we have no well authen-
ticated account of the details of the siege; which,
according to tradition, was replete with interesting and romantic incidents.

Nothing but the absence of historical records
can justify the insertion of the following popular
reports, the favourite theme of the followers of the
family, and by them handed down to the present
generation. It is said that the exertions of the
garrison, stimulated by the zeal and courage of the
Countess, were for a long time successful in re-
pelling every attack of the savage and infuriated
enemy. The Countess was seen in situations of
the greatest danger, animating by her presence
the almost exhausted spirits of the besieged, and
more than sharing the dangers and privations of
the meanest soldier. The honour of the gallant
defence is attributed to a gunner who directed
the artillery of the castle, and who, next to the
owner, held the principal command. Fortune
seemed to favour his exertions. Cromwell, wea-
ried with the length of the contest, was preparing

to retreat, he had already drawn off a part of his forces, and allowed some repose to the anxiety of the garrison. The countess had retired to rest without attending sufficiently to the wants and comforts of the heroic gunner, who, " the fight being done, breathless and faint," sent to request that suitable refreshment might be prepared for him: a drink of buttermilk was the unromantic return for his exertions, which so irritated his gallant spirit that he made signals to the retiring enemy, and, on their re-appearance, surrendered the castle !

Whether Cromwell acquired possession in the manner popularly reported, it is now difficult to determine, but there are indubitable proofs of his remorseless hand in the ruins of the castle and the adjoining church, one-half of which has been carried away by the explosion of gunpowder. —The winter season being now far advanced, Cromwell returned to his army, and proceeded, on the 2d of December, to the village of Kilmactho-mas. The river here was so greatly swollen by the land floods, that the entire following day was consumed in transporting the foot soldiers: this circumstance retarded the advance of the army, which was able to march only a few miles, and was quartered for the night in several small villages. On the morning of the 4th of December, Cromwell proceeded with his usual rapidity, rifling every place of consequence as he moved along, and, like his modern imitator, scattering his cannon shot with an unsparing hand.

Near Clonea many balls have been since found, which, it is supposed, were directed by Cromwell against the castle of Clonkoscoran.

Clonea

On his arrival at Dungarvan, which he reached on the evening of the 4th of December, he regularly invested the place, and while he impatiently awaited the result of his operations, a part of his army was detached to the neighbouring castle of Knockmoan, a place strong in its natural situation, being built upon a high insulated rock, and surrounded on all sides by a deep morass. A few days were sufficient to enable Cromwell to overcome all opposition. Knockmoan was taken by storm, and shortly afterwards Dungarvan surrendered at discretion.

Having ordered the inhabitants to be put to the sword, Cromwell entered the town on horseback, at the head of his troops, and as his merciless soldiers were about to execute his savage command, an incident occurred which deserves to be related. A woman, whose name was Nagle, advanced boldly to him as he was passing along, took his horse by the bridle, and, with a flagon of beer in her hand, drank to the health of the conqueror. This spirited conduct immediately struck Cromwell, who was not insensible to a daring and generous act: he took the cup and drank, and was so pleased with the conduct of the

Dungarvan Tale

female, that he revoked his former order, and not
only spared the lives of the inhabitants, but also
saved the town from being plundered by his
troops—the castle and church excepted.

Two days after the surrender of Dungarvan,
General Jones died there, and was carried to
Youghal, where he was buried with great pomp
in the chapel of the Earl of Cork.   Some circumstances connected with General Jones's death are
considered as strong proofs that poison was ad-
ministered to him by order of Cromwell.   Such
at least was the opinion of the time, and receives
some confirmation from the statement of a Mrs.
Chaplain, in whose house General Jones died;
who frequently declared, that it was confidently
believed he had been poisoned by Cromwell.—
Mrs. Chaplain died in 1730: she was the daughter of Andrew Chaplain, who was minister of the
town during the usurpation.

Cromwell's army, now greatly reduced by the
casualties of war as well as by the numerous de-
tachments which were to garrison the conquered
towns, retired for a short period into winter-
quarters; and being quickly recruited from the
revolted Irish troops, with men enured to the
climate, again commenced the campaign in the
month of February, 1650.

Previous to the commencement of active operations, Cromwell divided his army: one part was
commanded by himself in person, the other was

entrusted to General Ireton. Early in June of this year, Waterford was again besieged. On the approach of General Ireton, on whom the chief command devolved after the departure of Cromwell, Preston, the governor of the city, sent to inform the Lord Lieutenant that if supplies were not immediately forwarded to him, he should be compelled to surrender. The siege was not of long continuance; the garrison were soon reduced to the greatest distress, and must have readily yielded, had they been attacked with vigour, but General Ireton did not summon them to capitulate until the 25th of July, and, after a treaty protracted for a considerable time, the city was surrendered to him by General Preston on the 10th of August, 1650.

The terms granted to the citizens were favourable; their persons and private property were preserved. The violence of the parliamentary army was chiefly directed against the churches, works of art, and remnants of antiquity; even the tombs of the dead were plundered or mutilated by their savage hands, and in cases where they could not plunder, they were contented to destroy. The city of Waterford was, from this period until the year 1656, governed by commissioners appointed by Oliver Cromwell: the accustomed mode of government by mayor and sheriffs was abolished, and in its place was substituted the mere pleasure of the creatures of the usurper. But though not strictly guided by the principles of constitutional law, many public acts passed at this time, evince the wisdom and attention of those in power. The quay, the public buildings, the streets and roads, were all carefully attended to ; even in regard to comparatively unimportant objects there was a minuteness of attention shewn, which is not a little remarkable: this appears in the order to take care of the eight pieces of hangings belonging to the commonwealth, at Preston-House, Waterford.

The cruelty and vigour of Cromwell's administration may be clearly traced in the public records of the time. Courts of justice were held here for the trial of persons concerned in the massacres of 1641; but so many of those to whom this designation applied, had been since destroyed by sword and pestilence, very few remained to perish by the hands of the executioner. *1656*

Ireland was now completely subdued, and the possessions of the ancient proprietors very generally parcelled out amongst the followers of Cromwell. The war of extermination, which had been carried on for some years, was brought to a conclusion; even the principal abettors of this horrible scheme were ashamed of it, and forced to adopt a new expedient to uphold the views of the republican party; this was called the transplantation of the natives, and consisted in plundering them of their properties and expelling them from their homes, under circumstances of the greatest cruelty. The principle upon which this was done, was afterwards followed by other severe enactments: it was ordered, " that no papist be permitted to trade in the city of Waterford, within or without doors." And in the following year an order was issued by the lord deputy and council, " that the governor, Colonel Leigh, and the justices of the peace at Waterford, do apprehend forthwith all persons who resort there, under the name of quakers; that they be shipped away from Waterford or Passage to Bristol, and be committed to the care of that city, or other chief magistrates of that place, or other convenient places to which they are sent, in order to their being sent to their respective places of abode; and that they be required to live soberly and peaceably, and make honest and due provision for themselves and their families, according to their respective callings." We now look back with astonishment at these injudicious and intolerant enactments, prejudicial to the interests, as they were disgraceful to the understandings and hearts of those who adopted them: and while we reflect upon the fortunate results of a more generous and enlightened policy, we may indulge a becoming pride in the improved feeling which has arisen from the experience of little more than a century.

The restoration of Charles II., which was eagerly anticipated as a remedy for all the griev-

ances and miseries of the country, was found to
be destructive to the hopes, perhaps unreason-
ably, entertained by the most anxious well-wishers
of that measure. To effect an arrangement between the plunderers and the plundered, to satisfy
those who were contented and those who were
desirous of a change, was beyond the reach of
human ingenuity, and must have failed had it
been attempted. But it was an undertaking
which had no charms for a government, but
yet imperfectly established, and which was
inclined to sacrifice personal feeling to public
convenience, and to weaken the ties of affection,
rather than irritate the sullenness of discontent.
The collisions of the contending parties demand
our hasty view, only for the purpose of explain-
ing the origin of the enmity which afterwards re-
sulted from them, the effects of which it may be
hereafter necessary to relate. In the important
events which succeeded the restoration of the
family of the Stuarts, and which terminated in
their abandonment of, or expulsion from, the
throne, the magnitude and the general importance of the events have thrown all minor and local
concerns into complete oblivion: the history of
particular places is involved in the general history
of the country, and one cause, and one interest,
is found to have engaged universal and undivided
attention.

We may therefore omit all the circumstances

which preceded and accompanied the revolution, simply narrating the changes and the few remarkable events in which Waterford was particularly concerned. When James II. recalled the charter of Dublin, he proceeded in like manner to dissolve the corporation of Waterford, and to new model it in such a manner as best suited the object which he had in view.

On the 22d of March, 1687, a new charter was granted to the city, and the following persons nominated to fill the vacant places.

RICHARD FITZGERALD, ESQ. Mayor.

24 *Aldermen.*

Rich. Earl of Tyrone	Francis Driver, gent.
Sir S. Rice, chief baron	Richard Madden
Peter Walsh, esq.	Nicholas Porter
Thomas Wise, esq.	James White
Garret Gough, esq.	William Fuller
Thomas Sherlock, esq.	Michael Head
James Sherlock, esq.	Richard Say
Wm. Dobbin, esq.	Nicholas Lee
Nich. Fitzgerald, esq.	Dominick Synott
Thomas Christmas, esq.	Martin Walsh
Edw. Browne, merchant	Abraham Smith
Robert Carew, esq.	Peter Cransburgh

24 *Assistants.*

Tho. Dobbin, merchant | A. Brown, merchant
Patrick Troy, merchant | Tho. White, merchant
Rd. Aylward, merchant | Jos. Hopkins, merchant
Victor Sale, merchant | William Dobbyn, esq
J. Aylward, merchant | Henry Keating
Edw. Collins, merchant | Bartholomew Walsh
M. Sherlock, merchant | James Lynch
S. Leonard, merchant | Patrick Wise
Mat. White, merchant | Richard Morris
Francis Barker | Thomas Smith
Thomas Lee | Joseph Barry
John Winston | John Donnaghow

Sheriffs.

James Strong | Paul Sherlock

John Porter, esq. *Recorder.*

Daniel Mollony, *Town Clerk, Prothonotary, and Clerk of the Peace.*

William III

The triumph of King William terminated the short existence of this charter, which being set aside, the charter of Charles was again resorted to, and remains in force at the present time.

After the battle of the Boyne, the city of Waterford received the unfortunate James, exhausted in mind and in resources. On the day of the engagement he fled to Dublin, and on the following day rode to Waterford, and from thence sailed to France, abandoning his faithful, but unfortunate followers, to the mercy of their enemies, and quitting the dominions of his ancestors in disgrace, and for ever.

Waterford continued faithful to James, even after he had abandoned all claim to the allegiance of the citizens and when there appeared scarcely a chance of his success.   But serious opposition to the arms of the victorious party was fruitless, and therefore on the approach of a part of King William's troops, which marched from Carrick to Waterford, the citizens agreed to surrender, on condition that they should be allowed to enjoy their estates and the liberty of their religion, and that their forces, with their arms and ammunition, should be safely conveyed to the nearest garrison. These terms were refused, and orders given to bring down some heavy cannon and additional troops.   The garrison then asked liberty to march out with their arms, and to have a safe convoy, which was granted them; and they were conducted, with their arms and baggage, to the town of Mallow.   After the surrender of Waterford, King William went to visit it, and having left directions not to permit any unnecessary severity towards the inhabitants, embarked for England on the 5th of September, 1690.

We can easily imagine, that after the violent commotions produced by the rebellion, by Crom-

well's invasion and partition of the country, and
by the important events connected with the Revolution, the great mass of the people could not
quietly settle down into peace and contentment,
satisfied with their relative situations, and neither
devising nor desiring a change; but even now,
things were getting into a better state of adjust-
ment.   The first object of the Roman Catholics
was to obtain a fit place for the exercise of their
religion.   They had been dispossessed of Christ
Church at the Reformation, and were without a
place of public worship, until they obtained permission to assemble in an old building which was
situated opposite to their present chapel.   This
being unfit for the purpose, both in point of size
and accommodation, they petitioned the corporation to be allowed to erect a more suitable building.   Not only was their request acceded to, but
they were assisted in this desirable undertaking,
and a considerable space of ground was allotted
to them for this purpose at merely a nominal rent:
thus proving that, however rancorous the feeling
of enmity might have been at an early period, it
was at length beginning to subside.

But the Roman Catholics at this time (1700)
had still a great deal to contend against.   Such
of the tradesmen and artizans amongst them as
continued to reside in Waterford, were subjected
to many hardships: they were required to pay
what was called quarterage, for permission to

exercise their trade or calling. The persons by whom this tax was exacted were the Protestant tradesmen, who were formed into a regular body; and, from circumstances connected with their mode of levying their contributions, were designated by the familiar title of Hammermen.

During the Assizes, the company of Hammermen paraded through every part of the town, demanding the payment of quarterage from Roman Catholic shopkeepers; and in case of refusal, they signified their displeasure by nailing up the doors and windows of the house belonging to the party so refusing. The following is a copy of a receipt given by the master of the company, as a discharge for one of their illegal demands.

" Memorandum.—It was covenanted by the major part of the company, and likewise entered in the books, that Mr. Paule Keaton should be exempted from paying quarteridge for two years from the date underwritten, he paying forty shillings, which sum he has paid, as witness my hand this 15 day of June, 1704.

" WM. MORGAN, Master."

The early part of this century is remarkable, as having been years of suffering all over Ireland. Landlords were demanding exorbitant rents and large fines, which the people, not being able to pay, thought they were justified in resisting—the more particularly, as they had been deprived of what they had always looked upon as an inalien-

able right—the right of commonage. In addition
to these hardships, the people had to contend
against those occasioned by a deficiency in the
crops; for it happened now, as is too frequently *famine*
the case, that years of disturbance were followed
by years of scarcity.

In 1732 there was a tumultuous assemblage
in Waterford, the object of which was to prevent
the exportation of corn. There was another riot-
ous meeting of the mob in Waterford in 1744,
when Mr. Beverley Usher was mayor: the military
were called out, and several lives were lost.—
Both these riots were occasioned by a scarcity of
provisions. Some years afterwards corn was in
abundance; but, as happened on a recent occasion when England extended a fostering hand to
her brothers in Ireland, the inhabitants of Waterford and other towns were literally starving in the
midst of plenty.

Such being the state of Waterford, at the periods alluded to, it was not to be expected that
the people would remain totally passive specta-
tors of the numerous illegal assemblies which were
forming around them.

It is not the object of this sketch to do more
than merely allude to those societies in which the
misguided inhabitants of Waterford unfortunately
took a part. Some of them might have been, or
might have thought they were, justified in their
proceedings by the circumstances of the times;

but we now look back with regret at the formation of meetings which, however plausible their
arguments, were only calculated to keep up a
spirit of disunion and discontent, and to excite
feelings of ill-will where friendship ought to have
subsisted.

The " Catholic Committee," which was established in the middle of this century, is stated to
have been originally set on foot by a Dr. Curry
and Mr. Wyse, of Waterford. The first meeting
was held in Dublin in the year 1757, when only
seven gentlemen attended: it was not until the
year 1783 that they were formed into the de-
legated body which afterwards so much distinguished itself.

It was also about this period, (1759,) that the
association since so well known by the designation of the " White Boys," from their parading
about the country in white frocks or jackets, the
better to distinguish each other by night, first
made their appearance in the south of Ireland,
spreading insurrection over most parts of Munster. They were also distinguished by the title
of " Levellers," from their levelling such hedges
or ditches as they thought encroached upon commons, the chief support of the poor at that time.
It has been remarked, that they consisted of persons of different persuasions, and were by no
means disaffected to their king. They were succeeded, some years afterwards, by a set of insur-

gents called " Right Boys," who resembled them in every respect, except in the title which they assumed.   They bound· themselves by oath to assist each other, and so strictly did they adhere to this obligation, that one of them being con- demned to be whipped at Carrick-on-Suir, the then sheriff of Waterford could not procure a person to execute the sentence of the law, though he offered a large sum of money for that purpose; but was actually obliged to perform the duty him- self in the presence of an enraged mob.

A circumstance occurred in the year 1767, which it may be proper to notice, as showing the good feeling which was beginning to sub- sist between the Roman Catholics of Ireland and the royal family of England.   On the 20th of December of this year, prayers were publicly read in the Roman Catholic chapels of Waterford, and in the other chapels throughout Ireland, for King George III. and all the royal family, being the first time the royal family of England had been prayed for in this public manner by the Roman Catholics of Ireland since the Revolu- tion.

The year following this was remarkable through- out Ireland as a year of great bustle, occasioned by a general election.   That the city of Waterford was not an exception, may be seen by the follow- ing statement.

It was complained loudly by the citizens that

the freedom of the city had been conferred upon foreigners to the exclusion of those legally entitled to it. One of the gentlemen objected to by the corporation was Sir Joshua Paul, who was then lodging with his mother in a house in Lady-lane, in consequence of which, it was said he was not a resident. The matter was taken up in a very spirited manner by Mr. Shapland Carew, who, not content with merely stating the claims of the citizens, actually brought the question, at his own expense, into the Court of King's Bench, where, after much procrastination, it was at length decided in favour of the citizens.

The following was published in justification of the conduct of our chief magistrate on that occasion.

" An Address from Wm. Alcock, Esq. Mayor, to the Sons, Sons-in-Law, and Apprentices of the Freemen of the City of Waterford.

" Whereas there has been a false, malicious, and insidious report industriously propagated through this city, that I, William Alcock, was the only person of the council, who was determined to oppose the rights of the sons, sons-in-law, and apprentices of the freemen; and that I was resolved to carry on an appeal to England, in order to procrastinate any applications.

" Give me leave solemnly to assure my fellow citizens of Waterford, that nothing prevented me from vindicating myself sooner, but to have the transactions of the King's Bench properly laid before me. This was done last week. I immediately ordered a council to be summoned, which met last Monday, when I had the pleasure to move them in your favour, which occasioned the following resolution:—

"2d of January, 1769.

" Resolved unanimously,—That it is the opinion of this Board, that the sons and sons-in-law of freemen of this city, and also the apprentices of freemen of this city, having performed the usual and accustomed requisites, have a right to the freedom of this city. And that upon their preferring their petitions to this Board, setting forth that they are the sons, or sons-in-law of such freemen, or have served their apprenticehoods to such freemen, and proving the allegations of such petitions, that they shall accordingly be admitted, and sworn free of this city, paying the accustomed fees for such admission.—Now this is to give public notice, to all the sons, sons-in-law, and those who have a right by apprenticehood, to apply; that they give me their petitions as soon as they shall think convenient, in order that I may lay them before the council, to have them admitted to their freedom.

" WILLIAM ALCOCK."

In February, 1775, the citizens of Waterford presented a petition to the House of Commons, setting forth the fatal consequences that would result to that city in particular, and to the kingdom in general, from a continuance of the unhappy differences which then existed between Great Britain and the colonies: they stated, that in such case they would be deprived of the only branch of export which they were permitted to carry on with the colonies, that of their linen manufacture—" a misfortune," they added, " which we have already begun too sensibly to feel."

The year 1778 was a year of general complaint in Ireland, owing principally to the refusal of the English government to remove the restrictions which then so heavily pressed upon this country. In August of the following year, at the Summer assizes for the county of the city of Waterford, the high sheriff, grand juries, and principal inhabitants, met for the purpose of taking into consideration the then ruinous state of the trade and manufactures, and the alarming decline in the value of the staple commodities of the kingdom; and looking upon it as an indispensable duty they owed their country and themselves to restrain, by every means in their power, these growing evils, they came to, and signed the following resolutions :—

" Resolved, That we, our families, and all whom we can influence, shall, from this day, wear and make use of the manufactures of this country; and this country only, until such times as all partial restrictions on our trade, imposed by the

illiberal and contracted policy of our sister kingdom, be removed: but if, in consequence of this
our resolution, the manufacturers (whose interest
we have more immediately under consideration)
should act fraudulently, or combine to impose
upon the public, we shall hold ourselves no longer
bound to countenance and support them.

" Resolved, That we will not deal with any
merchant or shopkeeper who shall, at any time
hereafter, be detected in imposing any foreign
manufacture as the manufacture of this country."

A curious circumstance connected with the
celebration of the battle of the Boyne, occurred
in the city of Waterford. A miserable man, a
blacksmith, who had probably heard from his parents the principal events of the day, made it a
point to celebrate the anniversary with the ut-
most enthusiasm. The day was ushered in by
innumerable explosions from a rusty piece of iron
twisted into the shape of a gun barrel. Orange
lilies in merciless profusion, tied up with what
was intended to represent purple ribands, decorated the scene, when the officiating minister,
who concealed his sooty dress beneath a white
under-garment, received the congratulations of
his friends!

From the eccentricity of his manner, the mob
honoured him with the title of Bold Heart, under
which name he defied the world. In general, the
silly parade was beneath the notice of the people;

and Bold Heart was suffered to shout and shoot during the short remainder of his existence.

Another of those societies, of which Ireland is so fruitful, made its appearance in this part of the country about the period at which we have now arrived. It bore the imposing title of the " United Irishmen." Although their first meeting took place as early as the year 1791, it was not until 1797 that they first made their appearance in the province of Munster. At this period they had increased to a most enormous force—they had a directory for each province; in addition to which they had several newspapers completely under their controul. Every exertion was used by them to seduce the soldiery of the different towns; and so successful were they in this design, that it was at length found necessary by the military to offer rewards for the discovery and prosecution of any persons concerned in it. The following, among other regiments, offered these rewards: the Ninth Dragoons, the First Fencible Cavalry, and the militia of Waterford, Wexford, Kilkenny, and other counties. It has also been stated, that, at the battle of Ross, messengers were on the point of being sent there from Waterford by the treasurers of this society, to summon the people of the south to rise.

We are now arrived at a period (1798) of great importance in the History of Ireland, but which may be alluded to without exciting any angry feelings; for it is a period which no one can think of without regret, and an earnest prayer that such a time may never arrive again.

It is some satisfaction to the inhabitants of Waterford, that so far from their taking a leading part in the rebellion, it may be said they were actually compelled to join in this dreadful conspiracy. Its first appearance in the county of Waterford was in the latter end of the year 1797. It was not headed by any persons of education or fortune: their greatest opponents admit that the Roman Catholic gentlemen of the county remained loyal to the last; and even those of the peasantry who did join, were led away by the fear which prevailed all over Ireland, that the rebels would ultimately be successful. As it was, considering the disaffection which existed in other parts of Ireland, and particularly in the neighbouring county, it is remarkable how few suffered in the county of Waterford.*

It is to be regretted, that in the city the conspiracy assumed a more formidable appearance. There were several meetings of the United Irishmen, who showed great activity on this occasion.

* The amount claimed by the county of Waterford for losses sustained during the rebellion was only £1322 18s. 11d, whilst the claims of the inhabitants of the neighbouring county (Kilkenny) amounted to nearly £28,000, and those of Wexford to upwards of £311,000.

The conspiracy was first discovered by a person who happened to be in a public-house at Johnstown, where, through a thin partition, he overheard a number of conspirators conferring in the next room on the plot which was to be carried into execution on the eruption of the rebellion. The principal persons concerned were, Bohan, a baker, (leader;) Sargent, a publican; a person of the name of Quinn; and Carey, a stone-cutter. Sargent, who kept a public-house in Waterford, where the officers of the yeomanry corps used to sup, had conspired to put them to death. With this object, he signified his intention of giving a farewell supper, which would have afforded him an opportunity of securing their arms, and he was then to let in a party of rebels to complete the remainder of the deed.—The case of Quinn was rather remarkable. He had formerly been in the Artillery, and was now a servant to the Dean of Waterford, (Butson,) and in the greatest confidence of his master, insomuch that he was entrusted with the care of one of the cannon to defend the bridge at Waterford. He was in the habit of holding nightly meetings with the disaffected in the extensive vaults adjoining the deanery, where each communicated such information as had come to his knowledge in the course of the day. Sargent and Quinn were both apprehended, and found guilty of conspiracy; but, through the intercession of friends, they were only sentenced to be transported; and having been sent to New Geneva to wait the arrival of a vessel, were there permitted to effect their escape.

The conspiracy is stated to have been conducted with so much secresy, that a gentleman in Waterford had actually prepared an article in praise of the inhabitants for one of the newspapers, on the very day the conspiracy broke out. Waterford was evidently, at this time, in the most critical situation: there is little doubt that the fate of the city depended upon the success of the rebel army at Ross; and were it not for the gallant conduct of some of the gentlemen of the county on that occasion, the rebels would in all probability have been successful.

The next period deserving of notice in this sketch is, that important measure *the union of the two countries*. Considering that Ireland had suffered so much, it appears singular that so many obstacles should have been thrown in the way of an arrangement which, at all events, must have held out hopes of an amelioration.

The inhabitants of the county and city of Waterford were by no means favourable to the Union. They did not, as in many parts of the country, present a petition against it; but in signing the address to the lord-lieutenant they betrayed a reluctance tantamount to the strongest opposition. Notwithstanding the extraordinary exertions of the advocates of that measure, they failed in obtaining five hundred signatures to the address in favour of it, and many of these, as was afterwards proved by the parties themselves, were forgeries. The Union was also opposed by the representatives of the city in parliament; and so strongly did the Bishop of Waterford object to that arrangement, that he entered his protest against it on the journals of the Irish House of Lords.

The early part of this century brought with it new classes of disturbers, known by the designations of Caravats and Shanavests, who were particularly active in Tipperary, Waterford, and other parts of the south of Ireland. A violent animosity subsisted between these two parties, the cause of which has not been very satisfactorily accounted for; but their actions were similar, so far as assembling in arms by night, administring unlawful oaths, and using every possible exertion for the attainment of their illegal demands. The following extract from a report of a trial which took place before a special commission at Clonmel, in the year 1811, will give the reader some explanation of the names by which these formidable factions were distinguished.

James Slattery examined.

Q. What is the cause of the quarrel between these two parties, the Shanavests and Caravats? —A. I do not know.

Q. Do you know a man of the name of Pauddeen Car?—A. I do.

Q. He is your uncle; was not he the principal ringleader and commander of the army of Shanavests?—A. He is a poor old man, and not able to take command.

Q. (by Lord Norbury) What was the first cause of quarrel?—A. It was the same foolish dispute made about May-poles.

Q. Which is the oldest party?—The Caravats were going on for two years before the Shanavests stirred.

Q. Why were they called Caravats?—A. A man of the name of Hanly was hanged: he was prosecuted by the Shanavests, and Pauddeen Car said he would not leave the place of execution till he saw the *caravat* about the fellow's neck: and from that time they were called Caravats.

Q. For what offence was Hanly hanged?—A. For burning the house of a man who had taken land over his neighbour's head.

Q. Hanly was the leader of the Caravats?—A. Before he was hanged his party was called the Moyle Rangers. The Shanavests were called Pauddeen Car's party.

Q. Why were they called Shanavests?—A. Because they wore old waistcoats.

Considering the very extensive export trade of Waterford during a war of an unusually long continuance, it must not excite surprize that at the conclusion of it, there should be a general stagnation of business, attended by all those hardships and deprivations which an unexpected change from war to peace is sure to bring with it. Amongst other failures, the failure of the principal bank in Waterford, added to the hardships of the times. So firm a footing had this establishment obtained, not only here, but all over the south of Ireland, that its stoppage ruined many, whilst almost every individual in the county suffered in a greater or less degree. Persons were seen flocking from the country with what they had always looked upon as money in their pockets; but who, nevertheless, by this deplorable event, were deprived of the means of purchasing the common necessaries of life.

These clouds which have so long hung over the city, are at length beginning to disperse; and the people of Waterford have now reason to look forward, not only to the attainment of their former advantages over other parts of Ireland, but likewise to others derivable from the increased liberality of the times. The removal of the remainder of the Union duties—as also the establishment of steam packets between this port and Milford, by facilitating the communication between the two countries, will tend very much to the benefit of Waterford. Instead of the difficulty and delay which persons were formerly subject to in visiting this part of the south of Ireland, they may now calculate, almost to a certainty, on performing the journey, from London, in the short space of eight-and-forty hours; and when to this is added the advantages of cheap living, and the tranquillity of the county, which is in nowise affected by the disturbances in the adjoining counties, there can be little danger of disappointment in expecting that Waterford will experience, ere long, that extension of trade and commerce, of which she has proved herself deserving in times of danger and distress.

London to Waterford 48 hours
(2 days)

TOPOGRAPHY AND ANTIQUITIES.

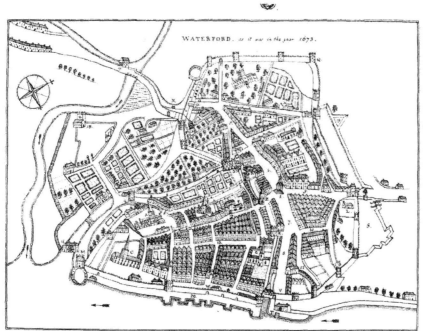

WATERFORD, as it was in the year 1673.

A. Christ Church	I. St. Stephen's Church	R. St. Patrick's Gate	1. The Cross	9. St. Patrick's Street	17. St. John's Mill and Bridge
B. Trinity Church	K. St. Michael's Church	S. St. Patrick's Fort	2. Lady's Gate	10. Little Patrick's Street	18. St. Catherine's Abbey
C. St. Frances's Abbey	L. St. Patrick's Church	T. Barry's Strand Mill	3. The Green Tower	11. St. Stephen's Street	19. The Bolt Works
D. St. Olave's Church	M. The Ring Tower Fort	V. Barry's Strand Gate	4. Colbeck's Gate	12. King's Street	20. The Quay.
E. Lady's Church	N. St. John's Fort and Bridge	W. The Great Quay	5. St. John's Street	13. High Street	
F. St. Peter's Church	O. St. John's Gate	X. Arundell's Castle	6. St. Michael's Street	14. St. Peter's Street	
G. St. Dominick's Abbey	P. Clove Gate	Y. Arundell's Gate	7. Broad Street	15. St. Olave's Street	
H. St. John's Church	Q. The French Tower	Z. The Guild Hall	8. Barry's Strand Street	16. Cole Pit Mill	

London: Published by John Murray, July, 1824.

SECTION I.

—◆—

THE CITY OF WATERFORD

—◆—

WATERFORD is supposed by some, to have been founded in the year 155, by others, and with more probability, in 853. The founder is said to be Sitiracus, one of three brothers, noble Easterlings, who about this time arrived in Ireland. The ancient name of the town was Cuan-na-Grioth, which signifies the harbour of the sun: the inhabitants at that time were Pagans, worshippers of the sun, and it was in honour of their deity, that the town received its primary appellation. There is a tradition still preserved, that on days of solemn worship, the people of the town were wont to march in procession to a high conical hill, in the adjoining county of Kilkenny, where, on its elevated summit, they worshipped and offered sacrifice to their God. The place alluded to is now generally called Tory Hill, but at that time, and even at the present day, it is only known in the Irish language, as the Hill of the Sun.

Another name which Waterford formerly enjoyed, was Portlargi, or the port of the thigh,
from the supposed resemblance which the river at
this place bears to that part of the human body.
In a very ancient history of Waterford, consisting
of only a few pages in duodecimo, the city is said
to have derived this name "from a spring in the
cellar of a house where Mr. Windever lived, in
High Street, which was called Portlargi." There
is no attempt to explain, or account for, this very
unsatisfactory etymology, which must therefore
be left to the conjectures of the curious.

Since the arrival of the English, the city has
been called Waterford, and here again we have
another difficulty to be surmounted, a difficulty
which, it is to be feared, is in this, as in many
other cases of antiquarian research, in the inverse
ratio of the importance. The name of Waterford
is supposed to be derived from a ford in the river,
but to this very simple manner of accounting for
the appellation, it is objected that the ford in the
Suir is at a considerable distance from the place
where the city is built. This objection, however,
may be removed by deriving the name from a ford
in John's river, which runs through the town into
the Suir.

I shall add one other conjecture, which deserves
attention from its ingenuity, as well as from the
respectable authority from which it proceeds.
According to this explication, the present name is

derived from Vader-fiord, which in the Norse
language, signifies a haven dedicated to Vader, a
Scandinavian deity. In the death song of Regner
Lodbrog, in the original Norse, the word Vader-
fiord is mentioned. This ode was translated by
Olaus Wormius, in latin verse: his latin for the
word is Vadræsinus, which is Vaders-haven. Part
of this ode is quoted in Mallett's Northern Antiquities: it may be seen at length in Blair's Dis-
sertation, prefixed to Ossian's Poems. It is reasonable to suppose that the city is indebted both
for its existence and its name to the capacious
harbour near which it is situated, or to the magnificent river, which, until it was confined by the
quay, flowed close to the foundation of the walls.

The Ostmen who founded Waterford, induced
to do so probably by the convenience of the situation for the purposes of commerce, were obliged
to protect their newly acquired dominion from
the violence and envy of the native inhabitants,
and for this purpose very soon encompassed it
with walls and ditches. They appear to have had
four stations for their fleets on the east coast of
Ireland, to which they gave Norse names. These
were celebrated *fiords* or havens, namely, Vader-
fiord (Waterford), Wessfiord or Westhaven (Wexford), Strangfiord (Strangford Bay), and Carlin-
fiord or Carlinshaven (Carlingford). As to Dublin,
the bay was too wide and unsheltered, to be classed
as a fiord or haven. According to the earliest

accounts, Waterford occupied a triangular space, having fortified castles at the angles. There is only one of these castles, a circular building, perfectly plain in its appearance, which still exists in good preservation: it is called Reginald's Tower, from the name of its founder, by whom it was erected in 1003 In some ancient documents, this place is called Dondory, Reynold's Tower, and the Ring Tower; the last is a corruption of the original name. Reginald's Tower, of which a print is annexed, is the oldest castle in Ireland.

The history of this remnant of antiquity is thus briefly summed up, on a tablet recently affixed over the entrance.

In the year 1003, this Tower was erected by Reginald the Dane—in 1171, was held as a Fortress by Strongbow, Earl of Pembroke—in 1463, by statute 3d of Edw. the 4th, a Mint was established here—in 1819, it was re-edified in its original form, and appropriated to the Police Establishment, by the corporate body of the city of Waterford:

Rt. Hon. Sir John Newport, Bart. Mayor.

Henry Alcock,
William Weekes, } Sheriffs.

Reginald's Tower, as appears by the above inscription, has been used for many and various purposes: originally a fortification, mounted with cannon, it was afterwards used as a prison, a royal

Drawn & Etched by W.H.Brooke.

REGINALD'S TOWER.

mint, a depository of public stores, and, more recently, a place of confinement, and a watch-house.
Under the name of Dondory, it was constituted
a royal mint, and is thus represented in several
statutes.

————◆————

It may be permitted here to offer a few observations on the subject of the *Coinage of Waterford.*

That the Danish kings coined money in Ireland
is now past all manner of doubt. The Anglo-
Saxon kings in England had a mint in almost
every town of their respective kingdoms. Whether
the monarch of Ireland only, or each petty king
in his province or territory, assumed the power of
striking money, does not clearly appear; but we
may well suppose that each prince in his kingdom,
in imitation of the Anglo-Saxon kings in England,
struck money of his own.

Simon, in his admirable Essay on Coins, gives
a description of a well-preserved silver coin of
Anlaf, which was in his possession; he was of
opinion that it was ANLAF, one of the Danish
kings of Waterford, for so he read the word
WADTER. which was on the reverse; it weighed
17¾ grains.

We are informed, that at a very early period,
when the communication between different parts
of the country was extremely imperfect, it was
found necessary to establish mints in various other
places besides the chief town or city, for supplying

the neighbouring districts with money for the purposes of trade and commerce. In the Wardrobe account of the 28th year of Edward I. may be seen a variety of charges for the expense of carrying money from one place to another; it was always conveyed on horseback, in baskets or panniers, and accompanied by a guard; according as the communication was opened and became more easy between distant places, the subordinate mints gradually sunk into disuse, and one in the metropolis was ultimately found to be sufficient for the supply of the whole kingdom.

The earliest coins of Waterford, which beyond doubt are known to exist, are those of John, who, while he was Lord of Ireland, enacted laws, granted charters, and coined money,—" Johannes filius regis, de dono patris dominus Hiberniæ, venit in Hiberniam anno ætatis suæ duodecimo." Of his money struck here, we have still preserved silver halfpennies, having on one side his head full-faced, with a diadem, or crown of five pearls, and this inscription, IOHANNES. DOM. (Johannes Dominus)—on the reverse a double cross, with a pellet or annulet in each quarter, and for inscription, the minter's name with that of the city, WILHELM. ON. WA.—ALEXAND. ON. WA. for Waterford. These halfpennies weigh from 10 to 10½ grains, and by wearing have lost from half a grain to one grain of their original weight.

When King John ascended the throne of England, he altered the stamp of his Irish monies, and ordered them to be coined in Ireland of the same weight and fineness as those of England. On his second visit to this country, in the year 1211, he caused pennies, halfpennies, and farthings, to be coined of the same standard as the coin of England, which were to pass equally current in both countries. He is represented on these pennies and halfpennies in a triangle, with his head full-faced, crowned with a crown fleurie, and holding in his right hand a sceptre with a cross fleurie, and having on the left side a rose of four leaves, with this inscription— + IOHANNES · REX—reverse in a similar triangle, a crescent and a blazing star, with three smaller stars in the angles, each point of the triangle terminating in a cross patee, and the like cross on each side above the legend— + WILHELM. ON. WA. The halfpennies are like the pennies, but instead of the blazing star, have a cross with the crescent; the farthings have likewise, on one side, his head full-faced with a crown fleurie, within a triangle, but want the sceptre and the rose, and have a small star in each angle; reverse, the blazing star in a triangle. These pennies weigh from 20 to 21½ grains, the halfpennies from 10 to 10¾ grains.

Edward I. is the next king who is known to have coined money in this city; his pennies and halfpennies have the sovereign's head in a triangle, full-faced, and crowned with a crown

fleurie, but want the sceptre, which from this
time is not seen on the Irish coins, they bear this
inscription— +EDW. R. ANG. D̄N̄S. HYB.—reverse,
the cross and three pellets in each quarter, and
round it CIVITAS WATLRFORD. The best preserved
of these pennies weigh 22 grains, the halfpennies
10 to 10½ grains.

With respect to Edward II. it does not appear
from history, that he coined any money in Ireland.
The pennies supposed to be of this reign, have the
king's head crowned in a triangle, with two dots
under the neck, and this inscription—EDW. R.
ANGL. D̄N̄S. HYB.—reverse, the cross with three
pellets in each quarter, and CIVITAS·WATERFORD—
they weigh full 22 grains.

The next king who coined in Waterford was
Henry VI. During his reign, many parliamentary regulations were made in Ireland relating to
money; but most of these acts, as well as those
of the three former reigns, are lost or destroyed.
His Waterford money has on one side, an escutcheon divided by a cross pommeté into four quarters, viz. 1 and 4, France; 2 and 3, England;
with this inscription—HENRICVS. DI. GRATIA. REX.—
and on the reverse, three open crowns in pale on
the like cross, inscribed CIVITAS·WATERFORD. It
is difficult to ascertain whether these coins were
struck before the year 1460, or subsequently to
1470 during the short time this prince had reas-
sumed the crown, but by the letter H, which is on

all the pieces with the three crowns, one might be induced to believe that they were coined during that short period, as it seems to be a distinguishing mark from those of Edward IV. struck before that time. These pieces weigh from 24 to 29 grains each: their original weight is supposed to have been 30 grains; and they were probably intended for three-penny pieces, though not worth above two pence.

Edward IV. appears to have been the last king that coined in the city of Waterford. We have more records concerning his money struck in Ireland, than we can find either of the preceding or subsequent reigns. In the first year of his reign, he directed that coin should be struck within the castles of Dublin and Trim, and the town of Galway, and this direction was subsequently extended, by act of parliament, to the cities of Waterford and Limerick. An extract from the said act is given in the historical part of this work. The Waterford mint is also noticed in an act for regulating the coinage, passed in a parliament held in Dublin, in the seventh year of this reign.

By an act passed in the fifteenth year of the same reign, all the mints in Ireland were abolished, except those of Dublin, Drogheda and Waterford.

Before the restoration of Charles II. and during the Commonwealth and Cromwell's government, no money was coined for the particular use of Ireland; but many persons in Dublin, and other cities and towns, in order to supply the great scarcity of small change, coined copper tokens, with their names and places of abode stamped on them, whereby they obliged themselves to make them good. All those tokens are made of brass or copper; and like so many promissory notes, were passed for one penny each, in the neighbourhood, and amongst the customers of those who issued them, whose names, together with the value 1ᴰ, and their coat of arms, sign or cipher, were imprinted on their respective pieces: which expedient was often put in practice in the subsequent reigns.

To give a minute description of such of those coins as belong to the city of Waterford, would be superfluous and uninteresting: when we take into consideration the circumstances under which they were coined, we cannot expect to meet with regularity as to size and weight, nor any thing worthy of notice as to execution; generally speaking, they are indeed rude pieces of workmanship, and must be classed below mediocrity.

Of those issued by the corporation we have still preserved some, having the arms of the city, with the words CITY OF WATERFORD, and the date 1658, on one side; on the other, a tower, (by some thought to be a representation of Reginald's tower,) and the words ANDREW RICKARDS, MAYOR. Others, dated in 1656, have a similar inscription for the city, and the name of John Heaven, Mayor.

Others have three gallies on one side, and a tower, (probably one of the city gates,) on the other; the inscription, CORPORATION OF WATERFORD, begins at one side, is continued to, and ends on the other.

Those which were issued by traders, are similar in many respects; the inscription on some extends to both sides, as on the last described, for example, DAVID OWEN OF WATERFORD: on the side which has his name is a device resembling wings;

on the other D $_*^{I\ D}$ O which means one penny, David Owen, 16$_{71}$.

St Martin's castle, which was situated at the western angle of the city walls, is partly preserved by being connected with a private dwelling, long known as the Castle. Turgesius's castle, which stood near the corner of Barron-strand street, is entirely removed, so that its exact site is now unknown.

Besides these castles originally connected with the fortifications of the city, there were other towers and places of strength, erected at the gates to protect them, and in some cases, built to perpetuate the names of private individuals.

These castles and towers are supposed to have been at least twenty in number; the very names of which are now, for the most part, forgotten.

Colbeck Street derives its name from a gate and castle so called, which opened into the church-yard of the cathedral; the entrance at this place was intended as a private way to the bishop's residence and to the church, and from its contiguity to the abbey, was sometimes called St. Catherine's gate. Here was the chamber of Green Cloth, or the chamber of Waterford, some time used as a place of confinement for refractory citizens, when the mayor was in the habit of exercising the ample powers vested in him by the charter. In Peter's Street were two castles, called after their founders, Magnus and Tor, sons of Turgesius. Arundel's castle occupied the present square of that name: here was also a college of the Jesuits, but no traces of these buildings are now visible, with the exception of a small part of the ruins of the Jesuits' college, which may still be seen from the summit of the tower of the Blackfriars.

Some years ago, there were several Danish semilunar towers on the walls of Waterford; but of these, that at the end of what is called the Ramparts, is now the only one remaining. Old John's gate was also Danish.

The Anglo-Normans soon covered the district, called the Pale, with castles; but their castles were all quadrangular.

The abbies and priories in this city were four in number, the abbey of St. Catherine, the priory of St. John, St. Saviour's, and the Franciscan

monastery. The priory of St. Catherine was considered the most ancient religious house in Ireland :
it was founded by the Ostmen, for Augustinian canons of the congregation of St. Victor, but at what
period is not exactly known. That it was built and
endowed previous to the year 1000, may be conjectured from the following circumstance. A dispute
having arisen in the year 1381, respecting ten
acres of land, then in the possession of the abbey,
it was proved that the grant of this land had been
made prior to the statute of Mortmain, which is
supposed to have been in force at least sixty
years before the Norman conquest. This abbey
was endowed by Elias Fitz Norman, in the year
1210, and in the following year, Pope Innocent
the Third took it under his especial protection,
and confirmed to the prior and canons all their
possessions, which he mentions by name. At the
time of the suppression of this monastery, Edward
Poer, who was the last prior, was possessed of
extensive and valuable estates, besides tithes and
advowsons, all of which were granted to Elizabeth
Butler, otherwise Sherlock, for a term of twenty-
one years. This abbey was situated to the south-
west of the city, adjoining Lumbard's Marsh, and
from the grant of Pope Innocent the Third, dated
14th May, 1211, it appears that the ground on
which it stood was then an island. A great part
of the building remained in tolerable preserva-

tion, until a few years since, when a part was demolished, to open a way to a bridge then built over John's river. An arched or vaulted room and a small portion of the foundation are all that now remain.

The Priory of St. John the Evangelist was founded by John, Earl of Morton, who arrived in Waterford in the year 1185, and established this house in the suburbs of the city, for monks of the Order of St. Benedict. In the Charter, by which certain lands were confirmed to this Abbey, the founder called it his alms-house, and made it a cell to the Abbey of St. Peter and St. Paul in Bath. This house received many grants and charters from the English monarchs, and was found at the close of the fifteenth century in possession of vast estates: the court baron within the bounds of the parish of St. John was also attached to this Abbey. Some time before the final suppression of this Monastery, there was found living in it one regular monk, with four sisters and three brothers, commonly called the Brethren and Sisters of St. Leonard; they were removed to other houses, and this Priory was at length entirely forsaken.

The order of Henry VIII. for the suppression of Monasteries was not carried into effect in the case of this Abbey, which retained its possessions until the nineteenth year of the reign of

Elizabeth, at which time this Priory, with the lands of Krydane, Ballymabin, and Lyssent, together with the rectories of Rathmoylan and Killea, the advowsons and presentations of the vicarages and the tithes of every kind of Kilcop, Ballygarron, Ballytruckle and Lumbard's land, together with sundry other possessions, were granted to William Wyse, Esq. and his heirs male, at the annual rent of a Knight's fee. The manor of St. John is still in the possession of this ancient family: there are no traces or records which can assist in discovering the situation of the Abbey.

Friary of St. Saviour.

Dominicans, or Black Friars, called Friars Preachers, being the first of the Mendicant order, were introduced into this city in the year 1226.

The citizens having determined to erect a monastery for their use, applied to King Henry III. who granted his royal approbation that their intended house should be built on a waste piece of ground adjoining Arundel's castle, on which stood the ruins of an ancient tower.

The Order quickly flourished here, and received a portion of an annual allowance granted to the Dominican Friars, established in all the principal towns. King Henry IV. was also a benefactor to the Dominicans of Waterford. This monastery was surrendered on the 2nd of April,

1541, at which time it contained within its site, a church, chancel and belfry, a chapel called our Lady's chapel, a cemetery, close, dormitory, chapter-house, library and hall, and two cellars beneath the same, a kitchen, store and bake-house, a chamber called the little hall, with two cellars beneath it, a chamber called the Doctor's chamber and a cellar adjoining the same, a chamber called the Baron's hall, with three cellars beneath the same, three small gardens, two small chambers, with two cellars beneath them. The building was then in a ruinous state, and considered of no value. It was afterwards granted, together with sundry parcels of land, to James White, in capite, for ever, at the annual rent of four shillings Irish money.

The number of distinct buildings within the precincts of this monastery, independent of the information derived from ancient maps, would be sufficient to prove the great extent of the original establishment. Nothing now remains except the chancel and belfry. The former is only in part preserved: the entrance is through an arched door way, highly ornamented with cut stone rope mouldings, over which is a spacious window. A curious circumstance connected with an inscription over the entrance may be mentioned here. Smith, in his history of Waterford, says, "over the door are those letters, P. E. E. D. I. F. I. E. D."

This is sufficiently perplexing, and no explanation or conjecture is offered. Having had the
stone cleaned, a younger, or perhaps a sharper
eye may clearly perceive that the first letter is
an R—and the inscription therefore signifies,
Re-edified.—(Date illegible.)—There are no stops
after the letters, as Smith has represented them.

The interior apartments, two in number, are
low and gloomy, each having a vaulted roof,
formed by groined arches, terminating in acute
angles, the bases of the arches spring from
large unornamented stones, which project from
the wall. The belfry is a lofty square tower,
having a flight of steps within the massy walls,
leading to the summit, where four bells were
formerly suspended. The view from this place
is commanding, and gives a good idea of the
ancient portion of the town : a small part of
the ruins of the Jesuits' college in Arundel
Square is here distinctly visible.

The burying ground was very extensive; it
lay to the south-west of the building, where its
locality has been distinctly traced, by the bones
and remnants of mortality, which appear in immense quantities on the most superficial removal
of the soil.

Franciscan Friary.

The ancient building in which the Holy Ghost
Hospital and the French Church are now situa-

ted, was formerly a Monastery of Franciscans or Grey Friars, founded in the year 1240, by Sir Hugh Purcell. The Franciscans, Grey Friars, or Friars Minors as they were commonly called, were divided into three classes, of which the first, or the Conventuals, were established in this Friary.

Soon after the foundation of this Monastery, King Henry III. granted the sum of twenty pounds sterling, payable annually on the feast of All Saints, to purchase tunics for the Friars Minors of Waterford, Dublin, Cork, Athlone and Kilkenny. Encouraged and endowed by succeeding monarchs, particularly by Edward I. the Franciscan Friary of Waterford flourished for many years, and at the time of the surrender, 2d April, 1539, was found to contain the following buildings : a church and steeple, recently used as the French Church, a cemetery, over which the present Holy Ghost Hospital is built, a hall, six chambers, a kitchen, two stables, a bakehouse and four cellars. A considerable portion of this venerable pile yet survives the assaults of time and the still more dangerous encroachments of man; but it has latterly been so much neglected, that the remnants of antiquity contained in it are nearly concealed by the falling ruins.

The exterior of this building is disfigured by a shabby modern front, built against the ancient wall, which entirely destroys the antique appearance and gives the idea of a wretched dwelling-house.

On passing a ruinous gateway the ancient entrance appears—a low gothic archway, of cut stone, without any particular ornament. Within appears the church, built in the shape of a cross, and having over the intersection, a lofty square tower, raised upon beautifully turned groined arches : the ogives of the arches, which are accurately cut and highly ornamented, spring from projecting stones at about twenty feet from the ground, and unite together in the crown of the arch, at very acute angles.

Near the entrance is the body of the church, beyond the tower is the chancel; the transepts were appropriated to apartments for the officiating priests. The chancel, for some time used as the French Church, is now unroofed. The eastern window, neatly ornamented with carved stone moulding, is composed of three gothic openings; underneath was the high altar. The body of the church—anciently a spacious building, the roof supported by transverse arches of hewn stone, and terminated by a magnificent gothic arch, over which the tower or steeple was built—is now deprived of all its beauty by the clumsy contrivance of comparatively modern architects, who have thrown a floor across the entire building at about fourteen or fifteen feet above the ground, by which the upper part of the church and cemetery are cut off, and converted into apartments for the use of the poor of the Holy Ghost Hospital.

The antiquary and the grave digger will now alone venture into this gloomy place, where however there are some monuments which deserve examination.

The most ancient, which could be deciphered, is a small and very narrow tombstone, nearly at the foot of the great altar: the centre is highly decorated with coats of arms and emblematical figures, in high relief. Around the stone is this inscription:

Hic jacet Honestissime. Fame. Mulier. Agnes: Lumbard. Quondam uror. Edward Walsh—die Octobris. ÃODṼI. 1570: et A^o. Etatis sue: 76. CVI^o. ÂIE. ET·c.

Nearly under the tower is a highly laboured monument, on which the traces of two figures are discernible, with this inscription:

Hic jacent Johannes Tew, filius . . . . quondam cibis cibitatis Waterford, qui obiit 1597 . . . . ejus uror . . . . 1599.

In the chancel is the tomb of John Skidy, who

was mayor of Waterford in 1635: the inscription is scarcely legible, the side wall projecting over the letters of the names, which are cut on the extreme edge.

𝔥ic jacet 𝕴ohannes 𝔖kydye cibis quondam et 𝔐aior hujus cibitatis 𝔚aterfordiae qui obiit 16 9ber. 1641. et 𝕴ohanna 𝔚hite ejus uxor quae obiit . . . .

The following is in very high pointed letters. 𝔥ic jacent . . . . 𝔗home 𝔐eyler et 𝕴sabella 𝔚alsh religione pe . . . . ac pietate non pauperes. 𝔔uisquis es . . . . . precor ora te. . . . . . obiit 𝔗homas

More interesting than any of the former is the tomb of one of the brave followers of the unfortunate James II. Sir Neal O'Neille, who was wounded at the battle of the Boyne and afterwards accompanied his sovereign to Waterford, where he died. The following inscription, in Roman characters, is on this stone.

HERE LYES THE BODY OF SIR NEAL O'NEILLE BARRONET OF KILLILAG IN THE COUNTY OF ANTRIM, WHO DYED THE 8TH OF JULY, IN THE YEAR 1690, AT THL AGE OF 32 YEARS AND SIX MONTHS. HE MARRIED THE SECOND DAUGHTER OF LORD VISCOUNT MOLYNEUX OF SEFTON IN LANCASHIRE, IN ENGLAND.

In the lower division of all the ancient monuments, are the letters, M R I A, placed in the angles of a cross: the workmanship is extremely smooth and good. Part of the floor was covered with small accurately shaped bricks, some of these, which were found in one of the vaults, appear as if recently made: they are perfectly sound, and their edges are exactly defined—the length is six inches, the breadth two.

Sir Hugh Purcell, the founder of this Monastery, was buried here in 1241, the year after the erection of the building. His tomb is described as having on it, the figure of a man in armour, in high relief, with a shield on his left arm, on which were three lions passant guardant in pale: no inscription. This tomb stood on the right of the high altar, but on the most minute examination at that place and throughout every part of the church, I was unable to discover it.

The Churches in this city are the Cathedral, St. Olave's and St. Patrick's, in which divine service is now performed, and the French Church, recently used as a place of worship for the descendants of the French refugees.

The Churches of St. John, St. Stephen, St. Peter, St. Michael and St. Thomas are in ruins: besides these places of worship, there were, Lady's chapel, Magdalen chapel and Bridget's chapel, of which there are no traces now existing.

The Cathedral.

Before entering on the description of the modern Churches, I shall give an account of the ancient Cathedral, as it is described by Ware, Smith and other writers, together with some historical notices chiefly extracted from a collection of ancient manuscripts, now in the possession of the very Rev. Ussher Lee, Dean of Waterford.

The Cathedral of Waterford, dedicated to the blessed Trinity, was built by the Ostmen, in the year 1096, when they first embraced the Christian religion. About the commencement of the thirteenth century, King John endowed it with lands, and at the same time, it is supposed, its first Dean was appointed. In 1210, Pope Innocent III. confirmed the possessions of the Dean and Canons.

In 1463, King Edward IV. granted to the Dean and Chapter of Waterford, a mortmain license to purchase lands of the yearly value of 100 marks.

A very ancient copy of this document is still in existence, but so defaced and torn as to be scarcely legible: it is written in Latin, in a very small character, and almost all the words are contracted.

It recites that the Dean and Chapter of the Cathedral Church of the Holy Trinity had presented a petition, setting forth that King John

had founded or repaired the said church, in honour of the Holy Trinity, and had endowed it
with possessions, as well spiritual as temporal, of
the value of 400 marks, for the support of twelve
canons and twelve vicars, who were to celebrate
divine service for the welfare of souls, but that
all these possessions had been so wasted or an-
nihilated by Irish and English rebels, that the
four dignitaries, viz. Dean, Præcentor, Chancellor and Treasurer, had nothing to support their
rank and dignity. After this preamble, permission is given to purchase lands of the value of
100 marks. This license is dated, 28th day of
June, third year of his reign. (1463.)

In the fifth year of the same King (1465) an
agreement was entered into between the Dean
and Chapter of the Cathedral and the Mayor,
Bailiffs and citizens of Waterford, from which
it appears that under the mortmain license of
Edward IV. the Corporation had purchased lands,
and now held them in trust for the Dean and
Chapter, and in consideration of retaining them
in possession, they covenanted to pay annually a
certain sum to the Dean and Chapter, which was
to be allowed them in their accounts delivered
into the King's Exchequer. The Dean and Chapter also covenanted not to demand the payment
of the original sum, so long as the annual pay-
ments were regularly discharged. This original

document is written in court hand, and has attached to it what appears to be the seal of the Corporation, a clumsy circular piece of wax, of which
a representation is annexed.

According to the terms of the original grants,
which were called the foundation of the property
of the cathedral, the Dean and Chapter were
restricted from letting their lands for a term of
years, and were in consequence subject to much
serious inconvenience. To remedy this evil, the
Dean and Chapter petitioned the Mayor, Bailiffs
and citizens assembled in Dearn Hundred, setting
forth the decay of God's divine service in St.
James's Chapel and in the Cathedral Church. It
was therefore resolved by the whole council in
the Dearn Hundred, "to the laud of God and the
Apostle St. James, and for the augmentation of
divine service in the said church," that the Dean

and Chapter should be permitted to grant leases for a term of sixty years.

This was done in the year 1535. From a consideration of many of these grants and agreements it appears, that the corporation had some sort of controul over the property of the cathedral, and were themselves accountable to the Dean and Chapter for rents arising out of lands and houses held under them.

The important changes connected with the reformation are very imperfectly handed down to us: the new liturgy was generally introduced in 1551, and at the same time the altars were every where abolished; a community of agreement, which Hume insinuates is mainly to be attributed to the desire of plunder. Commissioners were appointed to enforce the act, and to accommodate the appearance of the Churches and the forms of worship to the newly introduced regulations of the Reformers. These matters are not clearly recorded; it is, however, known that a vast quantity of valuable property was taken by the Commissioners appointed by Government to remove the relics and ornaments, with which the Churches were then crowded, and much of the wealth so taken was appropriated to the use of the Commissioners themselves. It was perhaps to guard against any such plunder of the property still left to the Church, the use of which was not allowed, that an agreement to the following effect was entered into, in the year 1577, between the members of the Cathedral and the Corporation. The Dean and Chapter gave to the Mayor, Sheriffs and citizens, and to their successors, the parcels following, viz. two candlesticks of silver gilt, weighing fourscore ounces, a cross of silver, double gilt, weighing 126 ounces, two candlesticks, of silver gilt, weighing 105 ounces, a standing cup of silver, double gilt, weighing 28 ounces, a cross of silver, double gilt, weighing 49 ounces, five censers of silver, whereof two are partly gilt, weighing 211 ounces, a monstrant with two angels of silver gilt, weighing 49 ounces, and other articles of the same description, amounting altogether to seven hundred, fourscore and seven ounces, at the rate of five shillings the ounce.

In return for this, the Mayor, Sheriffs and citizens of Waterford and their successors were bound to the Dean and Chapter in the sum of £400, the condition of which obligation was, that if the Dean and Chapter should be impleaded for the Church rights or lands, the Corporation should, from time to time, give them so much of the value of the jewels as should sustain their pleas at law. And if the Dean and Chapter should afterwards purchase any living for the use and maintenance of the Church, the Corporation should give them so much as remained in their hands. It was also conditioned, that if at any future time, the like jewels were allowed to be used in the Church, then the Corporation should purchase jewels of the same kind, equal in value to the sum remaining undisbursed. There was much contention afterwards respecting these jewels, as they were called; the value of which the Corporation refused to return, and a law-suit was instituted by the Bishop of the Diocess on behalf of the Dean and Chapter. At length— as appears from an order of council, an original document, signed by the Lord Lieutenant and some of the members of the privy council, and dated 25 May, 1637—judgment was given against the Mayor and Sheriffs, who were ordered to purchase for the use of the Church seven hundred, fourscore and four ounces of plate, it not having appeared that they had disbursed any part of the amount. A postscript to this order is directed to Richard Butler, Esq. Mayor, requiring him to restore certain copes and vestments, which it is alleged he had in his custody.

The Dean and Chapter were subsequently allowed to sell a part of this plate, to enable them to purchase tithes of the value of £30 per annum for repairing the choir. In November of the same year, (1637,) an agreement was entered into between the Dean and Chapter and the members of the Corporation, whereby the latter bound themselves to repair the Church, in consideration of the citizens having permission to bury within the walls of the Cathedral, without being required to pay any duties, save twelve-pence to the minister, six-pence to the clerk, and twelve-pence to the sexton. This agreement was approved and confirmed by the Lord Lieutenant and Council, dated the 29th December, 1637.

The events connected with the rebellion and wars of 1641, emphatically called, the troubles, are next to be noticed. It appears that the estates and moveable property of the Cathedral were entirely plundered by the enemies, and perhaps by the professed friends, of the establishment, who took advantage of the disordered state of affairs, at, and subsequent to this time, to appropriate the wealth of public bodies to private or personal uses. In consequence of the loss of agreements, leases, and other documents, the disputes which previously existed between the Dean and Chapter and the Corporation were again revived, and we learn from a petition dated 12th October, 1646, which sets forth the exhausted finances of the Cathedral, that the Mayor, council, and commons of the city of Waterford had refused to contribute to the repairs of the Church, to pay the Organist and to satisfy the annuity of ten pounds per annum, which, in consequence of the disturbances and also the poverty of the Corporation, had not been demanded since the year 1641. This is an important document, and from the course of proceeding adopted concerning it, will serve to show the degree of control exercised by the citizens over the public acts of the Corporation. At the foot of the petition we find this note.

> "Michaelmas Dernhundred,"
> " 12 Octobris, 1646,"
> "The contents hereof for soe " much as concerneth the Dignitaries and Orga- " nist are referred to the common Auditors to be " by them finally settled."
> " Per ord. Dernhundred,"
> " Nic : Lee."

In compliance with this order, the common Auditors reported, that the Corporation were indebted to the Dean and Chapter in the sum of £48: 9 : 10¾ which sum they ordered the Corporation to pay; and they also found that the Corporation ought to pay the Organist five pounds sterling, per annum, on account of a lot of ground held by them under the Dean and Chapter.

Upon the receipt of this report signed by the common Auditors, an order on the Treasurer, dated 28th September, 1649, for the payment of the money due, was signed by the Mayor, John Walsh, and Thomas Porter, Recorder.

Immediately after this, the Cathedral experienced new calamities in the revolutionary wars: the conduct of Cromwell, and of those under his authority, was particularly reprobated; they pursued the Church with the most unrelenting hatred, and plundered or spoiled whatever came within their reach. In a parchment roll of depositions, taken before Commissioners in Dublin, a variety of articles are enumerated, said to have been taken from the Cathedral in the year 1651, when the city was surrendered to General Ireton. Amongst the property which appears to have been most regretted, are the brazen ornaments of the tombs, grave stones and altars; the great standing pelican to support the Bible, the brazen eagle, two great standing candlesticks above man's height, and the great font of brass, to be ascended unto by three degrees, or stairs of massy brass, together with sundry gold and silver gilt vessels, the forms of which are minutely described.

The members of the Cathedral were loud and persevering in their complaints, as well as in seeking redress and the restoration of their rights; and there are numberless documents which show that their claims met with the most prompt and anxious attention from the government of the restored monarch. Commissioners were appointed to investigate the several claims, and on their reports the Sheriffs of the Counties were directed, by an order of the Lords spiritual and temporal in Parliament assembled, to restore to the Church all such possessions and lands as she was actually possessed of in the years 1640 and 1641, and whereof she had not been since ousted by due course of law. Some portion of the property of the Cathedral was thus recovered, but, in consequence of the loss of title deeds and other instruments, much inconvenience and confusion still prevailed. The repairs of the Cathedral were a fruitful source of contention; many petitions and orders of Council attest the persevering industry of the Church, and the tardy compliance of the Corporation. In a petition to the Lord Lieutenant and Council, the Corporation, endeavouring to excuse their neglect of two previous orders, set forth their great poverty, and after mentioning the scarcity of timber, a sufficient supply of which, it is stated, could not be procured in Ireland to accomplish the work, they solicit a reasonable delay before they shall be called on to comply with the last order. The question was at length set at rest by an order of the Earl of Essex, Lord Deputy, and Council, to the Mayor of Waterford, requiring the Corporation to contribute to the repairs of the Church. The original document is still preserved, and bears date 5th November, 1679.—It appears that the Corporation were to contribute two-thirds to the repairs and alteration of the Cathedral, the Chapter paying the remainder.

Having now brought down the history of the Cathedral to the period when its extent and appearance are most accurately represented, it will be necessary to introduce a description of the building. Like many of the ancient structures, which were added to and altered as convenience or bad taste suggested, the old Cathedral of Waterford was disfigured by a confused mass of buildings, attached to the original pile without regard to simplicity or unity of appearance. The three engravings of this Cathedral in Ware's Antiquities should be referred to, in order to enable us to understand the following description.

The Church consisted of a large nave, 45 feet long and 66 feet in breadth, the choir, 66 feet long, and two lateral isles. The roof was supported by large gothic columns and arches. Besides this which was the original building, there was at the back of the altar, Trinity Parish Church: on the south side of this church was the Vestry or chapel of St. Nicholas. On the south side of the nave was the bishop's consistory court, or St. Saviour's chapel; and on the north side, a chapel twenty-two feet square was erected in the year 1482, by James Rice, a citizen of Waterford, and was dedicated to St. James the elder, and the virgin St. Catherine. In the manuscript papers of the cathedral, this chapel is called St. James's, but it was more generally named Rice's chapel. Upon one of the gothic columns was an ancient monument, made of stucco or plaster of Paris, and very well executed. In the centre, a person on his knees in a praying posture, and on each side, a pillar of the Persic-or Caryatic order, on which were figures representing Truth and Piety. Underneath was the following inscription.

"Domine secundum actum meum noli me "judicare, nihil dignum in conspectu tuo egi."

Nobilis hic situs est Guilhelmus Clusius, ille
   Mercator fidus, cui Patria alma Brugæ
Cecropius, Cimonq; Cudonq; Corinthius alter
   Pectore munifico tum pietate pari.
Nec minor is Crœso, Mida, Crassove beatus
   Divitiis, placidus indole Plebicola.
   Obiit Waterfordæ Hiberniæ. MD.XLV.

Beneath this, the following verses, placed in two columns.

La Noble Renomee
Du mortel sans remoit
D'Art vive et animee
Triumphe de la Mort.

Le Noble de Le scluse
Jadis contre le tans
D'honneur, et grace infuse
Arma ses heurs et an's.

Je dis L'humain en somme
Periclitant c'a bas
Qui le sien Corp's consomme
Aux immortel's es bas.

Courtois et magnifique
Fut autant que Cimon
Clement et pacifique
Cent fois plus que Cydon.

Bruges ville Flandrine
. . . . more
. . . . peine
. . . .. faites decore.

De son hereuse race
A laisse un rameau
Qui Amplecte et embrasse
Virtu d'un Sainct Cerveau.

Au Temple de Memoire	Anvers, jout pour l'heure
Appendu est son nom	De ses pallons heureus
Bruges das rememoire	Illustrateurs J'asseure
A tout heur son renom.	De leurs noms vertueus.
Bruges crie et lamente	Le Ciel inaccessible
Apres son Citadin	Nous rechante hautement
Waterford s'en augmente	Del lencluse paisible
Daviour faict tel Butin.	Son duten Sautement.

This monument was much defaced by some of Cromwell's soldiers. In a niche in the south wall of the choir, is a tomb of one of the Bishops of Waterford, having the effigy of a bishop in his rochet, with a pastoral staff in his left hand, curiously cut in alto relievo.

The following words were legible.

Hic jacet Reverendus in Christo Dominus Richardus Anckel,—— Waterfordiensis Episcopus, qui obiit VII. die Maij Anno Dom. M.CCCCXLVI. cujus Animae propitietur Deus. Amen.

On a flat stone, near the east end of the cathedral, adorned with coats of arms, the cross and some other figures in basso relievo, are these words round the margin,

Hic jacet Franciscus Lumbard filius Nicolai quondam civis Civitatis Waterfordiae, qui in florido 33 anno aetatis obiit A. D. 1590, et 25 die Mensis Januarij.

𝕰𝔱 Katerina Walshe 𝔲𝔯𝔬𝔯 𝔢𝔧𝔲𝔰, 𝔔𝔲𝔬𝔯𝔲𝔪 𝔄𝔫𝔦𝔪𝔞𝔟𝔲𝔰 propitietu. 𝔇𝔢𝔲𝔰. 𝔄𝔪𝔢𝔫.

In the middle, on each side of the cross:

𝔏𝔲𝔪𝔟𝔞𝔯𝔡 𝔚𝔞𝔩𝔰𝔥𝔢.

On a flat stone in the chancel, adorned with the cross:

𝔥𝔦𝔠 𝔧𝔞𝔠𝔢𝔫𝔱 Patricius Whyte, 𝔣𝔦𝔩𝔦𝔲𝔰 Johannis, 𝔮𝔲𝔬𝔫𝔡𝔞𝔪 𝔠𝔦𝔟𝔦𝔰 𝔠𝔦𝔟𝔦𝔱𝔞𝔱𝔦𝔰 Waterfordiæ, 𝔮𝔲𝔦 𝔬𝔟𝔦𝔦𝔱, 𝔢𝔱 Anastacia Grant, 𝔢𝔧𝔲𝔰 𝔲𝔯𝔬𝔯, 𝔮𝔲𝔞𝔢 𝔬𝔟𝔦𝔦𝔱 ᐧ 𝔡𝔦𝔢 𝔐𝔢𝔫𝔰𝔦𝔰 𝔒𝔠𝔱𝔬𝔟𝔯𝔦𝔰, A. D. 1592.

On a copper plate fixed on the outside of the south wall, was this inscription.

Heic inter utramque Columnam Depositum
DANIELIS BURSTON, S. T. D.
Miseri
Peccatoris, et quondam hujus Ecclesiæ Cathedralis
Decani indignissimi, latet in spe Resurrectionis.
Tu qui Primitiæ es, Phosphore, redde diem
Tumulatus fuit octavo die mensis Decembris anno
Salutis humanæ, Millesimo Sexcentesimo
Septuagesimo octavo. Epitaphium hoc
ipse sibi dictavit vivus,
Atque hâc Tabulâ æneâ insculpendum; quam
Tabulam huc loci ponendam jussit. Cujus
mandato obsequentes
Tres ejus Executores eandem sic poni curaverunt.

These and many other ancient monuments pe-

rished beneath the hands of the gothic destroyers
of the ancient cathedral, and it is said, were cast
into a vault beneath the communion table of the
present church: the relics of antiquity which
were preserved, will be noticed hereafter.

At a meeting of a committee appointed by
the council of the corporation, held on the fourteenth of July, 1773, and assisted by the Bishop
of Waterford, and the Dean and Chapter, it was
resolved, that the old Cathedral Church should
be taken down and a new one built in its place.

The sum proposed to be expended was £4000;
the actual expense, including £150 for pulling
down the old building, was £5397, defrayed by the
Corporation, by the tithes of Cahir, the sale of
pews, and by private subscriptions.   The new
church was fit for service, though not completed
in 1779.

It is a matter of sincere regret to many who
recollect the ancient edifice, that the profane
hands of the last generation should have violated
this beautiful remnant of antiquity.   It was stated, as a plea for destroying the old building,
that it was become so much decayed, as to be
judged unsafe for the purposes of public worship; but there is some reason to doubt the correctness of this opinion, not only from the acknowledged strength of all the ancient churches,
but also from the extreme difficulty which the
workmen experienced in effecting its demolition.

From the ruins of the old cathedral, and with much of the same materials, arose the present building, without even the slightest resemblance to that which preceded it: the gloomy aisles, the gothic arches and pointed windows are replaced by the light and vivid beauties of modern architecture. The present church is capable of containing about eleven hundred persons. it is a light and beautiful building, entirely in the modern style: the aisles are divided by a double row of columns, which support the galleries on each side. The length of the body of the church is ninety feet; the height forty ; total length one hundred and seventy feet, breadth fifty-eight feet.

A portion of the western extremity of the building is appropriated to the grand entrance, on each side of which are the vestry and the consistorial court: over these are apartments for a library, and from this part of the building rises a steeple of considerable elevation, neatly formed and decorated, but extremely faulty in its proportions. Between the western end and the body of the church, is a lofty and spacious porch, in which are preserved some of the monuments of the old cathedral.

Adjoining the consistorial court, is the monument of Doctor Nathaniel Foy, Bishop of Waterford and Lismore.

Near this, on a very neat monument, a child is represented weeping over a female figure: both are executed in statuary marble; underneath is the following :

TO THE MEMORY OF MRS. SUSANNAH MASON,

DAUGHTER OF SIR JOHN MASON, KNT.

AFTER A LIFE OF EXEMPLARY PIETY, SHE DIED

AUGUST, MDCCLII, AGED LXV.

At this fair shrine let not a tear be shed
Till Piety and Charity are dead,
Nor let the great and good her loss deplore
While they pursue the path she trod before;
But should her bright example cease to shine,
Grieve then ye righteous, and ye poor repine.
No ostentatious hand this marble placed,
No flatt'ring pen the just encomium traced;
Such virtues to transmit, is only giving
Praise to the dead, to edify the living.

A monument which was erected in the old cathedral, in 1747, to the respectable family of Morris, is placed in the porch.

Adjoining it, is the monument of the May family, also taken from the old cathedral, where it was erected in 1686.

On the right hand, is a very splendid monument, erected by the family of the Fitzgeralds. In the front is a statue of Time, an inverted, broken hour glass in one hand, and in the other, a scythe. Piety, veiled, is bending over a medallion of the persons to whose memory the monu-

ment was erected. Over these statues are the
Fitzgerald arms, with palm branches and oak
leaves depending. The figures, which are in
Italian statuary marble, are represented standing
upon a tomb, over which is a pall, having on it
the following inscription—

IN THE YEAR 1770,

THIS MONUMENT WAS ERECTED TO THE MEMORY
OF NICHOLAS FITZGERALD, LATE OF KING'S MEADOW,
ESQ. DECEASED, AND OF JOHN FITZGERALD, LATE OF
THE CITY OF LONDON, ESQ. DECEASED, PURSUANT TO
THE LAST WILL AND TESTAMENT OF RICHARD FITZ-
GERALD, LATE OF THE CITY OF WESTMINSTER, ESQ.
DECEASED, THE ELDEST SON OF THE SAID NICHOLAS,
AND NEPHEW OF THE SAID JOHN FITZGERALD.

THE RIGHT HON. HARVEY LORD
   VISCOUNT MOUNT MORRES,
SHAPLAND CAREW, ESQ.
EDWARD WOODCOCK, ESQ. AND
THE REV. EDWARD WOODCOCK,
   CLERK.
} TRUSTEES.

The words CROM A BOO were originally
placed at the head of this monument, but have
since been removed.

A tablet, inscribed with the names of many
members of the family of Denis, one of whom
died in 1681, has been lately re-erected within
the present church. This monument was taken

down when, the old cathedral was demolished, and has been since carefully preserved by the representatives of the family.

Opposite the door of the vestry is a very plain flag, bearing the following inscription, written by the Rev. Arthur Stanhope, Dean of Waterford.

VIATOR
SISTE GRADUM PAULISPER.

TUA ENIM MAXIME INTERERIT NOSSE CUJUS SUB HOC

MARMORE

OBSEQUUNTUR RELIQUIÆ;

NEMPE EJUS SUNT, QUÆ, DUM VIXIT, FUIT

ELIZABETHA CHRISTMAS,

FŒMINA LECTISSIMA,

UXOR CASTISSIMA,

MATER PIISSIMA,

CONSORS JUCUNDISSIMA

QUINTUPLICI EO NOMINE SATIS UBIQUE NOTA

SCILICET HANC HABUIT UXOREM THOMAS CHRISTMAS,

DE CIVITATE WATERFORDIÆ

MERCATOR, DUDUM PRÆTOR, ET ETIAMNUM SENATOR

URBANUS.

FŒLICIOREM HUNC, QUOD TALEM NACTUS SIT

UXOREM, AN MISERIOREM, QUOD AMISERIT,

HAUD FACILE DIXERIS;

NISI QUOD EO NOMINE FŒLIX MERITÒ SIT DICENDUS,

QUOD TALEM NACTUS, NUMEROSAM EX EADEM

SUSCEPERIT PROLEM,

QUIPPE EX UTRIUSQUE FŒLICI COPULA, LIBERORUM
TERNÆ TRIADES, BINÆ FILIORUM, NIMIRUM,
RICHARDUS, JACOBUS, JOHANNES, CAROLUS,
GULIELMUS, JOSEPHUS.
ALTERA TRIAS FILIARUM, NEMPE MARIA, ELIZABETHA,
MARGARETA EMANARUNT.
NOVEM HOS CHARISSIMOS LIBEROS, SIBI SUPERSTITES,
MATER RELIQUIT MORIENS, QUOS, EADEM
QUA PEPERERAT, EOS SOLICITUDINE CURATOS
MARITO SUO MORITURA QUASI
COMMENDAVIT OBNIXE, SCILICET,

UT IS JAM QUASI UTRIUSQUE SEXUS PARENS FACTUS,
CONDUPLICATO
AMORE QUA MATERNO, QUA PATERNO, SINGULOS
USQUE
COMPLECTERETUR, FOVERET, SUSTENTARET, EDUCARET,
PUERPERA FATIS CESSURA, SIC (EXISTIMES) EAM
MARITUM SUUM ALLOCUTAM
EN (CHARISSIME) ULTIMUM NOSTRI FIDELISSIMI,
ATQUE CASTISSIMI AMORIS PIGNUS
QUOD TIBI JAM EDIDI.
ET SIC EDIDIT, ET SIC OBIIT
ANNO ÆTATIS SUÆ, ULTRA TRIGESIMUM, SEPTIMO,
MENSIS FEBRUARIJ DIE VIGESIMO SECUNDO, ET
SALUTIS HUMANÆ INSTAURATÆ ANNO MILLESIMO
SEXCENTESIMO SEPTUAGESIMO SEPTIMO.
HIC CUM TU (LECTOR) RESCIERIS, SICCIS (SI POTES)
OCULIS, HINC ABEAS LICET.

These are the only ancient monuments within the walls of the cathedral; but there are two in the church yard, at the eastern extremity, which to the antiquary are more valuable than all the others: they are exposed to the weather, and are decaying rapidly.

One is the monument of James Rice, who was mayor of Waterford, in 1469. This tomb was originally placed in the chapel which he founded, and from thence was removed into the body of the cathedral: it was afterwards erected in the burying ground, outside the church. On this monument, the effigy of Rice, in high relief, is represented lying on his back, having a shroud tied in a knot, at the head and feet; vermin resembling frogs and toads, are cut in the stone, as it were creeping out of his body. The following inscription, in the gothic character, runs round the figure.

Hic jacet Jacobus Rice, quondam civis
    istius Civitatis, et mandato istius
Sepelitur Katerina Broun, uxor ejus.
    Quisquis eris, qui transieris, sta,
Perlegenda plora, sum quod eris, fuique quod
    es, pro me precor ora. Est nostrae sortis
transire per ostia mortis, Nostri
    Christe, te petimus miserere, quaesumus,
qui venisti redimere perditos, noli damnare
    redemptos.

Figures of saints are represented round the sides of the tomb with the names over each.

The other tomb, placed in the corresponding angle made by the projection of the eastern extremity of the cathedral, was formerly supposed to have belonged to Strongbow. On this monument, the figure of a man in armour is represented lying on his back: there is no date or inscription, or any thing else to discover the name or quality of the person. It has been said, that these two monuments belonged to the same individual, who directed that at his decease his body should be represented as it then appeared, and that it should be again described on another tomb-stone, according to the appearance which it exhibited after the lapse of a year. This strange fancy, it has been supposed, will account for the representation of vermin and decay, which has so long perplexed antiquarians.

Among the recently erected memorials may be noticed the monument of Doctor Joseph Stock, bishop of this diocess, who died in the year 1813. In the body of the church, over a pew in one of the galleries, is a neat tablet in white marble, on which is represented a figure bending over a funeral urn. Underneath is the following inscription.

1813.

HIC SITUS EST

JOSEPHUS STOCK

EPISCOPUS WATERFORDIENSIS.

INTER PRIMORES ECCLESIÆ EVECTUS DIGNITATEM
MERITAM EMERUIT. FACULTATES EPISCOPALES SUMMO
ANIMI FERVORE SANCTISSIME ASSERVAVIT. RELIGI-
ONIS CULTOR VERAX, PIUS: PAUPERUM INOPIÆ SUBVE-
NIRE ENIXE PROPERABAT. ERUDITIONE IMBUTUS AD
MEDULLAM, THEOLOGIAM PERCALLUIT LINGUIS QUAM
PLURIMIS PRECIPUE QUÆ AD STUDIUM SACRÆ SCRIP-
TURÆ PERTINENT, INSTRUCTUS. TOTAM FERE PERA-
GRAVIT EUROPAM, UBIQUE FLORES VIRTUTUM DECER-
PENS, HINC AMŒNITATEM ET EXCULTAM CONVICTUS
ELEGANTIAM DERIVAVIT TANTA FESTIVITATE LEPORIS
PRÆDITUS, SOCIETATEM SIBI DEVINXIT: MORUM SIMUL
SIMPLICISSIMUS NUNQUAM DEI AUT AMICI OBLITUS
EST.

VITA ETERNA FRUATUR.

THIS SMALL MEMORIAL IS ERECTED BY HIS
AFFECTIONATE WIFE
MARY STOCK.

Another tablet of recent erection, within the
body of the church, is thus inscribed :

THIS MONUMENTAL TABLET IS DEDICATED BY CONJU-
GAL AFFECTION TO PERPETUATE THE MEMORY OF
JANE MORRIS WALL,

L

WIFE OF GEORGE MORRIS WALL, ESQ.

WHO DEPARTED THIS LIFE ON

THE 5TH OF OCTOBER,

1822.

AS A CHRISTIAN,

PIETY, FAITH AND RESIGNATION

ADDED LUSTRE TO HER

VIRTUE;

AS A WIFE, MOTHER AND FRIEND,

LOVE, AFFECTION AND SINCERITY

DICTATED HER CONDUCT.

The present church is a light and beautiful building, entirely in the modern style. The aisles are divided by a double row of columns, which support the galleries on each side. The length of the body of the church is ninety feet—the height forty feet. Total length of the church, one hundred and seventy feet. Breadth fifty-eight feet.

This church was nearly consumed by an accidental fire, occasioned by the neglect of some persons who were employed to attend a stove placed in the organ loft, for the purpose of airing it.

Happily the conflagration burst out early in the evening of a calm day, when after much difficulty it was extinguished, having however previously destroyed the beautiful ceiling, and much of the wood work of the church; and totally consumed a magnificent organ, the gift of the late Dean Harman, which, thirty-five years before, cost twelve hundred guineas. The fire occurred on the 25th October, 1815. At much expense the cathedral was restored to its original beauty, and had service performed in it on the 10th of May, 1818.

St. Olave's Church.

The church of St. Olave is in the immediate neighbourhood of the cathedral, to which it was probably intended to serve as a parish church: the date of its erection is not exactly known, but it is represented as having been in a ruinous state, at the commencement of the last century. It was shortly afterwards, almost entirely rebuilt, at the expense of the bishop of the diocess. A brass plate, at the western extremity of the church, has this inscription.

THAT THE INHABITANTS OF THE CITY OF WATERFORD MIGHT HAVE A CONVENIENT AND DECENT PLACE TO OFFER UP THEIR MORNING AND EVENING DEVOTIONS TO GOD, THIS CHURCH WAS RE-BUILT AND CONSECRATED ON THE 29TH DAY OF JULY, 1734, BY THOMAS MILLES, S. T. P. BISHOP OF WATERFORD AND LISMORE.

There is little worthy of particular notice in this building. Over the entrance the following inscription is cut in stone.

TEMPLUM HOC

Sᵗᵒ OLAVO REGI AC MARTYRI

DICATUM, RE.EDIFICAVIT A. D. MDCCXXXIII

THOMAS MILLES, S. T. P. EPISCOPUS WATERFORD.

QUI ETIAM CURAVIT UT ECCLESIÆ Sᵀᴵ· PATRICII

WATERFORD, DRUMCANON, KILOTERAN, RATHRONAN,

ARDFINANE, & KINSALEBEG,

REFICERENTUR.

ACCEPI LATERITIAM, RELIQUI MARMOREAM.

The pulpit and bishop's throne are of very fine black oak, chastely and handsomely carved.

Divine service is performed here twice every day, at hours intended to accommodate those whose time is for the most part occupied by daily labour.   Besides the money expended in repairing the church of St. Olave, Bishop Milles bequeathed £266 : 13 : 4, the interest of which was to be paid to a Lecturer of St. Olave's and St. Patrick's churches

The corporation, with whom this money was placed at interest, amply fulfilled the intention of the donor, by granting an allowance of one hundred pounds per annum to the Lecturer of St. Olave's, who is also master of the endowed school. The same benevolent prelate, in anticipation of an income left by Bishop Gore, but which did not come into his hands until 1723, had expended £1177: 15: 5, of his own, in repairing and building churches throughout the diocess: this last sum was left to his heirs, if it should be received out of the funds appropriated to this purpose.

The Church of St. Patrick is situated on elevated ground, to the westward of the city. It is a plain building, with a single roof, supported without the aid of pillars: the appearance is more modern than that of St. Olave's, though both these churches are mentioned in the year 1600.

In the churches of St. Patrick and St. Olave, there are no private pews: each of these buildings is capable of accommodating about 500 persons.

The French Church, of which some description has already been given, is situated in a part of the ancient Franciscan Monastery.

In addition to the inscriptions given in the account of that monastery, there are several others of an early date. The most curious of these is one in church text, cut on one extremity of a small stone on the *eastern* side of the French Church. As far as it can be deciphered, it is as follows:

Patritius tumulo
latet hoc cognomine
mobl ... .
corpora terra premit
spiritus astra petit.

The two following are also on the eastern side
of the tower·

Hic jacent corpora Thome Wise ac Mabelle
Walshe, Religione juxta pietate non in pauperes
charitate conspicuorum qui legis pro ipsis precor
ora referes mercedem tua obiit Thomas 19 Juli
1604 Mabella 5 ma

Hic jacet Petrus Walshe civis Waterfordiensis,
qui obiit 29 June 1622.   Et Maria Skidi uxor
ejus quae obiit . . . .

On the *western* side of the tower:

HIC JACET MICHAEL HORE CIVIS QUONDAM ET MAR-
CATOR CIVITATIS WATERFORDIÆ QUI OBIIT————ET
ANASTACIA WALSH UXOR EJUS QUÆ OBIIT———

Joanne Wa . . . . uxoris. eis q. vitam mo—
. .   . .
concesit quarto Idus Januarias A. D. 1582.

HIC JACET CLEMENT WOODLOCK GENEROSUS AC
CIVIS WATERFORDIÆ   ET MARIA WALSHE UXOR
EJUS. . . . .

Hic jacet Robertus Lincol filius Gulielmi civis
civitatis Waterfordie qui obiit 25 January anno
Domini 1630, et uxor ejus Margarita Browne quae·
obiit . . .

MARY DE-RANT ALIAS ALCOCK DIED Y^E 17TH OF
JANUARY 1716, AGED 33 YEARS—PETER DE-RANT
DIED Y^E 27 JANUARY 1756, AGED 81 YEARS.

On the *south* side of the tower of the French
Church, there is placed in the wall, a pretty high
monument of Matthew Grant, who was appointed
one of the sheriffs of the city, by Charles I.'s
charter in 1626, and subsequently filled the office
of mayor. It represents his coat of arms with the
motto over the shield, and various ornaments:
part of the inscription is totally illegible.

HIC JACET MATTHÆUS GRANT CIVIS WATERFORDI-
ENSIS QUI OBIIT————DIE—————ANO————
UXOR EJUS CATHERINE SKIDY QUÆ OBIIT 12 OCTO-
BRIS ANO 1627—————————CATHERINE PORTER,
QUÆ OBIIT———————————————————
——————— PER MISERICORDIA -——————————
—————— LAZARUS —————————————————

This church was granted by government in the
early part of the last century, for the use of the
French Protestants who settled in this country
in consequence of the revocation of the edict of
Nantz, and was endowed with sixty pounds per
annum, as a stipend to the officiating clergyman.
The lapse of time, and intercourse with the people
of this country, have long since had the effect of
naturalizing the descendants of the French refu-

gees: the regular congregation of this church has consequently been diminishing from year to year, and is now entirely broken up, by the death of the late respectable and venerated minister, who, in early life, officiated to a large congregation of his countrymen, scarcely one of whom remained to follow him to the grave.

The performance of divine service is now discontinued, and the salary withdrawn.

The Church of St. Thomas, situated on a hill bearing that name, is supposed to have been erected by King Henry II. or his son John, and dedicated to the memory of Thomas à Beckett as a testimony of regret for the murder of that prelate.—Part of the entrance still remains and exhibits a beautiful specimen of Saxon architecture.

ROMAN CATHOLIC CHAPELS, AND MEETING HOUSES.

THERE are four Roman Catholic chapels in Waterford. The principal one, in Baron-strand-street, supposed to be one of the largest buildings in Ireland, is capable of accommodating 11,000 people. It was built in 1793, at an expense of £20,000, which was raised chiefly by collections of halfpence at the chapel door. The chapel at

Ballybricken can accommodate about 3000 persons. The other two chapels are very confined, and can only afford room to about 500 each.

At the Reformation, when the Roman Catholics of Trinity Parish were dispossessed of Christ Church, they were prevented, for some time, from having any public place of worship; but were afterwards allowed to meet in an old building in the form of an L, at the rear of the house now occupied by Mr. Weekes, and opposite to the present great chapel. In 1693, they petitioned the Corporation, setting forth their great want of accommodation, and praying that they might be allowed to build a large chapel at the back of the houses in Baily's-lane, which was an obscure passage not much frequented by the inhabitants, by way of strengthening their application, they promised, that if permitted to erect a suitable building, it should be hid from the view of the Corporation, so as not to be offensive to them. Their request being complied with, they built the late great chapel, the entrance to which was from Baily's-lane. In 1790, the Roman Catholics applied a second time to the Corporation, who very liberally bestowed upon them all the ground in front of Baron-strand-street, from Baily's-lane to Mr. Charles Clarke's house, for 999 years, at the yearly rent of two shillings and sixpence. The old chapel, which had stood, nearly one hundred years, was then taken down, and the new one commenced.

The present building has a beautiful architectural front of hewn stone, of the Ionic order: only a few columns have been erected, and the entrance and portico are even yet in a very unfinished state.

The interior of the chapel is remarkable for lightness and grand simplicity. The immense roof is supported by columns of the Corinthian order, serving to diversify the appearance of sameness, which the undivided floor of the building might otherwise produce.

There are preserved here some magnificent dresses,* supposed to have been the gift of Pope Innocent III. to the cathedral of Waterford. These dresses, which are used by the officiating Priest, and his assistants, on the day before Easter Sunday, consist of various articles, as Copes, Vestments, Dalmatics, &c. &c. The copes are five in number: they are about four feet in depth, and six in length, and when placed across the shoulders, meet gracefully in front. Three of the Copes are of crimson and two of green velvet, and are almost entirely covered with gold embroidery, which, after the lapse of so many ages, is still bright and splendid, though of course much

---

* It is probably these dresses which are alluded to in an order of Council, as having been fraudulently taken by Richard Butler, Esq Mayor See the account of the Cathedral, page 136.

worn. A broad band of highly finished work, representing various parts of scripture history, occupies the longer side of the cope; the figures are admirably executed, and the countenances are remarkable for a great variety of expression. The Vestments, which are close dresses, are worn under the copes: the Dalmatics are like the Vestments, except that they have sleeves. Amongst the valuable plate belonging to the chapel, the following deserve notice. A tabernacle of silver, in which the consecrated elements are exhibited: this is a magnificent piece of workmanship of pure silver, richly chased; it bears the date of 1729, and this inscription, " Belonging to God and Paul White's heirs."—A silver crucifix, with the words "orate pro Dr. Laurentio. Carew, 1752." Several large silver candlesticks, and a splendid silver lamp, on which are the words, " This lamp was given by Thomas Nunezael to the most holy sacrament, 1738." A crucifix said to contain a portion of the true cross is shewn here; it is a plain piece of workmanship, and exhibits the appearance of great antiquity. Around the edge are these words, " Ista particula ligni sacratissimæ crucis pertinet ad Ecclesiam Cathedralem Sanctissime Trinitatis Waterfordie.

I.II.S. MAR."

At one extremity is the date, 1620.

There are two handsome monuments erected to the memory of Doctor Hussey and Doctor Power, Roman Catholic Bishops of Waterford. The former is outside the chapel, and it is to be regretted that it is exposed to the influence of the weather. it consists of a marble slab fixed in the wall, and bears this inscription.

D. O M.

HIC JACENT SEPULTÆ EXUVIÆ MORTALES

REVERENDIS: & ILLUSTRIS: DOM:

THOMÆ HUSSEY, S. T. D.

QUI PER SEPTEM ANNOS

ECCLESIAM WATERFORDIENS: & LISMORIENS: REXIT.

OBIIT ANNO 1803, DIE JULII 11MO.

ÆTATIS 62O.

REQUIESCAT IN PACE.

The monument of Bishop Power is exceedingly handsome. A female figure is represented kneeling on a sarcophagus, and holding an open book, on which is written in gold letters—"Thy prayers and thine alms are come up for a memorial before God." Over the head of the figure is a crown, with the words "Well done, good and faithful servant."

On the Sarcophagus—

SACRED TO THE MEMORY OF

THE RIGHT REV. DOCTOR JOHN POWER,

WHO FOR ELEVEN YEARS GOVERNED THE UNITED
DIOCESES OF
WATERFORD AND LISMORE.
IN HIS ZEAL, DIRECTED BY PRUDENCE AND KNOW-
LEDGE, WAS DISPLAYED THE PRELATE ;
IN HIS MEEKNESS, CHARITY, PIETY AND HUMILITY,
WAS EXEMPLIFIED THE CHRISTIAN ;
AND
IN HIS ENLARGED BENEVOLENCE AND UNWEARIED
EXERTIONS TO PROMOTE THE TRUE HAPPINESS OF ALL,
SHONE FORTH THE MAN.

HIS FELLOW CITIZENS OF EVERY RELIGIOUS DENO-
MINATION, AND HIS SORROWING FLOCK, LAMENTING
AS IF WITH ONE VOICE, THE LOSS OF SUCH A PASTOR
TO THE CHURCH, OF SUCH A MEMBER TO SOCIETY,
AND ANXIOUS TO PERPETUATE THEIR SENSE OF HIS
VIRTUES, HAVE ERECTED THIS MONUMENT.
OBIIT JAN. XXVII. MDCCCXVI. REQUIESCAT IN PACE.

The Meeting Houses in Waterford are very numerous—they are attended by Presbyterians,
Baptists, Quakers, Methodists and Independents.

PUBLIC BUILDINGS.

WATERFORD can boast of very few public buildings of any considerable antiquity: the most ancient of those recently used were the *Exchange*

and *Custom-house*; they were situated on the quay, mid-way between the extremities of the city, but being in a ruinous condition, it was found necessary to take them down.

The new Town-hall is a fine building, situated on the Mall, contiguous to the bishop's Palace, and having a view of the river Suir. The front, faced with stone, presents a good appearance, and is admired for its just proportions and the simplicity of its style. The principal entrance opens into the public hall, or exchange, which was formerly the resort of merchants, who assembled here to make contracts and transact other commercial business: a curious looking antique, somewhat resembling a nail in form, and about four feet high, stood in the old exchange: bargains were concluded by laying the stipulated money upon this stand or nail, and hence the origin of the saying, "to pay down upon the nail." Under the same roof with the town-hall, is a very neat *Theatre*, and also a handsome suite of rooms for public entertainments.

The Market House has recently been erected on a piece of ground immediately adjoining the river: as a place for the purposes of trade, it is commodious and well arranged; but its situation is ill chosen, as it breaks in upon the line of quay, which extends from one end of the city to the other, and which presents a view of little less than an English mile in length, along the banks of the river.

The Fish House, a neat building, is similarly situated, and obstructs the view in like manner. It is to be hoped that these two buildings may be made to give way to the beauty of the city.

The Bishop's Palace stands at the south side of the open space which surrounds the cathedral church. It is a magnificent building of hewn stone, having two fronts; that next the Mall is ornamented with a handsome portico, sustained by pillars of the Doric order. The top of the building is adorned with a handsome cornice. The other front, next the church yard, has the doors, window cases, and coigne stones of plain rustic work.

The Deanery House and a building for the accommodation of clergymen's widows are situated in the same open space.

The Widows' Apartment is built upon the site of the palace in which King John resided during his stay in Waterford. It consists of a neat range of houses, with two returns, facing the grand entrance of the cathedral. A marble slab placed over the middle door, bears this inscription.

" This Apartment founded by the Right Reve-
" rend Dr. Hugh Gore, late Lord Bishop of Water-
" ford and Lismore, for the use of clergymen's wi-
" dows, and was erected, in the year of our Lord
" 1702, by Sir John Mason, Knight, surviving exe-
" cutor of his Lordship's last will and testament."

The benevolent Hugh Gore, whose whole time
and property were devoted to pious and charitable pursuits, was created bishop of Waterford
and Lismore in 1666. He was a man of great
talents and great modesty, to which qualities
he united a liberality and charity which knew no
limits. At the close of a long life, spent in improving his diocess and relieving the afflicted,
he was seized by some Irish ruffians who broke
into his bed chamber at night and beat him severely; and it was only by entering a secret un-
derground passage leading to the deanery—a
passage still in existence—that he contrived to
effect his escape. He was however enabled to
survive this cruel treatment and retired to Wales,
where he died in 1691.

By his will, dated 30th September, 1690, he
bequeathed almost all his fortune to pious and
charitable uses, there was afterwards much difficulty in recovering this property, which was
taken possession of by some individuals, under
pretence of a subsequent will. It is said that a
vast quantity of gold, part of the bishop's pro-

perty, which had been secreted in one of the cellars of the palace, was subsequently discovered by some workmen engaged in repairing the premises.

Among the bishop's bequests are the following: £200, towards providing a ring of bells for the church of Lismore and beautifying the choir of it; £100, towards buying a ring of bells for the church of Clonmell; £20, to the English poor of Waterford. The impropriate tithes of the parish of Cahir, in the county of Tipperary, being the residue of his property after his bequest for clergymen's widows, is left to the bishops of Waterford, to be expended from time to time in rebuilding and repairing decayed churches. £1200 were bequeathed for building an asylum and purchasing lands for the maintenance of ten poor ministers' widows, to each of whom he allotted ten pounds per annum.

The nomination is vested in the Bishop and Dean, for the time being, with power to appoint a receiver of the rents, who is accountable to them. The bishop's property having been recovered after a tedious and expensive law suit, his executors erected the present building, and with the residue of the fund purchased lands in the liberties of Waterford.

The *Court House* and the *City* and *County Gaols* occupy a considerable space of ground, near to

M

the place where St. Patrick's gate formerly stood,
The court house was designed and executed at
the recommendation of the celebrated Howard,
by James Gandon, Esq. who died lately, at the
advanced age of 82.

These buildings have a handsome front, faced
with granite.   In the centre stands the court
house: the entrance opens into a hall, from which
is seen the interior of the county and city courts,
which are tolerably arranged and well lighted, but
too much confined to give suitable accommodation to the public.

The gaols, although recently erected, are very
inconvenient, and do not admit of the improved
prison discipline now so generally practised.

A *Chamber of Commerce* was incorporated in
this city by charter, in the year 1815.

The *Penitentiary*, or house of correction, situated in the suburbs, was erected in the year 1820,
at an expense of £4,990.   It seems to be built
on the plan of the Bury gaol.   An exterior wall
surrounds a quadrangular space of considerable
extent; at one extremity of which is placed the
governor's house, having the cells ranged in a
semicircle round it.   At the rear of the cells, and
within the walls, are gardens and ground where
the prisoners are employed in labour.   The internal arrangements of this prison are not yet

completed; but it has been made available for a considerable number of persons, no less than 269 prisoners having been received between June, 1821, and April, 1824. The annual expense averages about £260. The male prisoners are occasionally employed at a tread-mill, which has been recently introduced.

The *Waterford Institution* was established in December, 1820. It is situated in Lady-lane, and consists of a well selected and daily increasing library, a reading-room and a news-room. There are at present one hundred proprietors, who paid ten guineas each, and contribute one guinea annually. Subscribers, of which there are ninety, pay two guineas annually. The books of the " Waterford Subscription Library" have been added to this, in return for which the proprietors were granted an allowance of three guineas in the purchase of the new shares.

The business of the Waterford Institution is conducted by a committee, consisting of a president, vice-president, and seven members, together with the treasurer. The proprietors note down in a book such works as they consider deserving of attention, and it remains with the committee to make such selections from these as they may think proper.

The present stock of the Institution exceeds £2000.—There is a tolerable collection of minerals.

RIVERS, BRIDGES AND QUAY.

The *Suir*, a broad navigable river, presents many advantages to the inhabitants of Waterford, and has always rendered this city remarkable as a place of trade.

It takes its rise in the county of Tipperary, which it separates from the county of Waterford. After a course of about four miles, it passes Clonmel, and is navigable for boats to Carrick-on-Suir; and from thence vessels of considerable tonnage may proceed up to the quay of Waterford.

From Waterford the Suir flows by a circuitous course, and at the distance of about three miles is joined by the rivers Nore and Barrow, opposite the little village of Check-point. The united stream, now become almost an arm of the sea, flows past the town of Passage, and after a course of twenty miles falls into the ocean, forming the harbour of Waterford.

The depth of the water immediately in front of the city varies from twenty to sixty-five feet at low water. Vessels of nearly 800 tons may come up close to the quay—a circumstance particularly favourable for the embarkation of cavalry and military stores.

It was long a source of regret, that no steps

had been taken for the removal of the fords or banks, which had almost blocked up the entrance to the quay of Waterford, to the great prejudice of the trade of the city : of late years this business has been attended to, with a success which is highly creditable to all the parties concerned.

On the 20th of June, 1816, the royal assent was given to an act of parliament for " deepening, cleansing, and improving such parts of the river Suir, as constitute the port and harbour of Waterford, between Bilberry Rock and Hook Tower, including St. Catherine's, commonly called St. John's Pill—the appointment of a Pilot-office and Ballast-office in the said city of Waterford."

The grand object of the commissioners appointed under this act was to take measures for enlarging the channel, which had already been commenced through the fords, so as to make it two hundred and ten feet wide, and seven feet deep. This great undertaking is now nearly completed : when finished, the expense will be about £22,000, of which government has already granted £14,588 The depth of water now in the channel, at the fords, is twenty-one feet at high spring tides, and seventeen at neap tides. Vessels drawing eighteen feet can clear the fords at four hours flood tide.

In addition to the enlargement of the channel, through the upper and lower fords, the harbour commissioners have materially improved that most difficult and dangerous navigation, called the King's Channel, by placing therein and along its verge mooring and warping buoys, perches, rings, chains, and posts. This improvement of the King's Channel, where vessels of the largest class can now, at all times of tide, have a super-abundance of water, added to the cut of two hundred and ten feet through the fords, has removed all those impediments to the trade up to the city of Waterford, so frequently complained of by navigators. We are also indebted to the commissioners, and to the indefatigable exertions of their secretary, Mr. Brownrigg, for a considerable reduction in the rates of tonnage duty, ballast and pilotage, as well as for the improved rules and regulations which they have adopted, with the view of preventing the possibility of frauds being practised upon masters of vessels frequenting the port of Waterford—practices which prevailed to an alarming extent previous to the introduction of the act into this port.

There are now three excellently found pilot boats, two of thirty and one of forty tons register, stationed near the entrance of the harbour, for the purpose of furnishing all vessels with pilots; and no accident can happen to a vessel whilst in charge of a Branch pilot, without an investigation taking place before the committee, who never fail to punish the pilot if found guilty of neglect of duty, or impropriety of conduct.

The commissioners have likewise been instrumental in the erection of beacon towers at Brownstown and Newton Heads; and, after repeated solicitations, have at length succeeded in procuring the establishment of a floating light near the Saltees : by which two objects, the hitherto frequent loss of lives and property will at once be prevented.

John's River, which falls into the Suir, within the bounds of the city, has its source in the marshy lands between Waterford and Tramore, about three miles distant from the former place. It is a narrow stream until it approaches Waterford, when it is affected by the tides, and becomes, at high water, navigable for the largest description of boats.

John's River is traversed by three bridges, within the city of Waterford; two of ancient date, namely, John's bridge, and William-street bridge, and one, called Catherine's bridge, recently erected, near the old abbey of St. Catherine.

It is surprising that so considerable and so ancient a city as Waterford should not have had a bridge over the Suir until 1794 : for although it has been conjectured, from the discovery, a few years since, of some fragments of piles and framed timber, that the Danes had a bridge over the river at this place, we are without any record of the fact. In former times it was considered a vast attempt to erect a bridge over a river of such depth and breadth as the river of Waterford; we may therefore conclude, from these and other circumstances, that no attempt was made before that which has so fortunately succeeded.

The wooden-bridge connecting Waterford and the county of Kilkenny was undertaken, in 1793, by a company, (incorporated by act of parliament,) who subscribed £30,000 to complete the work, including the purchase of the ferry. The money was raised by loans of £100 each, the interest of which was to be paid by the tolls of the bridge. The work, having been completed for a less sum than was originally estimated, only required the payment of £90 on each debenture. The erection of a bridge has eventually become a good speculation; the debentures now sell for £170, and the company have a sinking fund, already advanced to a considerable amount, to repair or rebuild the bridge, as may be necessary. The tolls for the present year let for £4260.

The present bridge was built of American oak, by Mr. Cox, a native of Boston, who also erected the magnificent bridge over the Slaney, and also those of Derry, Portumna and Ross Cox advised the proprietors of the Waterford bridge to case one of the piers with stone until the whole were completed; but his advice was not followed.

Two tablets, affixed to the centre piers, give an account of the manner in which the foundation was laid, the date of the erection, and the materials of which it was composed. The inscriptions are as follow:—

In 1793,

A YEAR RENDERED SACRED

TO NATIONAL PROSPERITY

BY THE EXTINCTION OF RELIGIOUS DIVISIONS,

THE FOUNDATION OF THIS BRIDGE WAS LAID,

AT THE EXPENSE OF ASSOCIATED INDIVIDUALS

UNITED BY PARLIAMENTARY GRANTS,

BY SIR JOHN NEWPORT, BART.

CHAIRMAN OF THEIR COMMITTEE.

MR. LEMUEL COX,

A NATIVE OF BOSTON, IN AMERICA,

ARCHITECT.

ON THE THIRTIETH DAY OF APRIL, 1793,

THIS BRIDGE WAS BEGUN.

ON THE EIGHTEENTH OF JANUARY, 1794,

IT WAS OPENED FOR THE PASSAGE OF CARRIAGES.

IT IS 832 FEET IN LENGTH, 40 IN BREADTH,

CONSISTING OF STONE ABUTMENTS

AND FORTY SETS OF PILES OF OAK.

THE DEPTH OF WATER AT LOWEST EBB TIDES 37 FEET.

THIS WORK WAS COMPLETED, AND THE FERRY PUR-
CHASED, BY A SUBSCRIPTION OF THIRTY THOUSAND
POUNDS, UNDER THE DIRECTION OF THE FOLLOWING
COMMITTEE.

SIR JOHN NEWPORT, BART.

SAMUEL BOYSE, ESQ.	SIR SIMON NEWPORT.
THOMAS QUAN, ESQ.	REV. WILLIAM DENIS.
WM. PENROSE FRANCIS, ESQ.	THOMAS ALCOCK, ESQ.
	MAUNSELL BOWERS, ESQ.
ROBERT HUNT, ESQ.	HUMPHREY JONES, ESQ.
JOHN CONGREVE, ESQ.	THOMAS H. STRANGMAN,
JAMES RAMSAY, ESQ.	ESQ.

The *Quay*, unequalled by any thing of the kind
in Ireland, is an English mile in length—a continued line with scarcely any interruption throughout its entire extent. Between the houses and
the river there is a flag way for foot passengers,
and a road for carriages, the whole length of the
quay: the part immediately adjoining the river,
is divided off from the road, and forms a delightful promenade. The carriage way is now, and
has been for many years, formed on what is
called the Mac Adam principle.

For the advantages of this noble quay, we are
indebted in a great measure to David Lewis, Esq
in whose mayoralty, in the year 1705, the quay
was greatly enlarged, by throwing down the

CITY OF WATERFORD.

town walls. He also threw down Baron-strand gate; filled the great ditch, which then joined that gate and the town wall; and made a communication between the old quay and the new. The present quay and several of the fine buildings on it, including the exchange, were commenced in his time.

To see the the quay to any advantage, the observer should ascend the hill on the opposite side of the river, which commands a noble view of the city, the river, the quay, and much of the adjoining country, terminated at a great distance by Sleeve-ne-man and the mountains of Cummeragh. From this point of view a considerable portion of the Suir comes under observation: above the town, the picturesque castle of Granny hangs over the river; nearer are the high and precipitous hills between which the bridge is erected. All these objects, with the steeple and towers of the city, present altogether a beautiful and imposing landscape.

SCHOOLS.

EDUCATION has always been esteemed in Ireland. The Irish ever desired the character of a learned people; from the cloistered monk to the mendicant wandering through the country under the name of "poor scholar," learning has at all

times been zealously and enthusiastically cultivated.

Change of times and customs has effected little
alteration in this particular. The poor scholar indeed has suffered for the sins of his fraternity;
he who was wont to traverse from house to house,
professedly engaged in instructing others, but
really existing upon classic lore—himself as dead
as the learning which absorbed all his faculties—
is now almost banished: the idle and worthless
have assumed his character, and his place is seen
no more. A better system of education is now
adopted: the number of regular schools has increased considerably within the last fifty years,
and affords promises of much improvement in the
morals of the people.

The principal and only *Endowed School* here, is
under the patronage of the corporation, who give
a school-house and a residence for the master's
family rent free. The master, who is necessarily
a clergyman of the established church, has also
the appointment of Lecturer of St. Olave's, with a
salary arising from an allowance from the corporation, together with the interest of some money
bequeathed by Bishop Milles, amounting altogether to £100 per annum.

Amongst the schools established for the gratuitous education of youth, the first to be descri-

bed is that founded by Bishop Foy, and called the *Boys' Blue School.* This noble foundation was the gift of an individual, of whom a brief memoir is subjoined. Nathaniel Foy was born in the city of York, and educated in Trinity College, Dublin, of which university he was elected a fellow. He was next appointed minister of the parish of St. Bridgid, in Dublin, where he first distinguished himself as an able theologian. After the success of King William, he was promoted to the see of Waterford and Lismore, where he continued until his death, which took place on the first of January, 1707. He bequeathed £5 to his kinsman, Thomas France, for preaching his funeral sermon, with this singular condition, that he should speak nothing of his person, good or ill, and he directed that the charge of his funeral should on no account exceed thirty pounds. He left £20 to the poor of the city of Waterford, to the Blue-coat Hospital in Dublin, £10; and £7 to the church-wardens of the parish of St. Bridgid, to be disposed of in charitable uses.

He mentions that he had expended £800 in the improvement of the episcopal house at Waterford, and he bequeathed, that whatever should be got out of that sum from his successor should go to the mayor and corporation of Waterford, to be laid out on good security, the yearly profits to be employed in apprenticing out protestant children of the inhabitants of Waterford, either boys or girls, and he gave the nomination of the persons to be bound out, to the bishop, dean, and mayor of Waterford, or any two of them, whereof the bishop to be always one. After these provisions, he bequeathed the remainder of his property for the establishment of a school for the gratuitous education of protestant children. In the will it was directed, that fifty children should be instructed in reading and writing, and in the principles of religion. The salary of the master was fixed at forty pounds a year, and that of the catechist at ten pounds, with liberty to increase the salaries and the number of the scholars, as the funds should improve, in such a manner, that the number of scholars should be increased in the same proportion as the salaries. The nomination and removal of the master and the catechist were vested in the bishop alone: the mayor, three of the aldermen, and the sheriffs were to nominate the scholars to the bishop, for his approbation; but in case the bishop should disapprove of any of them he might nominate others in their room.

The executors under the will, having obtained from the corporation a grant of a piece of ground at the corner of Baron-strand-street, erected a handsome school-house, and, with the residue of the fund, purchased lands of the yearly value of £191: 2: 2; a further sum of £48 was shortly after, at the death of the bishop's sister, added to the income of the charity, when the master's salary was raised to £60, the catechist's to £15, and the number of boys was increased from fifty to seventy-five.

An act of parliament was subsequently obtained by the Rev. Nathaniel France, surviving executor, to perpetuate and regulate the charity. According to the provisions of this act, the ground conveyed by the corporation, and the lands purchased, together with a sum of £774 : 15 : 3½, then in his hands, were vested in this gentleman during his life, and, after his decease, in the bishop, dean, and mayor of Waterford, for the time being, in trust, that out of the yearly income they should maintain and repair the school-house, pay £5 to the receiver, £15 to the catechist and £60 a year to the master, who should be obliged to teach gratuitously seventy-five poor children of the city of Waterford.

The act further provided, that the master should have no other office, nor teach any other children, than the number mentioned, except his own; that the excess of income after these disbursements should be applied to clothe the seventy-five children, and if there still remained an overplus, that it should be expended in binding out the boys as apprentices. It appears from a report of the board of education, that the income of the charity, in the year 1788, was £523 : 11 : 0, and that there was then the sum of £1400 in money, lodged in private security, belonging to the trustees, and that seventy-five children were in that year on the establishment.

In the year 1808, an act of parliament was obtained for the better regulation of this charitable institution, by which the trustees were empowered to sell the school-house in Baron-strand-street, to erect a new school-house in a more convenient situation, and to raise the salaries of the master and ushers, the former to £100, the latter to £50 a year each.

The funds of the charity having increased considerably, in consequence of the determination of leases, and the accumulation of a sum of £4900 from the savings of former years, the trustees resolved to maintain, board and lodge the master, ushers, servants and children in the school-house; Bishop Foy, in his will, having limited his trustees to instructing and binding out the children only

The school was shortly afterwards established on the lands of Grantstown, within the liberties of the city, in a recently erected house, which, by numerous and rather unsightly additions to the original building, was rendered large and commodious.

The estates of the charity consist of about fourteen hundred acres of land, together with two or three small plots of ground in the city of Waterford.

Girls' Blue School.

A school-house for the education of female children was erected in Lady-lane, in 1740, by Mrs. Mary Mason, daughter of Sir John Mason. The building, which cost £750, is plain and rather gloomy, but sufficiently well adapted to the purpose for which it was intended. The arms of the Mason family, with the inscription of " PIETAS MASONIANA," are placed in the front.

When this school was first established, thirty children were clothed and instructed until able to go to service: the salary of the mistress was £10 per annum. The whole expense was defrayed by an annuity of £60, paid by the Corporation, on account of £900 given for this purpose by Sir John Mason, Sarah Mason, and John Mason, Esq.

In the year 1784, Counsellor Alcock left £1000 to the charity, the interest of which is expended in apprenticing the most deserving children.

Killoteran School.

The Charter School at Killoteran, within the liberties of the city, was built in the year 1744, and was endowed by the Corporation of Waterford with twenty-six acres of land, at a nominal rent.

N

An avenue shaded with large trees, and of considerable length, leads to the house, which is
situated on rising ground.   The school-room is
thirty feet in length, by twenty-one in breadth,
and is lighted by four large windows: there are
two dormitories of the same dimensions, lofty and
well ventilated.   The master's and ushers' apartments are in the centre of the house, and upon
the same floor with the dormitories.   There is
a small infirmary detached from the house, and a
room of recovery under it: the infirmary is well
ventilated by two windows, placed at opposite
sides.

The children are instructed in reading and writing and in the principles of religion; and are
occasionally employed in the garden and in agricultural labours.   There are at present forty-nine
children in the house.   The annual expenditure
varies from £700 to £800.

Sunday Schools.

There are several schools here, conducted according to the regulations recommended by the
Kildare-street association.   The Sunday School
in Lady-lane, under the patronage of Mrs. Strang-
man, and a similar establishment, under the superintendence of Mrs. Nevins, at Ferry Bank, the
opposite side of the river, are regularly and numerously attended.

The *Roman Catholic Schools* are very numerous: the principal private school is the College of St. John. In the city and part of the liberties there are no less than 3396 catholic children at different schools: of this number 1374 are females. The number of children whose parents pay for their education is 1376. The remaining 2020 are educated through the private charity of the inhabitants of Waterford, with the exception of one school for twenty females, which receives £10 a year from the Kildare-street society.

In the schools established by Edmund Rice, Esq. for the education of poor Roman Catholic children, we have a splendid instance of the most exalted generosity. This gentleman having, at an early period of life, acquired an independent fortune by commercial pursuits, withdrew himself from public engagements; and being strongly impressed with the necessity of giving to the lower orders a religious education, he devoted his time, his talents, and his fortune, to erect and endow schools for their use. Amongst a distressed and unemployed population, whose religious opinions militate against the system of education offered them by their protestant brethren, these schools have been of incalculable benefit: they have already impressed upon the lower classes a character which hitherto was unknown to them; and in the number of intelligent and respectable tradesmen, clerks and servants, which they have sent forth, bear the most unquestionable testimony to the public services of Edmund Rice. In the schools under the superintendence of Mr. Rice, there are nearly nine hundred boys. The teachers are young men, who, from religious motives, have devoted themselves to the instruction of the poor, and who act without reward. The principal female school is conducted by the nuns of the Presentation Convent, who instruct gratuitously four hundred girls. There is also a boarding school at the Ursuline Convent on the Newtown road,— a short distance from which, a school has recently been established for the gratuitous education of poor females.

It is much to be lamented that real or fancied obstacles should oppose the general and national support of establishments which might otherwise be available to the indiscriminate education of the Irish poor. The difference of opinion seems to be confined to two points. One party requires the use, perhaps the too general use, of the holy scriptures, and at the same time, insists on the total exclusion of religious instruction: the Roman Catholic, on the other hand, demands religious instruction as a paramount object, and confines the perusal of scripture within, perhaps, too narrow limits. Would it be unreasonable to expect concessions on both sides? that a portion of time prior, or subsequent, to school hours should be appropriated to religious instruction;

and that the perusal of the scriptures by the children should be confided to the discretion of their respective spiritual teachers ?

There are upwards of two thousand children gratuitously educated in this city alone, and were all impediments removed, and suitable assistance afforded, the present number might be greatly increased.

CHARITABLE INSTITUTIONS.

Holy Ghost Hospital.

AFTER the suppression of the monastery of the Franciscans, or Grey Friars, the master, brethren, and poor of the Hospital of the Holy Ghost were incorporated in their place, by patent dated 15th August, 36 Henry VIII. (1546.) We may collect from this patent, and another of the same monarch, dated 7th of September, of the same year, that Henry Walsh had purchased the house or monastery of the Franciscans, together with all the property which anciently belonged to it, in trust for the master, brethren and poor of the hospital, who were to pay annually for the same eight shillings Irish money, in addition to a former sum of £150 : 13 : 4, the consideration for which the grant was made. According to the

terms of the first patent, the master and his successors, with the advice and consent of the mayor,
bailiffs and four senior of the common-council,
had power to nominate and elect, from time to
time, three or four secular priests for celebra-
ting divine service in the hospital, of which
they were to be considered as brethren, and to
be removable for just cause: they had also the
nomination of sixty at least of the sick, infirm
and impotent poor of both sexes, of the city of
Waterford; and all those persons, thus elected, together with the master, were to be a corporation
for ever.   They were to be allowed to possess
land to the value of £100 per annum and no more.
" And further," it is added, " of our more abun-
" dant grace, we give " certain possessions for the
support of said master, brethren and poor, " in
" order that they may pray for our prosperity
" while we live, and for our souls when we shall
" depart this life, and for the souls of all our pro-
" genitors, and for the prosperity of the said
" hospital, and for the soul of Patrick Walsh,
" and for the prosperity of Catherine Sherlock
" his wife, and for her soul, and for the souls of
" all the faithful."   They were also permitted to
enjoy the offerings of all persons residing within the
precincts of the late monastery; to bury within the
church or cemetery, and to administer all kinds
of sacraments.   By the original patent, the election of a master is vested in the heirs of Patrick

Walsh, with the consent of the mayor, bailiffs and
four senior common-council-men, for the time
being.

Queen Elizabeth, by patent dated 26th June,
24th year of her reign, confirmed the former
grants.

The exterior of this hospital consists of a shabby
modern front, built against the ancient monastery,
without any regard to architectural beauty, or
even regularity of appearance. Over the entrance is the following—"The Holy Ghost Hospital, founded by Patrick Walsh in 1545, and
was repaired and enlarged in 1741 and 1743, by
William Paul and Simon John Newport, Esqrs.
Mayors. Simon Newport, Master."

And on a tablet over the entrance to the cemetery—" Thomas Smith, Alderman, Master of the
Holy *Gost* Hospitell, 1718."

On each side of the entrance, two flights of
steep stone stairs conduct to the apartments of
the hospital, which are situated over the cemetery
of the Franciscan monastery. On the right hand
is a long narrow room, lighted from above, having
beds partitioned off the sides, throughout its
whole extent: this, and an inner chamber, raised
a few feet above the exterior apartment, occupy
one wing of the building. The upper parts of
two gothic arches terminate these rooms and give
them a singular appearance. In this place are
some curious ancient images and a font for holy

water, which stood in the chapel of the monastery. This font, which appears to have been fixed in the wall, has on it the coat of arms of the Walsh family, on each side of which are the names, Jacobus White, Helen Walsh, and, underneath, the date 1426. The other wing of the hospital consists of one long room, partitioned off with beds like the former: at the extreme end is an altar decorated with some curious ancient images; this is the chapel of the hospital in which mass is regularly celebrated, in compliance with the directions of the founder.

The figures over the altar are intended to represent the Creator, holding a world in his hand, the Saviour in the centre, and on the left, St. Patrick, the favourite saint of Ireland. Higher up is the figure of John the Baptist. On a small table in the same room are representations of the decapitated head of John the Baptist and some grotesque ancient figures. There are sixty poor assisted by this charity, all of them females.

The property of the charity is in the hands of nineteen leaseholders: the earliest lease is dated in 1791.—By a return presented to Parliament in 1811, it appears that the old yearly rents had risen from £76 : 12 : 6 to £355 : 19 : 6 ; but still the funds are represented as in a very deranged state, owing in a great measure to debts formerly incurred—the arrears of rent remaining due at that period being £448 : 0 : 9½.—The present income is about £385 per annum. An allowance of £12 a year is granted to a clergyman, who is also overseer: the master has the same allowance as he had two hundred years ago—£6: 13: 4; the clerk, £2 per annum.

House of Industry.

This house was erected in the year 1779, at an expense of £1500. It is under the management of a general board of governors, the Bishop of Waterford president; and by the Acts 11th and 12th Geo. III. is formed into a corporation, under the denomination of the " President and Assistants instituted for the Relief of the Poor, and for punishing Vagabonds and Sturdy Beggars, for the County and County of the City of Waterford."

A general meeting of the corporation is held on the first Thursday of every month, and oftener if necessary, for the purpose of examining such vagrants and other improper persons as may have been sent into the house during the preceding month, by committals from different members of the corporation; and who either confirm the committals of such persons, or discharge them, if they are found to be irregularly committed, or if they give security to behave better for the future, or, if strangers, they promise to go to their native places, and be no longer troublesome to the city. The business of these meetings is also to examine such paupers as present themselves for admission, and select such as, from the dread pre-eminence of old age, poverty or infirmity, are best entitled to be admitted; and to make such rules, orders, and regulations for the government of the house, as from time to time may be necessary.

Subordinate to the monthly meeting there is a regulating committee, composed of nine governors, (or members of the corporation,) appointed for one year, who meet once a week, and to whom is confided the whole management of the institution: they order necessary repairs, see that the directions of the monthly boards are carried into execution, inspect the clothing of the inmates, and, where wanted, direct new clothing to be supplied, examine the weekly accounts of the superintendent, give orders on the treasurer for payment of bills, or for the current expenses of the establishment, and direct the purchase of necessary articles in proper season. Each member of the committee takes his turn to be visitor of the house for one week. The visitor is expected to attend every day, and minutely inspect the entire house, see that it is sufficiently clean and well ventilated, and report, in a book kept for the purpose, on the general appearance of the house, and whatever he may think deserving of observation.

One of the governors of the charity is appointed treasurer for one year. There are also two emi-

nent physicians who attend the house : two clergymen (one of the Protestant and the other of the
Roman Catholic persuasion) attend on Sundays
and holydays, and visit the sick at all times when
requisite. And all these gentlemen act without
any other recompense than the gratification of
their own benevolent feelings, which prompts
them to the exercise of works of charity.

An apothecary is paid, to supply the charity
with medicine, and to give daily attendance.
There are also a superintendent and two house-
keepers, who reside in the establishment, and
on whom the subordinate duties of directing
the concerns of the charity more immediately
devolve.

Numbers in the house, 11th of February, 1824.

Infirm Poor, admitted on petition	201
Vagrants - - - - - - - -	20
Lunatics and Idiots - - - - -	79
Prostitutes - - - - - - -	33
Children - - - - - - - -	2
Total	335

On a stone tablet on the front of the house, over
the hall door, is the following inscription:

FOR THE PROMOTING INDUSTRY, AND PUNISHING
VAGRANTS, THIS HOUSE WAS ERECTED, IN PURSUANCE
OF THE ACT OF PARLIAMENT, WITH THE AID OF
SEVERAL SUBSCRIPTIONS FROM THE NOBLEMEN AND

GENTLEMEN OF THIS CITY AND NEIGHBOURHOOD, AND WAS OPENED IN THE YEAR 1779.

SIMON NEWPORT, ESQ. MAYOR.

THOMAS PRICE, ESQ. ⎰
⎱ SHERIFFS.
SAMUEL KING, ESQ. ⎰

JOHN ROBERTS, ARCHITECT.

The inmates are employed (such as are able) in cooking, washing, cleaning the house, &c.; some in preparing clothing, as tailors, weavers, shoemakers, and flax spinners; others in spinning wool and doubling and twisting worsted for hire: they are allowed one-third of their earnings, as a stimulus to their exertions.

A school has recently been established for the improvement of the prostitutes, about twelve of whom are receiving instruction in reading and writing: they are attended two days in the week, for two hours each day, by a few benevolent ladies, who devote their time for the purpose, and from whose care and exertions much good is expected to result.

The institution has derived great benefit from the introduction of a tread-mill; previously to which, the house had no terror for vagrants and prostitutes, who were frequently confined at their own desire.

Fever Hospital.

An hospital, for the reception of persons afflicted with contagious fever, was established here in 1799. This was the first institution of the kind in Ireland, and the second in the empire. Previous to the existence of this charity, the poor, residing in crowded and confined parts of the city, suffered severely from fever, and it is well ascertained, that many streets, lanes, and lodging houses were, for many years, never entirely free from it. Struck with the fatal effects of this dangerous malady, some benevolent individuals exerted themselves to restrain its progress, and from a very small beginning raised this charity to its present extent and importance. A small house, called the turret, on John's Hill, was first used as a fever hospital, and when the funds increased, the present building, capable of accommodating 200 persons, was erected on its site.

During the prevalence of fever in 1816 and 1817 there were frequently 500 patients in the hospital. The average number of persons in fever, even during the most healthy seasons, varies from twenty to fifty.

The Waterford Fever Hospital is an admirably conducted establishment, possessing every requisite which the ingenuity of man can devise, as likely to contribute to the comfort and recovery of its unhappy inmates.

The *Charitable Loan*, a charity which has since been extended to different parts of the country, was originally established in Waterford by Arch-

deacon Fleury and the late Mr. Hobbs, on the
5th of January, 1768; and out of a capital of a
few hundred pounds (which arose from the produce of a little harmonic society) has, since its
commencement, lent to 14,173 persons the sum
of £32,669 : 15s. 1d. interest free.

It is to be regretted that the funds of this charity do not admit of its affording assistance to a
greater number of persons than the few now on
the list; and were it not for the praiseworthy
exertions of the late Mr. Hobbs, the industrious
poor of Waterford would not now have even this
small fund to resort to in time of need.

When it is considered how extensively beneficial a charity of this description might be in
such a country as Ireland, where the smallest
sums of money may, by management, be rendered available to the greatest emergencies, it is
to be hoped the citizens of Waterford will not
permit a charity to die away which they may look
upon as one of their own creating.

A *Dispensary* was established in Waterford in
the year 1786, for the purpose of affording to the
sick poor of the city medicine and medical advice. For a short period, previous to the erection
of the Fever Hospital, a few patients were received
into this institution.

At the present time, all who are recommended
by governors receive medicine and medical advice

at the Dispensary; or, if unable to attend there, at their own houses, where they are furnished with such other charitable assistance as their necessities may require.

This charity has been of incalculable benefit to the poor, relieving annually about 5500 patients, at the comparatively trifling expense of £250 per year.

The income arises from subscriptions, and from an annual presentment of the city grand jury, who are empowered, by act of parliament, to present a sum equal to the amount of the subscriptions received.

A donation of ten guineas, or an annual payment of one guinea, constitutes a governor. The physicians and surgeons afford their assistance gratuitously.

The *Leper Hospital* was founded by King John, in the early part of the thirteenth century. It has been stated that it was established by an individual of the name of Power, but this is evidently a mistake, and one which probably originated from the circumstance of a particular ward of the hospital, which was set apart for incurables, having been supported by the Waterford family, one of whose ancestors left a sum of money to be appropriated to that purpose.

The foundation of this hospital has been attributed to the following circumstance:—The king's sons, during the time they remained at Lismore, were so feasted with the fine salmon and cider of that place, that they lived almost entirely on them, which caused eruptions to break out on their bodies, supposed to be the leprosy; of which the king being informed founded the Hospital for persons labouring under leperous complaints, and granted a charter of incorporation by the name of the Master, Brethren, and Sisters of the Leper House of St. Stephen's, in the city of Waterford. He also granted the Corporation a Seal, which the master of the hospital holds, and with which he seals the leases of the lands, &c. of the hospital, which leases he is empowered to make, with the consent of the brethren and sisters of the hospital.

The King endowed the hospital with the Leper House, and several other holdings in St. Stephen's parish, and with the oblations, obventions, offerings, &c. of the said parish. Also with lands at Poleberry, without John's-gate, (which gate was formerly considered the boundary of the hospital,) and also the lands of Leperstown, in the barony of Gaultier.

In the middle of the last century, when leprosy had become of very rare occurrence in Ireland, the corporation of Waterford, on the grounds that the funds were intended solely for lepers, shut up the house. The impropriety of this measure being perceived, the Rev. Doctor Downes, an individual since well known for his extended charities, instituted legal proceedings, and at length obtained a decree requiring the corporation to employ the funds of the charity in relieving the sick and maimed poor. The first appropriation of the income was for the relief of fifty indigent persons, who received an annual allowance. An infirmary was subsequently established for their reception, and the property afterwards increasing, a magnificent hospital was erected in the suburbs of the city, capable of accommodating four or five hundred persons.

The master of the hospital is appointed by the corporation, to whom he is accountable, and removable at the pleasure of that body; as are also the medical attendants as well as the housekeeper and inferior attendants, who are appointed by the master, subject to the controul of the corporation.

The rent-roll of the hospital is about £1300— the actual receipts about £600;—out of which they have to pay for salaries, wages and subsistence, about £280 per annum. The physician and surgeon have £60 a year each. The number of patients varies from twenty to thirty-four.

Besides the charitable institutions already enumerated, there are several others in Waterford which are equally beneficial. The *Lying-in Cha-*

rity relieves poor women at their own houses, supplies them with medicine and medical advice, and such articles as their situation may particularly require. Of late years the funds have become totally inadequate to relieve one fourth of the persons applying for assistance.

The object of the *Stranger's Friend Society* is to relieve persons labouring under temporary distress, and to advance money to carry them to their respective places of abode.

There are two *Associations for the Relief of Destitute Orphan Children:* one for Roman Catholics, and the other for Protestants; both on the same plan. The Protestant Orphan House was established in the year 1818. A new school-house has recently been erected, calculated for the reception of fifty children. It is situated within a mile of the city, at a place called Gaul's Rock, on a piece of ground the property of John Fitzgerald, Esq., who very liberally made a gift of it to the association. A donation of £100 has also been granted by the late Sir Francis Hassard towards the expense of the building. There are at present twenty-eight children in the asylum: the expenditure for the building and other extra demands have hitherto prevented the association from extending the charity to the number for which the building is calculated.

There are also *Alms-houses* for the relief of Roman Catholics.

A *Mendicity Society* was established in Waterford in the year 1820. Previous to this period, the streets were infested with beggars, the greater part of whom were strangers to the city. This nuisance has been abated in a great measure by the exertions of the association, who expended the first year upwards of £1000; and, within the short period of three years, afforded relief to 1300 individuals. At present there are about two hundred on the books.

TRADE AND COMMERCE.

WE are indebted to two of our chief magistrates for a considerable improvement in the trade of Waterford. According to an ancient MS. " In 1695, when Richard Christmas, Esq. was mayor, he exerted himself very much, in conjunction with John Mason, Esq. in advancing the interests of the citizens. One measure was resorted to which had a very beneficial effect—admitting traders of all descriptions, and from all parts, to the freedom of the city: this was determined on by two separate acts of Council, dated the 11th September, 1704, and 26th February, 1705. In consequence of this encouragement, several merchants from Italy, Spain, France, Portugal, Holland, and elsewhere, came and settled in Waterford; houses were repaired, ships built, trade began to flourish."

These exertions were followed up by Mr. Mason, on his succeeding to the mayoralty, in 1696. To use the words of the same manuscript—" the houses were in ruins, the streets uneven, full of rubbish and dunghills;—he caused those nuisances to be removed—the high roads leading to the city to be levelled and new paved, and bridges made in many places of the said roads, to carry off the sloughs and superfluous waters, insomuch (the writer continues) that they were a pattern for the whole kingdom."

Waterford has never been very celebrated for its manufactures. In early times, when agriculture was much neglected, trading in cattle was the staple commodity—much attention was likewise paid to the butter business, and in both these articles a brisk trade was carried on, not only with the English settlements, but also with several of the ports of Spain. Of late years, however, owing to the West Indies getting their live stock from America, the Irish trade in that line has considerably decreased.

Cheese, made from skimmed milk, and called *Mullahawn*, was formerly an article of commerce in Waterford, and was exported in large quantities, but it was of such a hard substance that it required a hatchet to cut it.

Salt was another article of trade in Waterford, and was made in considerable quantities. The first salt-house was established in William-street, by the patentee and the late John Greene, Esq. of Greeneville.

There was also in the city a manufacture of woad, a material used by dyers; but this has long been discontinued. Waterford was also famous for a narrow woollen-stuff, which was circulated all over Ireland, and a considerable quantity exported to other countries. The weavers of this article had a hall, which also answered for an inn: it was situated in Michael-street, opposite to New-street, and had for its sign a spinning wheel. The persons known by the name of hammer-men had also their hall; and it is not more than a few years ago since their plate was sold.

This city has also been celebrated for making red or smoked sprats, which at one period were exported in large quantities. It has been remarked, that they were generally manufactured by shoemakers, who pretended that the paring of the leather gave them a peculiar flavour.

A considerable trade was carried on by the late Thomas Wyse, Esq. who attempted the manufacture of articles of various descriptions, such as japan-ware, all kinds of tools and articles of cutlery. That gentleman had also a fine corn-mill at the Manor, and also a wind-mill, the walls of which remain to this day · he received so many premiums from parliament that he named a street after that assembly.

The linen manufacture was introduced into Waterford by a family of the name of Smith, who brought with them a number of weavers from the north of Ireland. They had a factory and two

bleach greens—one at Ballytruckle, for thread
—the other at a small place, called Smith Vale,
about three miles from Waterford, for linen. The
thread manufactured here was celebrated all over
Ireland; nevertheless the concern failed, and
there is now no trace of it.

A glass-house for manufacturing bottles was
situate nearly opposite Ballycarvet: this also has
gone to decay. A glass manufactory, of a superior description, was established in Waterford, in
1783, by the Messrs. Penrose. It is now conducted by Messrs. Gatchell and Co. who have a
large export trade, particularly to America: the
number of persons employed average seventy
weekly.

There were two distilleries formerly in this
city; the first established by Messrs. Dobbs and
Hobbs, the second by Messrs. Ramsay and Bell.
At present there is not a single distillery in Waterford, with the exception of a rectifying one, on a
small scale, in Thomas-street.

The brewers of Waterford have brought the
manufacture of beer and porter to such perfection,
as to supersede the necessity of any importation
from England.

There is a starch and blue manufactory here,
established by the Messrs. Whites; and two iron
founderies. Until very recently, there was also
an extensive manufacture of glue, which was exported in large quantities to England.

Waterford has for many years been much distinguished for the extent of its exports in the articles of provisions. These amounted, in 1813, to no less a sum than £2,200,454 : 16 : 0. The average for the last few years scarcely exceeds one million and a half sterling; but the decrease is attributable more to a falling off in the value of the articles, than to a reduction in the quantity exported.

It is to be regretted that there should be such a want of capital in Waterford, where there is so wide a field for speculation, and where English capitalists might lay out their money with advantage to themselves and benefit to the country.

Notwithstanding the extensive export trade of the city and port of Waterford, it is not a little remarkable, that the merchants and traders have never invested property to any amount in shipping. British vessels have been mostly employed in conveying our produce to England and other parts, and bringing us the usual imports, a circumstance which is much to be regretted: for had the trade, or even a considerable part of it, been carried on by our own ships, the building of such vessels and their outfit in this port, would have opened new sources of industry, and by keeping at home the immense sums that have from time to time been paid to strangers, for freights, the benefits resulting from such a rational system would have been incalculable.

The primary cause for not building and repairing vessels in Waterford, was the want of proper accommodation: for until within these four years, this port laboured under the great disadvantage of being one of the worst in Ireland, in that respect, so much so, that only dire necessity caused any vessels to be repaired here.

These great disadvantages have been completely removed by the spirited exertions of Mr. White, whose establishment opposite the city bids fair to be one of the most complete in Ireland.

By a simple combination of wheels, and an inclined-plane, vessels of almost any size can with the greatest facility be drawn completely out of the water;—and, by that means, can be examined and repaired with the greatest ease imaginable.

The vessels which have been built at this establishment are much admired for beauty of model and soundness of workmanship;—and in justice it must be added, that there seems every convenience in the concern, which an owner or master of a vessel can desire.

NEWSPAPERS.

THE earliest newspaper known to have been printed in Waterford, was entitled " *The Waterford Flying Post, containing the most material News, both Foreign and Domestick.*" It was printed on a sheet of common writing paper, the head ornamented with the Royal Arms and those of the city of Waterford. One number, dated Thursday, August 21st, 1729, is still in existence: it has neither number nor price affixed to it, but the latter is supposed to have been one halfpenny, from the circumstance of a receipt having been seen for a shilling, as a quarter's subscription to a paper published twice a week, at a much later period.

In November, 1766, "The Waterford Journal" was established by Esther Crawley and Son, and sold at the Euclid's Head, in Peter-street, at the moderate price of one halfpenny. It was published twice a week, contained three columns in each page, and was continued for at least six years.

Ramsay's Waterford Chronicle was in existence at this period. A second series of it was commenced in 1769: it contained three columns, and cost one shilling a quarter. In 1778 a larger paper was used, containing four columns—the price of this was three halfpence a number. Ten years afterwards the price was two-pence half-penny; it was only two-pence in 1791: in 1800 it was four-pence; ever since it has been five-pence.

There were one or two other papers published in Waterford, of which very little is known. One was "*The Waterford Advertizer*," of which Mr. William Murphy was the proprietor. This

was succeeded by " *The Shamrock*," established
by Dr. Hearn: The " *Waterford Mirror*" was
commenced in 1801.

A weekly newspaper was started a few years
ago, but was abandoned. At present there are
three newspapers in Waterford: the *Chronicle*,
the *Mirror*, and the *Mail*.

It would appear by a recent popular publication, that there were only three newspapers in
Ireland, in the year 1782 ; but this must evidently
be a mistake, as there were two in Waterford as
early as 1770, and it cannot be supposed that
there was only one newspaper in all the other
towns in Ireland. The first newspaper in this
country was commenced in the year 1641, under
the title of " *Warranted tidings from Ireland*."

GOVERNMENT OF THE CITY.

BEFORE entering into an account of the charters
which have at various times been granted to the
city of Waterford, (a subject on which, at present,
very little is known,) it may be as well to offer a
few general remarks relating to the government
of the city as at present constituted ; merely pre-
mising, that any rights or privileges that have
been granted to the citizens by the early charters,
remain in force at the present time.

Like most other towns, the government of this
city is incorporated under the denomination of the

mayor, sheriffs, and citizens. The corporation
consists of a mayor, two sheriffs, a recorder,
eighteen aldermen, and nineteen assistants or
common-council men; and the whole together
are named the common-council of the city.

The mayor is selected out of the aldermen; and
the sheriffs from amongst the assistants. There
are also—a sword-bearer, who is authorized to
carry a sword of state before the mayor, unless
the king or his heirs be present; four serjeants at
mace; a public notary; a coroner; clerk of the
crown and peace; town clerk, &c.

By the present charter of Charles I., the mayor
and recorder may hold a court of record twice a
week, for actions of debt, &c. to any amount; and
a court-leet twice a year. The mayor, recorder,
and four of the senior aldermen, are empowered
by this charter to be justices of gaol delivery, and
to determine all felonies and other offences committed in the city and liberties, treason alone excepted.

They have power to hold an admiralty court
within the limits of the harbour, and are not to
be disturbed therein by any other admiralty
court in England or Ireland. They may also hold
a court of orphans once a week, with the same
power as that of the city of London; and can
appoint a seneschal, who may hold a court of pye-
powder.

In cases of absence or sickness, the chief magistrate may appoint a deputy from amongst the

aldermen; and in all cases of election by the council, the mayor must be one of the majority. The charter expressly mentions that no suit once commenced in the mayor's court shall be removed before it is determined. All returns of assize, precepts, bills and warrants are to be made by the mayor and corporation. The mayor and recorder, with the four senior aldermen, are justices of the peace within the liberties and also for the county of Waterford; but are not, as such, to proceed to the trial of any treason, felony, &c., to the loss of life or limb, which the charter authorizes them to do in the city.

The mayor and council have power to tax the citizens, towards defraying any necessary expense. He and the town-clerk may take cognizance of debts, according to the form of statute-merchant and the statute of Acton-Burnel. The mayor is conservator of the waters, and may punish according to the statute in that case provided. Without his license, no ship is to load or unload in any other part of the harbour but at the quay of Waterford; those of the burgesses of New Ross the county of Wexford, excepted. The mayor and council may make a guild in all respects similar to that of the city of Bristol; no guild or fraternity to make by-laws without a license from the mayor.

The CHARTERS of Waterford form a subject of an important nature, and, independent of the rights and privileges which they confer, they contain some curious particulars relating to the early periods at which they were granted.

Of these valuable documents, the only one of which even the corporation of Waterford has any knowledge, is the charter of Charles I., under which the city is at present governed: all the other documents prior to the year 1680 were destroyed by fire, and no steps have since been taken to supply their place.

The following is a list of all the charters that have been granted to the city of Waterford, from the earliest period to the present time.

	Dated at				Anno Regni		A. D.
John - -	Markebridge	-	3 July	- -	7	-	1205
——— - -	Dublin	-	8 Nov	-	9	-	1207
Henry III. -	Woodstocke	-	16 June	-	16	-	1231
——— -	Westminster	-	14 Nov	- -	30	-	1245
——— -	do.	-	4 Aug.	-	45	-	1260
Edward II -	Langley	-	16 June	- -	2	-	1308
Edward III. -	Westminster	-	14 Nov	-	30	-	1356
———	do	-	21 Feb	- -	38	-	1364
Richard II. -	do.	-	26 May	-	3	-	1379
Henry IV							
Henry V. -	do	-	6 May	- -	1	-	1413
——— -	Dublin	-	15 Jan	- -	3	-	1415
Henry VI. -	Westminster	-	20 March	-	5	-	1426
——— -	do	-	1 March	-	20	-	1441
———	do	-	8 April	- -	26	-	1447
Edward IV. -	do.	-	20 Nov.	- -	1	-	1461
Richard III. -	- -	-	25 March	-	1	-	1483
	- -	-	-	- -	2	-	1484
Henry VII. -	Westminster	-	14 May	-	2	-	1486
——— -	do		12 May	-	3	-	1487
Henry VIII.	do.	-	12 Sept	-	2	-	1510
Edward VI. -	do	-	17 April	-	2	-	1548
Philip and Mary	do	-	2 June	2d & 3d	-	1554-5
Elizabeth -	Westminster	-	8 Feb	- -	11	-	1568
——— -	Norhambury	-	16 July	-	16	-	1573
———	Westminster	-	12 March	-	25	-	1582
James I -	Dublin	-	10 July	-	7	-	1609
Charles I	Westminster	-	26 May	-	2	-	1626
——— - -	do	-	19 Feb	-	7	-	1631
James II	- -		22 March	-	4	-	1688

The charter of John, as being the earliest, is undoubtedly the most important. It fixes the exact bounds of the city as decided by the oaths of twelve men living within the walls and twelve living without, in compliance with a former precept of Henry II. Connected with the tenures of the city, it gives up all fines, amercements and redemptions of contempt to the citizens, with some peculiar regulations. In cases of differences or disputes between the citizens, it directs that there be no duels, but that the point in question should be decided by the verdict of twelve men.

By this charter a hundred court was to be held twice a week, on Mondays and Fridays, and as much oftener as might be necessary : it also regulated the proceedings in this court, and the rights attached to it. No citizen was to be impleaded for lands which did not pertain to the hundred. Twelve of the principal citizens, and others specially appointed, were to elect annually a provost on the day of the festival of the Exaltation of the Holy Cross, who, on his being duly sworn, was to have cognition of all pleas in the hundred of the city, and the citizens were to have cognizance of all causes tried before the said provost. It also orders, that no person should be judged touching any money except according to the hundred of the city.

Among the other privileges contained in this charter, the citizens were to have liberty to give their children in marriage to foreign merchants without obtaining the permission of their lords. They were to have the same " reasonable Guilds" as the burgesses of Bristol; to be free from pontage, murage, &c.

This charter likewise grants to them all the tenures within and without the walls of the city, to be disposed of at their pleasure in messuages, &c.—to be held by burgage tenure, by reasonable payment, to wit, ten marks which they pay within the walls of the city. It also grants that each person may erect buildings on the banks of the river, provided they do not injure the city or town; that the citizens should have all lands and waste places to be held and built on at their pleasure; and leave was also granted to them to sell wholesale and retail to Irish enemies and English rebels, as well in peace as in war.

Neither the Templars nor the Hospitallers were to have any maintenance or dwelling in the city, except one within the prescribed bounds; nor was any foreign merchant to purchase within the city of Waterford any piece of merchandize from any person but a citizen; and, as an encouragemen to trade, the citizens had permission to grant " safe conducts" to all rebels and felons who came there for that purpose. No person was to be bailiff of the city unless he held of the king in capite. Justices were expressly commanded not to harass the citizens.

The charters of Henry III. confirm the two

former charters, with the exception that the hundred court should be held only once a week.

By these charters, the citizens were to have all the tenures within and without the walls, to be disposed of at their pleasure, by the assembly or common council of the city. *They were to have the election of the mayor*, who was to be sworn before his predecessor in office and before the council of the city assembled in the Guildhall.

There was to be no assize or gaol delivery by barons of the King's Bench without the mayor being present; and in case the barons were unable to attend, then the mayor and two or three of the more worthy and discreet citizens, and one or two lawyers might deliver the gaols. There was to be a Guildhall and also a prison with wards in which to confine robbers and felons, *apart* from the other citizens: liberty was also granted to choose a coroner from amongst the citizens.

It was also ordered that there be in the city one common seal, according to the form of the statute of Acton-Burnel, of which seal, the greater part should be in the hands of the mayor or guardian of the city, and the smaller part, in the hands of the clerk; both parties to affix their respective parts of the seal in confirmation of certain deeds.

The charters of Edward II. and Edward III., Richard II., Henry IV. and Henry V., confirm the former charters, the principal parts of which, are quoted at some length. Edward the Third's charters provide that no mayor, either in war or in peace, should compel any of the citizens to go out in a warlike manner against his own will, but that they might, of their own accord, go forth with flying colours, &c. against rebels. The mayor, &c. may make convenient rules and regulations, with the consent of the council and citizens in their guilds or assemblies.

Henry the Sixth's charters recite that, whereas the mayor and citizens of Waterford had declared to him, that many rebels, malefactors and plunderers, &c. in the counties of Kilkenny, Tipperary, Wexford and Waterford, had assembled an armed force, perpetrated sundry murders, robberies and other intolerable crimes; the mayor, council and their successors, might collect an armed force and march or ride with horsemen and footmen and with standards in martial array, at such times as they might think proper, and might plunder, burn and destroy their enemies and all those aiding and assisting them.

The charter of Edward IV. contains a recital of all the previous charters. "And whereas some grants and immunities contained in former charters are not clearly expressed, these being represented to us, and knowing that the city of Waterford has in front four hostile counties, *Waterford*, Kilkenny, Tipperary, and Wexford. we, willing to show our affection to the citizens, &c , and to the praise of the holy and undivided Trinity and the blessed Virgin Mary, mother of our Lord, and of St. George

P

the Martyr, and St. Patrick the Confessor, and of all the saints, confirm all the liberties and privileges and that the city should consist of one mayor, two bailiffs and citizens, under the name of mayor, bailiffs and citizens of Waterford, and that they have perpetual succession and have power to plead and implead, and have a common seal and be capable of acquiring property.

"And further that the said city may become more famous and honourable, the mayor, &c. may have a sword with an ornamented sheath, to be borne before them, in such manner as the sword is borne before the mayor of Bristol, at all places within the bounds of the city, except in the presence of the king, in case of which presence, the mayor is to present a sword and a silver gilt key, as is the custom in Bristol." After alluding to the privileges conferred by the early charters, he thus concludes: "taking into consideration all these causes and others, as well as the humble petition of the mayor, bailiffs and citizens, we grant to the mayor and citizens thirty pounds annually towards the repairs of the walls, &c.; and further that the city be one of our chambers, and we receive the citizens into our especial favour. And moreover we will and grant, that if the above recited charters are invalid or informal, our chancellor shall make them perfect and every thing in them shall be determined favourably for the mayor and citizens."

Richard the Third's charters also confirm the previous charters. His last one recites several of the others very minutely.

It would occupy too much space to enter into a lengthened description of the remainder of the charters granted to the city of Waterford. With the exception of one of Henry's, the four subsequent charters are merely confirmations of the former. Philip and Mary's charter sets out almost all the charters at full length, confirming them in the fullest manner. The three granted by Elizabeth are new charters; they occupy much less space than any of the former. By the second charter (1573) the office of sheriffs was first created, as also the county of the city of Waterford.

During the first ten years of James's charter, there was no settled form of government in the city: it was not till the year 1626 that the citizens were restored to all their former privileges by Charles the First's great charter which remains in force at the present day. The charter of James II. can scarcely be considered as having been ever in force; on the restoration of the protestant government it was immediately set aside.

While on the subject of the charters of Waterford, it may not be uninteresting to give an account of a curious paper which is lodged in His Majesty's State Paper Office. It is supposed to have been written in the time of Henry VIII.; the following is a copy of it.

Patrick Strong, Town Clerk,
Waterford, tempore Henry 8

God of his goodnes praysed that he be
For the daylie increase of thy good fame,
O pleasant Waterford, thou loyall cytie,
That five hundred yeres receavest thy name
Er the later conquest unto thee came,
In Ireland deservest to be peerelesse,
Quia tu semper intacta manes.

Therefore Henry the Second, that noble kinge,
Knowinge thy prowes and true allegiance,
Assygned thy franchess and metes namyng,
All thy great port with each appurtenaunce,
Commanding his son theyre honor to advance
With gifts most speciall for thy good ease,
Quia tu semper intacta manes.

John, I do meane the first named Lord,
Elected governor to rule all Ireland,
For thine amorous truth and loyall accord,
In the first seysed of all this land,
In thy charters large he did comand,
Of his bounteous grace the for to pleas,
Quia tu semper intacta manes.

To the was granted that every shipp
Entring this port so wyde and large,
Only in thy presence for great worshipp,
Ever thereafter shoul lade and discharge,
And no where else, no vessell nor barge,
By thy charters noble it doth expresse,
Quia tu semper intacta manes

Anno 24 Eliz 1573 the city had sheriffs

And of thy sadge citizence chose thow must
A Provost yearlye thy people for to guyde,
That by aucthorytie when hym lyst,
Saff conduct may give to lands wyde
To encrease thine honer att every tyde,
By this noble King that knew nathlesse,
Quia tu semper intacta manes.

Then Henry, his son affirmyng the same,
Granted thy fee fearme for a yearly rent,
And of each shipp to encrease thy fame
That enter shall with wyne thy port so potent,
The prysadge of them this he did consent
Thyne honer to conserve without distress,
Quia tu semper intacta manes.

And Edward the First a maior to the did grant,
His son confyrmed the same in every case.
Edward the Third, of tryumph most abundant,
Granted that all pleas by speciall grace
In thee shall be tried, and in no other place,
For ease of thy people and great prowes,
Quia tu semper intacta manes

The staple estatute assigned he had by name
Unto thee by grant with gyftes many moe
Kilkenye and Casshell ought to obey the same
Weixford and Ross Dongarvan allso,
And each other townes adjoynynge thereto
Within this sayd bound these for thine ease.
Quia tu semper intacta manes.

The King first by Rosse falsely seduct
To make her a giant contrary to his will
Then att thy request of newe he did product
All thy noble giantes and hirs did he spill
The law did assent for he knew by skill
Of thy true love and service nott the lesse
Quia tu semper intacta manes.

Richard the second of his abundance
Confyimed the same and in the took place
Trusting thy fydelytie and true allegiance
Which allwa}s shall continue and never deface
And Henry the fourth followeth his tiace
Thy grants knytting to put the in piess
Quia tu semper intacta manes.

The lusty Henry that conquired Fraunce
In the did creat by his grantes ioyall
All offycers nedeful the to advaunce
In honour and ease with aucthoritie speciall
Precluding others to kepe thee fiom fall
And by high Parliament did geve release
Quia tu semper intacta manes

Henry the holly that boine was in Wyndsoie
Collected thy Chaiters then unyting in one
Every poynt dystinctly that Kinges befoie
Did grant unto the for like I know none
Confirmyng thy loyalltye and true subjeccon
Fiom the said conquest that never did sease
Quia tu semper intacta manes.

Then Edward the strong the same did know
Of which he was glad then for thyne ease
Committing of newe thy grants to shewe
And the same regranted the for to pleas
Enlarging thy libertye thyne honour to increase
Called the his Chamber of allegiance peerles
Quia tu semper intacta manes.

Submytt art thou under his proteccōn
Agaynst all wronges the for to save
Not giving thy honour in oblivyon
A Sword of justice to the he gave
Thyne equitie knowen and thy good lawe
With other large giantes the for to please
Quia tu semper intacta manes.

Henry the valiant famous of memorye
Well did he know by true experyence
Thy great fydelytie in tyme of victorie
When Lambert was crowned by false adveitence
And Perkin allso with no lesse reverens
Then only of this land thou were Empresse
Quia tu semper intacta manes.

Thy prowess therefore and renown so prudent
His Grace remembring exempted thy port
From pondadge and subsidy by letters patents
That thereby all strangers shoul gladlyer resort
For thy true legeance to thy comfort
And thy people in quietnes to redresse
Quia tu semper intacta manes.

And of thy Gaole the full delyverance
To thee he gave with execucōn
Thy Church with anuall rent he did advance
Thine honour allso with retribucōn
Confyrming thy giants from resumpcōn
In his high Parliament for thyne increase
Quia tu semper intacta manes.

And his noble son Henry the tryumphant
Beholding thy virtue in eache degree
Of his gracious favor most abundant
All grantes affirmed granted unto thee
By his progenetours noble and free
Under his great sele it doth expresse
Quia tu semper intacta manes.

His bounteous grace revolving in mynde
Thine old fydelytie and perfect allegiaunce
Affirmed in thee of duty and kynde
Without wemb or spott and dyceaveraunce
Accepted had newe thy perseveraunce
With hearts infallible that allways shall cease
Quia tu semper intacta manes.

And to the Waterford in speciall token
Of his princely favour he lately sent
The Sword of justice of which is spoken
No less honour than worthy is the present
The gyft well followed his gracious intent
To comfort them that he find faultlesse
Quia tu semper intacta manes.

With triumph gladnesse and great honoun
Thy cityzence all with humble obedyence
On Easter day att a convenyent houre
In their best maner with good observaunce
Hath this received with letters in affirmaunce
To have them in protecōn both more and lesse.
Quia tu semper intacta manes.

O joyful tyme o day and feast most pleasant
In which thy people illumyned was
With loyalltye true and love ardeant
Adverting thy swete favor and great grace
Of our tryumphant King to our sollace
Avoyding all dowbt fytt he know nathelesse
Quia tu semper intacta manes.

O Citizence all this knott surely ye knytt
In last allegiance your name to conserve
And your ancestors heartes and nott permytt
Your famous loyalltye sclander deserve
By corrupt matters but truly observe
Your Princes will from it do nott digresse
Quia tu semper intacta manes.

Now God we pray that three art in one
Preserve his high Grace in royall estate
And kepe this cytie from dyvysyon
In true allegiaunce without debate
And our hertes in the same to sociate
Then Waterford true shall never decrease
Quamdiu vere intacta manes.

By the following curious document which has also been discovered in the same department, it would appear that the arms of the city of Waterford have undergone a very material alteration since the time of Henry VIII.

"*The emblasing or displaying of the ensigne or armes of the Auncient and Noble Citie of Waterford.*

" The Noble and Auncient Citie of Waterford for the ensigne thereof beareth wavy of argent and azure *three gallies* fardled or a chest of England supported by a lyon of the sonne and a dolphyn of the moone: the crest upon an healme a lion sejeant holding an harpe topaze set on a wreth of pearle and rubie; the mantle gules doubled argent, and for an apothegme is added—Fidelis in æternum—True and trustie for ever, &c."

In the Harleian collection of manuscripts in the British museum, there is a sketch of the Waterford arms, of which a fac simile is annexed.

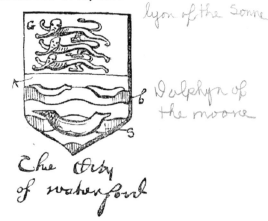

The present arms of the city consist of—a field vert, party per fess: three lions proper, passant gardant, in pale; and an eight oared galley. Crest, a lion rampant, resting on a harp. Supporters, a lion and a dolphin. Motto, *Urbs intacta manet Waterfordia.*

LIBERTIES OF THE CITY.

According to the charter of Charles I. the city of Waterford, that part of the county of Kilkenny which is contained within the bounds of the parish of Kilcullheen, also the great port of the city of Waterford, which enters between Rodybanke and Rindoane to Carrick by water, and all the lands within Ballinakill, Killure, Kilbarry, and Killoteran constitute the county of the city of Waterford and are entirely distinct from and independent of the county of Waterford and the county of Kilkenny. Within the liberties of Waterford, there is little which demands much notice. From the lofty hills on the north of the river, the city appears to the greatest advantage: the accompanying view is taken from Cromwell's rock, of which, in passing, it may be observed, that, if history may be depended on, Cromwell was never at that place. On the south of the Suir, are the ruins of two houses or preceptories of the knights of St. John of Jerusalem. One of these buildings, situated at Killure, was founded in the twelfth century, for the templars, it was afterwards given to the knights hospitallers and became a commandery. At Kilbarry, another preceptory was founded, about the same time, for knights tem-

plars, and was afterwards given to the knights of
St. John of Jerusalem. The plan of these two
buildings was the same :- they were originally of
considerable extent and consisted of a dwelling
and place of worship, which were probably connected together. The chapel, which may be distinguished by its standing east and west, joined
the dwelling at right angles. These two preceptories also resemble each other as to site, being
built on gently rising ground in the immediate
vicinity of a marsh and in both cases standing to
the south west of the low ground.

On a tombstone amongst the ruins of the preceptory at Kilbarry, there is the following inscription.

1598

TM—CIAS

Ancient ornamented cross underneath

MUNITUS HOC SIGNO TUTUS LRIS

I II S

Crest

Arms

QUID CLARIS SOL..

ORATE PRO ANIMA AMABILIS AYLMER UXOR.
NICOLAY FITGERALD DE KINGSMEADOW ARIMIGERI
OBYT SECUNDO MAY ANNO DOMINI 1708
ÆTATIS TRIGESIMO SECUNDO.

In the valley of Kilbarry there is a large tract of land of from two to three hundred acres, covered with water for eight or nine months in the year, and now lying worse than useless, the vapour arising from it at certain periods being exceedingly unhealthy. Two methods have been proposed by Mr. Musgrave, civil engineer to the harbour commissioners, for draining this valley, by either of which, this land might be rendered the best in the county, while at the same time it would afford 70 or 80 per cent. to persons undertaking the work.

At no great distance from Kilbarry, but on the opposite side of the marsh, may be seen a magnificent cromlech or Druids altar, consisting of an immense flat rock, until very lately supported by three upright pillars.

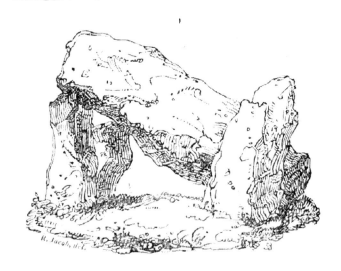

The dimensions of the incumbent stone are

length   -   -   -   21 feet
breadth   -   -   -   18
thickness   -   from 1 to 3 feet.

A farmer who cultivated the adjoining lands, in attempting to remove this noble relic, precipitated it from its original position, but in consequence of the immense weight was unable to accomplish his barbarous intention. One extremity is still firmly supported, the other rests upon the ground; the face of the rock is consequently greatly inclined, a circumstance which detracts much from the regularity and picturesque beauty of the mass. This Cromlech is in the angle of a field, within one or two hundred yards of the bridge of Couse-ma-keal, on the road to Tramore.

In offering some remarks upon the geology of this district, it is only intended to state general and leading facts: an accurate examination of all the minerals found here, independent of the difficulty of the subject, would not be suitable to the present work and would involve dry and tedious details. The prevailing rock in the vicinity of Waterford, and indeed throughout the entire county, except where limestone is found, is argillaceous schistus, varying in hardness and colour, and in many places combined with a portion of silex. The summits of the hills are composed of siliceous breccia, over which red sand-stone frequently occurs. On the sea coast near the

231

rate
ach
ght
elve

ord
un-
ose
oad
ind
gh-
n a

ck-
rry
uir
gy
d a
he

ty-
ole
te,
re.
so
ry
en
al-
in
th

Conglomerate.

Red Sand Stone.

Pudding Stone.

Quartzose Porphyry.

Porphyritic Hornstone.

Argillaceous Hornstone Schistose.

Porphyry Hornstone.

Porphyritic Schistus.

Metallic Vein

Vitreous Slate.

Bituminous Slate

Transition Slate

Red Slate

Green Slate

Black Slate

Bituminous Slate

Copper Iron ore

Graphite with Veins of Quartz

Clay Slate.

RIVER SUIR.

Conglomerate or Pudding Stone.

Red Sand stone alternating with Pudding Stone- and Millstone Grit.

MOUNT MISERY.

Clay Slate with Iron Grits.

Quartz veins

GEOLOGICAL · SECTION · OF · BILBERRY · ROCK ·

P. S. Foley del.

harbour of Waterford, the siliceous conglomerate and sandstone are found interstratifying each other, the thickness of the beds, sometimes eight or ten in number, varying from two to twelve feet.

In the immediate neighbourhood of Waterford the following rocks occur in considerable abundance: sienite and hornblende at Kilronan; talcose slate near Knockhouse, lydian stone on the road to Annstown; hornstone and jasper are found alternating with flinty slate, in the same neighbourhood; serpentine may be seen resting on a bluish black quartzose rock at Knockhouse.

Clay iron ore appears in a small bed at Knockaveelish strand. A view of a section of Bilberry Rock as it is laid open by the course of the Suir will give a concise illustration of the mineralogy of this district; but it may be as well to add a few explanatory remarks by the Author of the Sketch.

" There are several veins of quartz in the clay-slate of Bilberry, in which there is a considerable quantity of micaceous iron ore and scalygraphite, both passing into oxyde of iron and jaspery iron ore. These ores are, in some places of these veins, so intimately blended with quartz as to form jaspery iron stone, which is extremely beautiful when polished. Beautiful specimens of brown crystallized quartz may be collected in small trusses in the clay slate, some of which are intermixed with minute crystals of chlorite. Red-ochre is abundant; this is formed by the decomposition of carburet of iron, and acts so forcibly through the several strata of the hill as to give them a spotted and variegated texture. A small portion of sulphate of barytes is mixed with the micaceous iron ore in several parts of the quartz Oxyde of titanium is also found alternating with the jaspery iron ore; this appears of a blood red colour. The bituminous shale contains 25 per cent. of carbon, its fracture is obliquely fibrous and iridiscent, in consequence of the metallic matter which passes throuhg it. The variegated texture of the talcous slate depends on the same principle. Round the metallic vein, marked in the above section, the talcous slate and indurated green earth are intermixed with arseniemat of iron, which is gradually decomposing by the action of the atmosphere."

In all the ancient ruins, a soft sandstone, resembling Portland-stone, is found in great abundance: the ornamental parts, the cut stone arches and light pillars are composed of this material. In the lower parts of the old cathedral, which still exist and form the foundation of the new building, this whitish soft stone may be seen in the turnings of the arches and windows. This rock does not occur near Waterford and was probably brought here from a considerable distance.

SECTION II.

———

THE COUNTY OF WATERFORD.

———

THE County of Waterford is divided into seven baronies,—Gaultier, Middlethird, Upperthird, Decies without Drum, Decies within Drum, Coshmore and Coshbride, and Glanaheiry.

GAULTIER.

THE barony of Gaultier,* the most eastern division of the county, derives its name from an Irish word which signifies the land of the foreigners.

The Ostmen, Danes or Easterlings, were very early settled in this district, and from its contiguity to the ocean and its almost insular situation, were enabled to protect themselves against the violence of the natives. The Danes, who had

---

* Gaultier is bounded on the north by the Suir, on the west by the liberties of Waterford, part of the barony of Middlethird, and the bay of Tramore, on the east by Waterford bay, and on the south by the ocean. It contains the parishes of Ballynkill, Ballygunner, Kil St Nicholas, Faithleg, Crook, Kilmacombe, Killea, Rathmoylan, Kilmacleague, Killure, and Kilcaragh. According to an ancient record, this barony was divided into nine parishes — See Report on the Records of Ireland, for 1818, p. 21

Q

expelled the more ancient occupiers, some of
whose works are still existing in this barony,
were themselves expelled by the English settlers,
who considered it essentially necessary to secure
a place of embarkation.

When Henry II. was preparing to land his
forces, the only opposition he experienced was
from an Ostman Lord, who vainly attempted to
impede the disembarkation by drawing a chain
across the river.—Passing the bounds of the city
and following the course of the Suir, as it de-
scends towards the sea, the first object which deserves attention is the Little Island—a portion of
land which appears to have been originally connected with the county of Kilkenny, and afterwards insulated by the waters of the Suir partially
effecting a shorter course.

This conjecture is strengthened by the discovery of a large tree, which, with its root and
branches, was found at the depth of some feet
beneath the bed of the river at this place.

The Little Island is about three quarters of a
mile in length and nearly the same in breadth,
and contains one hundred and eighty acres.

This delightful spot is well situated, and commands a fine view of Waterford, the course of the
Suir, and the adjacent counties of Kilkenny and
Wexford, terminated by the lofty and picturesque
mountains of Tory and Shevekielta. On the
island is an ancient castle, to which a comfortable

farm-house is attached: the natural beauties of
the place are heightened by an improved and
thickly-planted neighbourhood. The castle, a
square building, with lofty battlements, evidently
intended as a place of strength, is still in tolerable
preservation : it is supposed to have been erected
in the sixteenth century, and was for many years
occupied by the proprietors of the adjacent lands.
The external appearance of this building denotes
the unsettled state of the times when it was first
inhabited. The principal, and indeed the only
entrance, a small gothic door-way, is defended
by a projecting window, which commands the
approach, and is, at the same time, protected by
a sloping battlement against remote assailants:
there is an aperture in the stone-work, through
which molten lead, boiling oil, and the various
warlike missiles of the time were wont to be cast
upon the heads of the hapless invaders. A human
face rudely cut in stone, and an almost defaced
escutcheon, are inserted in the wall at a few feet
from the door-frame. Narrow windows and loop
holes, at regular distances, afford a faint light to
a flight of stone steps, which, winding through
the massy walls, conduct to the summit of the
building, from this place the view is singularly
grand and extensive. This castle has, at different
times, been fitted up as a place of residence, and
it is said to be the intention of the present proprietor of the soil, John Fitzgerald, Esq to repair

it again, and use it as a summer retreat when he visits his Irish property.

The various windings of the river open new scenes as you advance towards its embouchure: from one point, Waterford appears as if rising out of the river; as you proceed, the towers and steeple of the city are almost concealed by the green and gently sloping hills. The view from the hill of Faithleg is magnificent. In the direction of Waterford, the Suir is seen descending its winding channel, deeply sunk between cultivated hills, at a little distance from the town, the river, dividing into a double stream, incloses the Little Island, and, uniting again, proceeds to receive its tributary waters: further on, as if stretched out immediately beneath, may be seen the confluence of the rivers Suir, Nore, and Barrow, which here unite their waters with a fulness and rapidity that might be taken for the violence of the ocean: the breadth at this place is nearly three miles. To the North, the back ground is terminated by Mount Leinster: Tory-hill, Slieve-kielta, and the Wexford mountains complete the outline, until the view is bounded by the ocean toward the south. Three miles below the Little Island, and at the confluence of the rivers Nore and Barrow with the Suir, is a small village, called Check-point, formerly the packet station, and the scene of much generous but unprofitable speculation. Mr. Bolton established a cotton

manufactory here, but this and many other projected attempts of the same spirited individual
were, unhappily for the country, unsuccessful.
Nearer to the sea is Passage, built on a narrow
neck of low land between the river and a lofty
and precipitous hill which overlooks the town:
the streets are confined, and the houses poor and
neglected, exhibiting evident marks of a declining
place. The church is situated on the summit of
the hill, imposing upon its attendants from the
town an involuntary breach of Sabbath repose.
The river here offers commodious shelter and an-
chorage for vessels of large burden, which may
without difficulty unload at the quay. At Crook,
in the vicinity of Passage, there is an ancient
castle which belonged to the Knights of St. John
of Jerusalem, and was founded in the thirteenth
century by the Baron of Curraghmore. The lands
connected with this preceptory must have been
considerable; for we find that, in the year 1565,
27th Queen Elizabeth, a lease of them was granted
to Anthony Power, for a term of sixty years, at
the annual rent of £12 : 11s. 10d. Irish money.
It is believed, that the Knights of St. John had
nine houses in Ireland, three of which were situated in the barony of Gaultier. At a short distance from the coast, and between Passage and
the sea, are the barracks and the village of New
Geneva. It was originally contemplated by the
government of Ireland to establish at this place a

colony of Genevese, who were obliged to leave
their own country in 1785: fifty thousand pounds
were granted by parliament, half of which was to
defray their charges in removing, the remainder
to be appropriated in aid of their establishment,
and every reasonable encouragement was held out
to induce them to remain; but it appears that they
required certain privileges and immunities which
could not be conceded, and in consequence the
projected settlement was abandoned. The Genevese were, for the most part, industrious me-
chanics, whose zeal and talent would have well
repaid the hospitality of the country which received them. A military barrack was afterwards
erected here, in which one or more regiments were
stationed during the war. the " piping times of
peace," and a love of economy, have now reduced
this establishment, the buildings have been taken
down and the materials sold. — After passing
Woodstown Strand, within a mile of New Geneva,
the coast is bold and precipitous, with lofty headlands stretching out into an arm of the sea, which
forms the harbour of Waterford.

Nearly at the entrance of the harbour is the
village of Dunmore, formerly a place of resort for
fishermen, but now a delightful and fashionable
watering place. The village is situated in a
valley, with a gentle slope towards the sea; the
houses are built irregularly, without regard to
site or uniformity of appearance, except that

they all look to the same point—the Hook Light-
house, on the opposite coast. Most of the cot-
tages are built of clay and are thatched with
straw, and generally let during the summer season from one to three guineas a week. On the
hill, which forms the back-ground of the picture,
are the ruins of a church. Dunmore has latterly
been much enlarged; it is now a post town and a
station for the packets which carry the mails
between England and the south of Ireland. By
an act passed in the 58th year of Geo. III. cap. 72.
the limits of the harbour of Dunmore are defined
to be " from Shannoon Point, otherwise called
Black Nobb, to Ardnamult Point." This act also
regulates the duties to be charged on vessels ar-
riving at, or sailing from, the harbour: it also
authorizes the appointment of a harbour-master.
In order to have a convenient and secure asylum
for the packets, a pier has been built on the adjacent coast. On the road leading to the pier,
there is a handsome church, which, with the neat
white houses interspersed among highly cultivated fields, present a pleasing view to vessels
approaching the coast.

The pier of Dunmore is situated on the southern
shore of the bay of Waterford, where the haven
joins the Atlantic Ocean. The harbour for the
packets is formed under Dunmore head by the
projection of a mole, which is carried to a considerable distance into the sea. The object being

to reduce the fury of the waves, which, when im-
pelled by the south and west winds, dash against
the coast with inconceivable violence, a mole, supported by an immense breakwater, was commenced from a little within the head of Dunmore.
By vast exertions, and by procuring rocks of
great size, this mole was extended 800 feet into
the sea, which, at the place where the breakwater is formed, is from four to five and six
fathoms deep.   The mole is raised on an inclined surface between forty and fifty feet above
low water mark, roofed or paved with great
masses of stone, imbedded in a species of mortar
which becomes hard under water; the inclination
is such as to allow the fury of the waves to ex-
pend itself before reaching the parapet, which
surmounts the whole, at an elevation of seventy
feet perpendicular above the foundation.   The
pier and quay for the shipping are erected inside
of the mole, and present a most beautiful specimen of masonry.   This pier, or quay, is 600 feet
in length: the depth of low water at the entrance
is twenty-five feet, and at the innermost part
eighteen feet.   The greatest part of this noble
quay under low water has been built by means
of the diving bell, of which useful machines there
are two here, on very improved principles.

Under the superintendence of skilful engineers,
the workmen (untaught peasants) soon learned to
move vast rocks with admirable dexterity: few

of these were less than five or six tons weight, and some exceeded ten tons. These immense mountain masses, torn from the solid rock, were transported with apparent ease, on inclined planes and iron railways, to the place where they were squared with the greatest exactness; they were then disposed in their places, accurately fitted and joined together without the clumsy iron bolts and bands, which are at the same time laborious and expensive.

This great work, now nearly completed, offers obvious advantages. The packet harbour, ranging N. E. and S. W., is protected by the mole and Dunmore Hill against the most formidable and prevailing winds, the West and South West. It is also sheltered from the N. E. by another promontory, called Dunmore West, and from the East by the peninsula on which Hook Light-house stands.

The material of which the pier is principally composed is silicious pudding-stone, and a rather fine-grained sand-stone, which was found in regular strata: much of the latter was chiefly used in the mason work, the pudding-stone, broken into large irregular masses, served as a foundation.

Two neighbouring hills having been almost entirely cut away, and the stratified sand-stone being exhausted, it became necessary to seek elsewhere for stones to face the work, and these could not be

had, with the advantage of water carriage, nearer
than the lime-stone quarries of Dunkit, in the county of Kilkenny, distant about twenty-five miles. It
appears from an " Estimate of the expense of forming a packet harbour near Dunmore," extracted
from the Parliamentary Papers of 1814, that the
cost of the originally projected work was calculated at £19,385.   Various alterations and improvements, subsequently effected, raised the estimate, in 1821, to £42,500 : now (1824) £85,000
have been actually expended; and it is supposed
that £15,000 more will be required to complete
the work, making the total expense £100,000.
By hastening the works, a considerable saving
would be made in the expense of engineers, over-
seers, and other officers, at the same time affording employment to a greater number of persons.

Steam packets sail every day between Waterford and Milford, and afford a cheap and expeditious conveyance : the passage is usually effected
in about nine hours.* The time occupied in conveying the mail between London and Waterford

* The Cinderella, the first vessel of this description on this part
of the coast, performed the passage in a little better than seven
hours.   She left Milford at half past nine in the morning of the
16th of April, and arrived at Dunmore a quarter before five the
same evening.   The usual hour of arrival is between seven and
eight ; but it is expected that when the arrangements are completed, the packets will arrive three or four hours earlier.   The
packets do not leave Dunmore now until twelve o'clock at night.

48 hours

rarely exceeds eight and forty hours. On the arrival of the packet at Dunmore, in the evening, a
well appointed mail coach is to convey the passengers to Waterford; and from thence coaches
proceed to Dublin and Cork, where they arrive
on the following morning.

There are many spas in this barony, principally
chalybeate. At Monamintra, a spring strongly
impregnated with iron has been found useful in
many cases: at the foot of the rising ground, at
the rear of the new church and near the " Fairy
Bush," there are also mineral waters, which have
been proved to be very efficacious in giving health,
or, at all events, occupation to those who frequent
them.

The only remnant of Celtic superstition in this
barony is to be seen on the hill of Kilmacombe,
distant about two miles from Dunmore, it consists of five large stones, placed side by side, and
enclosed in a circle of stones about thirty yards
in diameter: it is supposed to have been a seat
of justice, or probably the grave of some hero.
Within three miles of Waterford, where the road
branches off to Passage and Dunmore, a stone
is pointed out as a Cromlech, or Druid's altar,
and has given the name of Mount Druid to the
seat of Mr. Reynett; but it is altogether too minute to deserve the appellation with which it has
been dignified. On the coast of this barony there
are several caverns, all of which appear to be na-

tural formations, and therefore more remarkable for grandeur and extent than for regularity of appearance. In the projecting headland which separates Woodstown Strand from Credan, there are three caves of considerable dimensions, which branch out into various chambers, consisting of natural arches of great symmetry and beauty.

They should be approached at low water: the rock out of which they are excavated is a coarse pudding-stone, which appears to have yielded readily to the influence of a descending stream. In the little bay of Dunmore, a fissure in the rock, of no great extent, is called the Cathedral. To the westward of Dunmore, near a promontory called Red-head, in a field adjoining the cliff, is an immense hole, styled the Bishop's Cave: it is one hundred and five feet long, and twenty-four feet wide; and, although eighty yards from the sea, it may be approached in a boat at high water. There are several other caves in this neighbour-hood, as at Rathmoylan, Ballymacaw, and at Brownstown-head.

The natural advantages which this barony derives from its proximity to the sea have not yet been made available to its numerous and peaceful population. The villages of Portally, Rathmoy-lan, Ballymacaw, and Summerville, which are principally occupied by fishermen, and which, with suitable encouragement, might be made thriving and industrious places, are now the re-

sidence of a poor and almost unemployed peasantry, vacillating between agriculture and fishing, and consequently unsuccessful in both. From
the prevalence of south and south-west winds, to
which this coast is directly exposed, and from the
want of convenient harbours, these villages are
unprofitable as fishing stations during the greater
part of the year.

On the appearance of foul weather, the fishermen are obliged to draw up their boats on the
beach, and are thus limited in their operations by
this additional labour, as well also as by the fear
of violent and unexpected storms, against which
they have no resource: had they a safe anchor-
age, into which they could run in bad weather,
they might, with little trouble or apprehension,
venture into the deep sea, where fish is always to
be found.

From the pier at Dunmore to Brownstown-head
the coast is rocky, and in stormy weather almost
inaccessible : at the projecting headland called
Fileskirt or Swinehead, there are sunken rocks,
nearly covered by the sea at high water, which
render the approach at this place particularly
dangerous. Brownstown-head forms the eastern
promontory of the bay of Tramore, and, from the
similarity of its appearance, has been frequently
mistaken for the land at the entrance of Waterford
harbour. To enable mariners to distinguish, and
consequently to avoid, the dangerous bay of Tra-

more, beacon towers have been recently erected, at the earnest solicitation of the harbour commissioners, who had much opposition to contend against: two of these towers are situated on the eastern, and three on the western promontory. The intended establishment of a floating light, near the Cunny Rocks, in the neighbourhood of the Saltees, will also tend most effectually to put a stop to the frequent losses of life and property on this part of the coast.

Near Tramore is a very ancient seat, called Summerville, the property of the Earl Fortescue. At the eastern extremity of the bay is the little harbour of Rhineshark. To vessels embayed in Tramore, the only chance of safety is to be sought by running directly into the harbour of Rhineshark. The stream which flows into the sea here is very inconsiderable, except when swelled by the winter rains; it takes its rise from several small springs, and is occasionally supplied from an extensive lake situated near Woodstown, and called Bellake.

MIDDLETHIRD.*

The barony of Middlethird adjoins the barony of Gaultier; the western boundary of the parish of Kilmacleague, and the eastern boundary of the

* Middlethird contains the following parishes Drumcannon, Kilbride, Island Icane, Don Isle, Reisk, Newcastle, Kilmeaden, Ballycashen, Lisnekil, Loughdahy, and Kilronan.

parish of Drumcannon, mark the line of separation between them. The bay of Tramore is situated about four miles to the west of the harbour of Waterford.

Between the promontories of Brownstown and Newtown-heads the coast is a dead flat, and presents a surface of level beach, three English miles in length. A bar, or mound of sand, raised by the united influence of the tides and the land streams, prevents the further encroachment of the sea. The part thus separated from the open bay, is called the back strand; it contains about a thousand Irish acres of. improvable land, and offers an inviting spoil to those who would wrest it from the dominion of the sea. The practicability of enclosing the back strand is now unquestionable, and the advantages to be expected are abundantly sufficient to repay the probable expense: it is therefore to be hoped that, within a short time, this enclosure will be undertaken, and become a mean of giving employment to the numerous surrounding population.

At the western extremity of the bay is situated the village of Tramore. Protected from the prevailing winds, commanding a magnificent view of the sea, and enjoying the advantages of a hard and level strand of great extent, Tramore possesses within itself everything which can recommend a sea-bathing place: there are good markets and commodious lodging houses. The great hotel is a spacious building, elevated considerably above the village, and admirably adapted for enjoying the invigorating breezes from the sea. The proximity of Waterford, distant little more than five miles, and the facility of communication by means of a countless multitude of indescribable vehicles, render this village the favourite summer retreat of the citizens of Waterford. The strand is about three English miles in length, and throughout perfectly hard and level: in the summer season there are regular races here, which are encouraged by the proprietors of the village and by private subscriptions. At one extremity of the beach, immense heaps of sand have been cast up by the sea, and compose what is called the Rabbit-burrow. These sand hills are partially covered with natural grasses and with a few plants, as asparagus, pansey, scurvy grass, &c. From this place the bay of Tramore may be seen in all its grandeur, either smooth and glassy as an unruffled lake, or, when agitated by the west wind, exhibiting the frightful magnificence of convulsed nature.

In the month of January, 1816, the Sea-Horse transport, having on board the second battalion of the 59th foot, was driven by a raging tempest into this inhospitable bay. It occurred in the day-time, the shore was crowded with people, who were aware of the inevitable fate of the crew, and had no possible means of relieving them. As the vessel neared the shore, those on board were distinctly seen, awaiting in agony the dreadful catastrophe. Husbands and wives, parents and children, (there were many women and infants in the ship,) were plainly observed in some few instances encouraging each other, but for the most part clinging to the timbers, or folding their arms round those they loved, that they might die together. Their anticipations were but too well founded: the vessel struck and went to pieces, when two hundred and ninety-two men, and seventy-one women and children, perished in sight of the assembled thousands. All that courage and the most devoted gallantry could do, was attempted to save them; and there are some splendid instances of successful exertion, in which the preservers nearly shared the fate from which they had rescued others. The calamity was almost general: only thirty men were preserved. A few days after the shipwreck, nearly sixty corpses, some of them the remains of women and children, were carried on the country cars from the coast to the burying-ground, at two miles distance. The wretched survivors accompanied the melancholy procession, and witnessed their companions and relatives deposited in one vast grave. A handsome mausoleum was ordered to be placed over their remains: the work is now finished, but the expense of it being still unpaid, it has not yet been erected The following inscription is on the stone.

BENEATH THIS TOMB

ARE DEPOSITED THE REMAINS OF

	AGE.		AGE.
Major *Charles Douglas*,	29	Lieut. *William Gillespie*,	19
Captain *James Macgregor*,	23	Ensign *Andrew Ross*,	19
Lieut. & Adj. *Abraham Dent*,	26	Ensign *Rowland F. Hill*,	19
Lieutenant *William Veal*,	21	Surgeon *James Hagan*,	30
Lieutenant *Robert Scott*,	23	Assistant Surgeon *Lambe*,	26
Lieutenant *James Geddes*,	21	Quart.-Mast. *William Baird*,	38

Of His Majesty's 2d Battalion 59th Foot,
Who perished in the Bay of Tramore,
On the 30th day of January, 1816,
By the wreck of the Sea-Horse Transport.
To their revered Memories
This testimonial is erected by
Lieut. Colonel AUSTIN, Lieut. Colonel HOYSTED,
And the other surviving Officers of the Battalion;
Also a Monument at the Church of Tramore.

Returning to their native Land,
Where they looked for solace and repose,
After all the toils and dangers they had endured,
For the security of the British Empire,
And the deliverance of Europe,
Their lives were suddenly cut short
By the awful dispensation
Of an all-wise but inscrutable Providence:
But the memory of those gallant achievements,
In which they bore so distinguished a part,
Under the guidance of the
ILLUSTRIOUS WELLINGTON,
Will never be forgotten, but shall continue to illuminate
The historic page, and animate the hearts of Britons
To the most remote period of time.

In the burying-ground of the new parish church in the village of Tramore, a monument was erected by the surviving officers. The principal circumstances of the melancholy event are recorded in the following words:

On the south side—

> LUGO, *6th & 7th of January*, 1809.
> CORUNNA, *16th of January*, 1809.
> WALCHEREN, *August*, 1809.
>
> ————
>
> This Monument was erected by
> Lieut. Colonel AUSTIN, Lieut. Colonel HOYSTED,
> and the other surviving Officers
> of the 2d Battalion of His Majesty's 59th Regiment,
> as a testimonial of their profound sorrow
> for the loss of their gallant Brother Officers,
> who perished by the wreck of the Sea-Horse Transport,
> in the bay of Tramore,
> on the 30th day of January, 1816;
> and as a tribute to the heroic and social virtues
> which adorned their short but useful lives.

N. B. The Mausoleum at Drumcannon Churchyard.

On the east—

> VITTORIA, *21st of June*, 1813.
> ST. SEBASTIAN, *31st of August*, 1813.
> BIDASSOA, *7th of October*, 1813.
>
> ————
>
> On the 30th day of January, 1816,
> the Sea-Horse Transport, Captain GIBBS,
> was wrecked in Tramore bay;
> upon which melancholy occasion,

12 Officers and 264 Non-Commissioned Officers & Privates
of His Majesty's 2d Battalion 59th Regiment,
together with Lieut. ALLEN, R. N. 15 Sailors, and 71
Women and Children,
perished within a mile of the shore.
Of the hapless inmates of this ill-fated vessel,
only 4 Officers, and 26 Soldiers and Seamen
were providentially rescued
from the raging Ocean!

On the north—

NIVELLE, *10th of November*, 1813.
NIEVE, *9th, 10th, 11th, § 12th of December*, 1813
BAYONNE, *February § March*, 1814.

———

SACRED TO THE MEMORY OF

Major CHARLES DOUGLAS,   Lieut. WILLIAM GILLESPIE,
Captain JAMES MACGREGOR,   Ensign ANDREW ROSS,
Lieut. & Adj. ABRAHAM DENT,   Ensign ROWLAND F. HILL,   Age 19
Lieutenant WILLIAM VEALL,   Surgeon JAMES HAGAN,
Lieutenant ROBERT SCOTT,   Assist. Surgeon LAMBE and
Lieutenant JAMES GEDDES,   Quarter-Master W. BAIRD,

Of the 2d Bat. 59th Regt. who were lost by the wreck of
the Sea-Horse Transport.
Your heroic deeds, Brave Warriors!
will never be erased from the page of history: and though
cypress instead of laurels encircle your temples, your ceno-
taph is erected in the bosoms of your Countrymen.

On the west—

WATERLOO, *18th of June*, 1815.
CAMBRAY, *21th of June*, 1815.
SURRENDER OF PARIS, *6th of July*, 1815.

The 2d Battalion of the 59th Regiment
commenced their Military Career in the Autumn of 1808,
when they accompanied Sir David Baird to Corunna,
and were conspicuously brave in the arduous campaign
under Lieut. General Sir John Moore.
They partook of the fate of the Expedition to Walcheren:
They also bore a distinguished part in the principal Actions
that were fought on the Peninsula in 1813 & 1814,
under the command of
THE ILLUSTRIOUS WELLINGTON;
and finally participated in the renown of the
ever-memorable day of Waterloo, and the
second surrender of the French Capital.

A considerable number of soldiers were inter-
red in the sand, at the distance of a hundred yards
from the sea: it was in agitation to erect a monument over their remains, but this has not been
accomplished.

The bay of Tramore, justly described in charts
as " notorious for shipwrecks," has at length engaged the attention of scientific and practical men;
and through them, of the public bodies, whose
duty it is to improve the navigation of our coasts.

A benevolent and spirited individual,* with
much labour and at some expense, has made a
survey and measurement of the bay, and has suggested improvements, which, it is to be hoped,
will be readily adopted by the proper authorities.

These improvements consist in the formation

* W Wolseley, Esq. Admiral of the Blue

of two secure harbours, one at the western and
the other at the eastern side of the bay : the harbours to be formed by the erection of small piers,
projected from the extremities of two fishing coves
within the entrance of the bay. The most obvious advantages arising from such works would be
these : fishing boats could sail to and return from
the Nymph-bank, during the continuance of the
prevailing winds ; and the bay being only about
two miles distant from the inshore fishing ground,
all engaged in such pursuits would have a secure
retreat in stormy weather, and could, without the
loss of time now necessarily incurred, return to
sea when the danger was over. These ports would
be stopping places for coasters, and would much
benefit the agriculture of the country by affording
facilities to the landing of lime and coals : but the
principal and paramount advantage would be the
security which they would give to vessels embayed within this dangerous place ; and which,
in the existing circumstances, have not a shadow
of safety. In the numberless cases of shipwreck
which have occurred here, the loss of life has been
invariably attributable to the want of a harbour,
into which to run the vessel. In great national
concerns, where commerce and human life are
concerned, expense should not be too narrowly
considered—such has not been, nor ever will be,
the conduct of the government : in the present
case, the probable expenditure is insignificant,

the estimate of the proposed works not exceeding
ten thousand pounds. To enter further into this
matter would be unsuitable to the present work,
the arrangements and detail belong altogether to
professional men.

The land in the vicinity of Tramore, from its
exposure to the sea breeze, has always been un-
propitious to the growth of trees. The face of
the country exhibits little improvement in this
respect, during the last century; and were it not
for the increase of tillage occasioned by the war
prices, the coast to the westward would still present a wild and uncultivated appearance.

Amongst the many advantages which the spirit
of geological research has conferred upon this
part of Ireland, perhaps the most generally useful is the discovery of limestone, on the coast of
the barony of Middlethird, at a place which had
hitherto been considered destitute of this valuable
mineral.

This stone is found in the immediate vicinity of the village of Tramore, at a place called
the Lady's Cove, where it is embedded in indurated clay slate. The rocks on both sides of the
limestone effervesce with acids, and hence it appears that they contain some portion of calcareous matter, which is probably the cause of their
exhibiting a tabular structure. Sulphuret of iron
is found crystallized and granular, in small veins
running through limestone next the indurated

clay slate; it is also found in the alluvial matter.
On examining some of the clay which is situated
over these rocks, calcareous matter was discovered to be a chief ingredient, and hence it appears, that all the substances, both rocks and
earth, partake largely of the nature of limestone.
The limestone is of the primitive kind, and is capable of receiving a very fine polish: it is, however,
chiefly valuable for agricultural purposes, and in
this point of view that the discovery may be considered a public benefit.

Arrangements are already made for the erection
of lime-kilns, which must tend immediately to
increase the value of land in this neighbourhood;
for lime, though perhaps used for ages as manure,
is still found beneficial to the soil of this country,
which, instead of being exhausted by its stimula-
ting qualities, is found to increase in fertility
after repeated applications.

Previous to this discovery, limestone was not
known to occur nearer to Tramore than eight or
nine miles.

Within a short distance of the village, are the
ruins of the castle of Cullen, formerly a place of
defence, and the residence of some warlike chieftain: an isolated rock is the foundation or ground-
work of the building, which, before the general
use of artillery, must have been almost impreg-
nable.   Tradition has preserved nothing of the

history of the place, or its inhabitants; like many
other works of art, Cullen has outlived the memory of its founders.

It is generally supposed that the castles and
fortified houses, the ruins of which are still to be
seen in great numbers, were the work of colonists,
whom the policy of the English monarchs induced
to settle in Ireland.

From the time of Henry II. lands were freely
offered to settlers at trifling or nominal rents: some
individuals of rank and consequence, who received
these extensive grants, very frequently neglected
to fulfil the conditions attached to them; and instead of bringing over a number of followers, and
affording their own personal influence and counsel,
they sold their interests to the old possessors,
neglected to provide for the defence of their properties, and, in some instances, abandoned them
altogether.

Succeeding monarchs endeavoured to obviate
these evils, by affixing certain conditions to the
grants, in proportion to their extent.

The lands to be planted were divided into three
proportions; the greatest to consist of two thousand English acres, the next of fifteen hundred,
and the least of one thousand. The undertakers
of two thousand acres were to hold of the king
in capite; they were to build a castle and inclose
a strong court-yard or bawn, and they were to
place upon their lands, within three years, forty-

eight able men, of English or Scottish birth: they
were besides to retain six hundred acres in their
own hands, and for five years, to reside constantly,
or to keep such agents as should be approved of
by the government. The same or similar conditions were attached to the smaller grants. The
holders of fifteen hundred acres were required to
finish a house and bawn within two years : a bawn
or strong inclosure was all that was required of
the third class.

From the bay of Tramore to Dungarvan, there
is little shelter for vessels of any description;
the shore is rocky and precipitous, and offers only
a few recesses or coves, precarious retreats for the
boats of the fishermen. The rocks along the
coast appear to have been violently disrupted,
the beds being heaped irregularly, and meeting
together, in the greatest confusion. Clay slate is
here also the prevailing rock; occasionally pudding-stone occurs, and, in the neighbourhood of
Annstown, a species of green-stone. Contiguous
to the coast in the parish of Icane, there are several small islands, which are only masses of rock
separated from the main land ; they are partially
covered with grass, and, except to the mineralogist, offer nothing worthy of observation.

Proceeding to the westward, a range of rocks,
possessing a columnar structure, are observed
jutting out into the sea, the colour is dark, approaching to black, extremely hard, and with a

faint lustre : the columns are irregular in shape and in the number of their angles, but are mostly terminated by five sides. There are several indications of mineral veins, and a variety in the rock formations, exceedingly remarkable in so confined a space.

The village of Annstown, distant about three miles from Tramore, is built on the western side of a valley which extends from the sea to a considerable distance inland. There are a few lodging houses for the accommodation of summer visitors, who are sometimes attracted by the retired situation; but the want of regular markets, and the distance from Waterford, have rendered Annstown little frequented as a bathing place. A handsome church has recently been erected here. The situation and appearance of this village are striking and picturesque. With few improvements or works of art to recommend it, Annstown possesses within itself many natural beauties: amongst these may be considered, a bold and magnificent coast, stupendous rocks rising abruptly from the sea, and headlands extending into the ocean and exhibiting natural arches of vast extent. To the east, the islands of Icane bound the view: the headland of Dungarvan is seen stretching away to the south-west. The prospect on the land side is chiefly remarkable for an ancient ruin, the castle of DonIsle, which stands above the ravine that extends

from the sea to the interior. The castle of Don-
Isle, or Donhill, as it is usually called, situated
about an English mile from the sea, is discernible
at a considerable distance, the rock on which it
is built being almost detached from the range of
hills which forms one side of the ravine. As you
approach the ruin by the road leading from Waterford to the demesne of DonIsle, the view is
impressive and romantic.

Having descended from the main road, through
a plantation of ·flourishing trees, the castle, a
square tower of great elevation, is seen, over-
hanging a river, here crossed by an antique
bridge. In ancient times, it was the property of
the family of Le Poer, from whom the present
Marquis of Waterford is descended. So far back
as 1346, this family held a distinguished rank in
this county: in that year John Le Poer, and others
of the same name, gave security to the Lord
Justice Birmingham, at Waterford, for themselves
and all others of their name in the counties of
Waterford and Tipperary, for their peaceable behaviour to the king and his ministers.

The castle of DonIsle might be considered inaccessible on two sides; and where it was liable
to be approached, its defences appear to have
possessed a considerable degree of artificial
strength

The only vulnerable part was well defended by
a strong wall and deep fosse, which inclosed a

court-yard of about fifty yards square: the mason work of the wall can still be traced through its whole course. After entering the court-yard, the passage to the castle was ascended by a steep flight of stone steps, which led to a gate defended by a portcullis; the arch of the gate, and the groove of the portcullis, being still discernible. You then enter into a small court-yard, which appears to have contained several out-offices belonging to the castle, and turning to the left hand into a still smaller inclosure, of about twelve feet square, the door of the castle is at length seen. All the various approaches already mentioned are carefully defended by loop-holes and embrasures; and on entering the castle itself, the usual square trap-door is observed over the passage, which gave the last opportunity of defence to the besieged, and from which, in the obstinacy of despair, they poured down on the assailants large stones, boiling water, or any other means of annoyance which the danger might suggest. The walls of the castle are still perfectly upright, not having yielded in the least to the encroachments of time: the castle, however, evidently suffered considerably from the violence of man, having been subjected to the force of gunpowder; but the square tower which crowns the summit, and which now can only be ascended by a ladder, the stairs having been designedly destroyed, is as perfect as if erected within these few years. The

Church at Don Isle

church, which lies at the distance of about 300
yards west of the castle, and which was evidently
attached to that building, appears to have been
subjected to the same barbarous violence, as the
rocky firmness of the masses which formerly composed it, and which now lie scattered in various
directions, clearly prove.

In one instance, an entire staircase remains perfect, but the wall in which it was built has been
thrown a considerable distance from its original
position: the only part of the wall which remains
perfect is the arch which separated the chancel
from the aisle.   On digging among the ruins of
this church some years ago, a statue, cut in sand-
stone, and bearing on its head a coronet, was
discovered: it is now to be seen, set upright
against the wall at the west end of the church.

A very ancient tombstone has also been discovered in the burying-ground; it is without any
inscription, and simply decorated with a coronet.
It is supposed to have been the tomb of the
Countess, who perished when the castle was taken
by Cromwell.

A considerable range of high land extends from
the sea, through the parishes of DonIsle and
Reisk.   The rock is mostly pudding-stone and
clay-slate, and occasionally large masses of jasper:
some of the specimens are very beautiful.   Along
the coast the rocks are rich in minerals: lead and
copper have been found at Annstown and Bon-

mahon, where mines of these substances were worked to a considerable extent, and at no very remote period. The elevation and abruptness of the coast afford some facility in discovering these minerals, veins frequently appearing where the earth has been washed away by the encroachments of the ocean. Various circumstances concur to induce the belief that mines might be advantageously worked here. The course of the veins is east and west; the ore is heavy, and has a rich appearance, and there is besides the advantage of water-carriage. The range of hills passing through the parishes of DonIsle and Reisk divides into two branches in the latter parish: the intermediate low land is partially covered with water, which forms the lake of Ballyscanlan. The bottom of this lake is still thickly covered with fragments of trees, which were probably displaced by the water at no very remote period. After leaving Reisk, the high land extends to the vicinity of Waterford.

At Sugar-loaf Hill, so called from its abrupt and conical appearance, there is a very noble Cromlech, or Druids' altar, the most perfect of these antiquities, which is to be found in the county.

Four oblong masses of rock, elevated on their extremities, support a table-stone or altar of considerable magnitude, the height of which is about twenty feet The workmanship is altogether

rude and unpretending. Within the space inclosed by the uprights or pillars, a single stone
stands entirely detached from the sides and covering of the altar. This relic of ancient days is
situated to the south-east of the range of hills,
which, through its entire course, is covered with
fragments of rock, varying in size from field stones
to immense mountain masses. Connected with
this relic, we have here an indisputable instance
of the policy of those who first introduced Christianity into this country; and who, in every case,
endeavoured to engraft the pure religion upon the
heathen superstition which preceded it. The
neighbourhood of a Celtic monument was selected
as the site of a Christian church, which now in
its turn affords protection to its neglected rival.
The church is gone to decay, the altar remains in
all its rude perfection: the combination is striking;
there is something grand and romantic in these
ruins of remote and dissimilar periods, which
cannot fail to impress the mind with admiration,
and which leaves upon it a pleasing though melancholy feeling.

It is probable that the church, the ruins of
which adjoin the altar, was erected shortly after
the introduction of Christianity into this country:
it was only at that period the Celtic monuments
were considered as giving sanctity to the place on
which they stood, though it might be supposed
that some veneration was still attached to them,

the Irish expression for, going to worship, literally signifying, going to a stone around which people assembled to worship. A view of the rocks throughout this range, and of the uncouth forms and grotesque positions which they sometimes assume, leads to the belief that the elevation of cromlechs, or altars, is not always to be attributed to the physical exertions of man. It is impossible to conceive such immense blocks to have been raised in rude times by uncivilized men; and the absence of regularity in the position, and in the number of the stones employed, strengthens the supposition that they are natural formations. In this neighbourhood, some other large and flat rocks might be made to exhibit the same appearances, by removing the earth on which they rest, and exposing to view the irregular, and frequently perpendicular, pillars beneath them.

There is another altar near DonIsle inferior in magnitude and beauty to that at Sugar-loaf. There is no similarity observable in the direction or inclination of the stones in these antiquities. In that at Sugar-loaf, the direction appears to be east and west, the upper or table stone dipping to the east; at DonIsle, the table stone is supported by three uprights, the direction is north and south, and the inclination to the south. The rock of which these altars are composed, is siliceous slate; the flat stone or covering at Sugar-loaf is chlorite slate

s

In an open space between these wild and irregular elevations is a small conical hill, called
Cruach or the Heap, in which is an exceedingly
rich mineral vein containing lead ore combined
with a considerable proportion of silver: this mine
was formerly worked to a great extent, as appears
from the still remaining shafts which were excavated with care, and propped and supported with
timber which was only recently removed.   Near
to this place, beds of sand occur in large quantities, and there are some indications of limestone,
which will probably be found on the lands of
Gaulstown.

There is a romantic wildness in the country
about Pembrokestown which is totally unlike any
thing to be seen in this barony.   The hills, which
rise precipitously, are covered with singularly
bold and rugged rocks, and immediately adjoining
and between these irregular elevations, small
patches of the finest land, watered by a clear
stream and sheltered from every wind, present a
retired and quiet landscape, which even from
contrast must be considered interesting.   A slight
improvement in the farmers' dwellings, and some
judicious planting, would supply all that is wanting to render the scenery perfect.   It would be
surprizing if, in such a place, some traces of the
Celtic inhabitants of Ireland were not discernible:
there is here all the romantic interest and natural
grandeur which these people loved, and the simple

monuments which still remain to us incontestibly prove that this was a favourite haunt. A round hill or rath, which commands no distant view, could only have been a residence or retreat; besides this, there is a cromlech which consists of five upright stones supporting a flat stone or covering. The entire is inconsiderable in size, and possesses no remarkable beauty.

At Whitfield, the property of Mr. Christmas, the coarse slate passes into roof slate: a quarry of this material has been worked to some extent; but, in consequence of the smallness of the slates, is now disused. Probably, were the quarry sunk to a greater depth, the slates would be found larger.

Near Knockaderry, a subterraneous passage is hollowed out of the rock, and seems to have had some connection with the Druidic superstition. A curious sepulchre was discovered here beneath a cairn or heap of stones; it consisted of six square stones joined together in form of a box, and contained human bones, some of which appeared to have been burned.

Near Whitfield were lately discovered two stone chambers, somewhat resembling the monument at New Grange near Drogheda, described by Ledwich.

On the removal of a vast heap of stones which lay for ages on the side of the road, and from which portions were taken away from time to time to be used in repairing, a large flag was observed, which, when removed, discovered a circular opening into an arched or vaulted apartment constructed in the shape of a bee-hive. It was composed of flat stones, the higher projecting beyond the lower, and tapered into a point which was covered with a flag. On entering into it, a narrow passage was discovered, leading from one side, but it was almost filled up with rubbish and clay: another chamber was found at no great distance. These buildings are about five or six feet high, and are supposed to have been used as tombs.

The village and neighbourhood of Kilmeaden were formerly places of some consequence; but the castle and the ancient private residences are long since gone to decay, and in their place only one considerable residence has been built, at Mount Congreve, the property of John Congreve, Esq.

In the churchyard of Kilmeaden is the tomb of John Ottrington, Esq. who purchased part of the property of the Le Poer family, which was seized by Cromwell. The monument was erected by Elizabeth, Viscountess Doneraile.

At Phair Brook, on the lands of Cullinagh, in this parish, and six miles to the west of Waterford, there is a most extensive paper manufactory, carried on with great spirit and judgment by the

respectable proprietors, Messrs. Phair and Har-
dums.

Notwithstanding all the disadvantages under
which this species of manufacture has laboured
from enormously high duties, and the frequent
and vexatious visits of revenue officers, who are
personally interested in making the discovery of
illicit practices, this establishment has gradually
and progressively succceded so as to arrest the
attention of even the most superficial traveller.

The steadiness and regularity with which the
business is conducted, the excellence of the ma-
chinery, the constant adoption of every species
of improvement, and the unwearied attention
evinced in every department, have placed this
manufactory on the firmest and most durable
basis.   About 140 men, women, and children are
kept in constant employment, and thus the beneficial effects of Phair Brook mills are felt for
miles around.   This neighbourhood is peculiarly
fortunate in the occupation of the peasantry. Mr.
Malcomson, of Clonmell, a spirited and enterprising merchant, has lately become tenant to the
mills of Pouldrew, where there was formerly an
extensive iron manufactory carried on by Messrs.
Wyse. He has already expended much money
in repairing the old bolting mill, and is about to
erect a mill and corn stores, which will be of
great service to this part of the country.

These two establishments are situated on the

same stream, which unites itself with the river Suir at a little distance from Pouldrew.

UPPERTHIRD.*

The barony of Upperthird consists of two irregular portions of land, extending across the county from the Suir to the sea, except where the northern division is separated from the southern, by the parish of Rosmeer, a part of the barony of Decies. This barony is of considerable extent at the northern boundary, but is contracted as it approaches the sea-coast: it contains no town unless we include a part of the town of Carrick on Suir. The face of the country adjoining the sea is altogether wild and uncultivated, almost entirely destitute of trees, and, except near the village of Bonmahon, unimproved by any respectable residence. The coast labours under the same disadvantages as were before enumerated in the account of Middlethird, and consequently the fishery is at present comparatively unproductive. It is to be hoped, that the peasantry residing on the coast of this county, will shortly receive some portion of the assistance intended by government for the fisheries of Ireland.

* Upperthird contains—near the sea, the parishes of Kilbarrymeaden, Monksland and Ballylaneen, near the Suir—Gilcagh and Coolfin, Clonegam, Fenoagh, Mothill, Deseit and Kilmoleran This barony was formerly divided into eleven parishes.

The parish of Kilbarrymeaden derives its name from a church which was built here by St. Baramedan. The Irish word *cill*, pronounced *kill*, signifies a church, abbey or place set apart for religious purposes. The land which belonged to this church has long been highly venerated by the common people, who attribute to it many surprizing qualities. It is said that a notorious robber, whenever he passed through this place, used to wash his horse's hoofs and legs in the first water which he chanced to meet, lest his haunts should be discovered in consequence of his being guilty of sacrilege, in carrying away a portion of the holy clay. There is a well here, sacred to St. Baramedan, frequently resorted to by pilgrims, who ascribe many virtues to its waters. Murina, a sister of this Saint, and equally esteemed for piety, also resided in this parish. A church, the ruins of which are still discernible, built by her near the sea, gives to the place the name of Kilmurrin. An image of this saint, rudely carved out of a rock, may be seen in a cave near Dunbrattin: the place is often resorted to by the neighbouring people.

A recent discovery of limestone at Tankardstown, near the sea coast, promises great advantages to the neighbouring country.

At Dunbrattin, a term which signifies the fortification of the Britons, it is supposed that the first English invaders landed in this county : a small mound, with a circular entrenchment, is still pointed out as their earliest acquisition. The contiguity of this place to DonIsle, or as it is sometimes called, Dondrone, is supposed to countenance this idea.

To the west of Dunbrattin is the village of Bonmahon, consisting of some handsome private residences and several convenient lodging-houses, generally occupied during the summer season. The river Mahon, which rises in the Cummeragh mountains, and after a course of seven or eight miles here meets the sea, is crossed by a light wooden bridge, which adds to the picturesque appearance of the place.

Much has been done by the proprietor of Bonmahon, to render it a popular and fashionable bathing place: a circular race-course, a convenient strand and public rooms are among the inducements which this village offers to the public. The mines at and near Bonmahon, deserve particular attention, and, whether we consider their importance, and the advantages derivable from them to the country generally, or to the unemployed population of the adjoining district in particular, it must be admitted that a faithful inquiry into their extent, value and facilities for working, is much to be desired. This can be effectually accomplished only by those practically acquainted with the business of mines. The following observations are offered, with the hope of arousing public attention to the subject. It appears from a manuscript of the Bishop of Clogher, in the college library, that valuable mines were known to be in this neighbourhood, at a very early period: the situation of Knockdry and Powers-country, in which places, silver and lead were said to be found, cannot now be exactly ascertained; but it seems probable that the latter place was somewhere near Bonmahon or Annstown, where the representative of the family of Power formerly resided. The mines of Bonmahon, under which denomination are included the mines in the vicinity, produce copper, lead and silver; veins have already been opened in many places, and worked to a considerable extent. In the year 1745, a company rented these mines from Lord Ranelagh, for a term of thirty-one years, under an agreement to render to his Lordship one eighth part of all the ore obtained. The works were carried on for eight or ten years with great spirit and tolerable success, but a want of union among the members of the company, injudicious arrangements, and, above all, unfaithful managers, checked the progress of the undertaking and it was at length abandoned. One hundred and thirty tons of copper and thirty-five tons of lead ore, are mentioned in an old document as having been raised in a few months.

Mr. Wyse subsequently worked these mines

with three hundred men, and obtained large quantities of ore: a heap, which was thrown aside as of little value, was afterwards shipped to England on speculation, and produced near four hundred pounds. In 1811, Lord Ormond undertook to renew the works, but was obliged to desist after a considerable expenditure had been incurred, and when there appeared every probability of ample remuneration.

The value of the mines is described in the most glowing colours, by an individual who had the management of the works at this time: solid copper is said to have been found exceeding eight inches in thickness, and extending through a space of more than thirty yards; while the situation of the veins is represented as the most favourable for the operations of the workmen.

The rock in which the mineral veins occur is clay slate: the veins are found in some cases within a few feet of the surface, and none have been worked at any time to a greater depth than twenty-five yards. Persons walking along the beach may observe copper ore in many places; but the course of the principal veins is known only to miners residing at Bonmahon.

At the strand of Kilmurrin, lead ore is found among the sand, and amply repays a number of country people who are constantly employed in seeking for it by turning up the surface with their spades. This ore has produced from thirty-eight to forty ounces of pure silver per ton. Very many veins of lead and copper ore have been discovered besides those which were worked at Bonmahon, but the property in them being reserved by the lord of the soil, the occupying tenants are averse to their being publicly known, conceiving that the operations of the miner would interfere with their interests, while they would be entirely excluded from any participation in the profits. Mineral veins are known to occur at Temple Bric and at Carrig Castle. The principal mines are on the property of the Earl of Ormond, and on a part of the see lands of the Bishop of Waterford.

The central part of the barony of Upperthird is traversed by a range of high land, called the mountains of Cummeragh, which extend from the river Suir to the neighbourhood of Dungarvan. The Cummeraghs, as they are called, are composed of an irregular chain or series of hills, only partially connected together, and varying in direction, in some degree, though having a general tendency from north to south.

The sides of these mountains are extremely wild and precipitous, and present a singular appearance when viewed at a little distance; the lofty rocks and deep precipices exhibiting great masses of light and shadow. Clay-slate forms the base or mountain mass of all this range. On Monevullagh, large beds of hornstone porphyry are found: there are also several veins of quartz and pink felspar, in which micaceous iron ore and iron glance show themselves. The clay-slate which forms the mass of this range, is, in some places, of a beautiful purple colour: over this are found a close grained sandstone of a light grey colour, argillaceous red sandstone, and slaty conglomerate. The slaty conglomerate is exceedingly beautiful: its base is fine argillaceous sandstone, in which very small quartz and hornstone pebbles are occasionally blended with fragments of purple slate, pink felspar, and indurated green earth. The purple slate is, however, the chief constituent of this rock.

These rocks are all tabular, but irregular· they are placed in a vertical position, and hence the ruggedness of the mountains as you ascend toward their tops. At and near the junction of the several streams which form the river Mahon, veins of quartz are to be seen, in which granular galena is found. There are several lakes on the summit of the Cummeraghs; they are called the Cummeloughs and the Stillogues In the former a remarkably fine species of trout is found, but the fish in the latter are very little esteemed. The views around the lakes are highly picturesque, and in some places magnificent. Porphyritic rocks occur here, and there are also indications of iron ore, particularly iron glance. At the White-horse hill, a very beautiful white sandstone, resembling Portland stone, is quarried for building, but as this stone is decomposed rapidly by the action of water, it should not be used where great durability is required.

The mineralogist who expects variety in the rocks in this district will be grievously disappointed; in fact, clay slate, purple slate, roof slate, and slaty conglomerate, are the principal formations. The tourist, however, who visits these mountains to see and admire the beauties of nature, will be amply recompensed by the sublime and romantic scenery which everywhere presents itself. These wild and lonely mountains, enveloped during a great portion of the year in mist and fog, and seldom visited except by the sportsman and summer tourist, were, for a long period, the retreat of General Blakeney, an eccentric being, who " loved not man nor woman either."

After a continuance of some years in the gaieties of the world, and while still in the prime of life, this gentleman constructed a dwelling on one of the hills which compose this range, and, with a single male attendant, for he never admitted females into his residence, retired to live here in solitude

How he passed his lonely hours is not exactly known: the servant partook of the taciturnity of his master, and few ever visited where they felt that their presence was an intrusion. The recluse was mostly engaged with his fishing rod or gun;

and was often seen, clad in an apparently impenetrable garment, braving storm and rain, even in the wildest weather. He was seldom known to leave his solitude, and never sought or enjoyed society, except when obliged to give shelter to a benighted sportsman; and, on such occasions, his manner and behaviour were kind, though reserved and distant—as if to show that he did not regret the demand on his hospitality, though he wished that the same necessity for it might not occur again.

General Blakeney is represented as an intelligent and well informed man; and it is, therefore, the more unaccountable, that no reason should have been assigned for his singular retirement. He continued on the mountain until his death, and, according to his own wish, was buried near his residence, with his dog and gun.

Passing from the south to the north division of this barony, the contrast is truly singular. In the former, all is sterility and desolation; a rude, naked, and uncultivated soil, without trees or improvements of any kind: in the latter, the face of the country and even the climate appear more favourable, and in some places there is a richness and a magnificence of scenery which is rarely surpassed. Of course the former observations do not apply to the parts of the southern division which are fortunate in enjoying the residences of wealthy individuals, around whose seats nature

and man wear a more kindly aspect. It is in
those places where gentlemen's mansions are
" few and far between," that the truth of the remark is undeniable; and it is after having wan-
dered over miles of unimproved country, that we
fully perceive the value of resident proprietors.

There are, however, capabilities of wealth and
prosperity in this quarter, which should stimulate
exertion. Independent of other advantages, the
mines and the fisheries may be made of incalculable benefit to the country, opening a vast field
of enterprize, and affording capital to some, and
profitable employment to a now wretched multitude.

In this barony was situated the principal part
of what was called Powers-country, under which
denomination was also included the adjoining
portion of Decies and part of the neighbouring
barony of Middlethird. The representative of the
family of the Powers, or Poers, still retains a commanding influence here; and includes, within his
magnificent mansion at Curraghmore, a part of
one of the castles of his ancestor of former centuries.

Curraghmore, the seat of the Marquess of Waterford, is situated at the distance of about ten
miles and a half from Waterford, and about two
miles south from the river Suir, in a valley formed
by the waters of a mountain river called the Clodagh This river discharges itself into the Suir,

and is navigable for about one mile, as far as the
bridge of Portlaw.

At the distance of eight miles from the city of
Waterford, at the stream and ruined church of
Kilbunny, the grounds of Curraghmore may be
said to commence; and from this place the pe-
destrian traveller may enjoy the luxury of a most
romantic and retired walk, which leads, without
any interruption, to some distance beyond the
house of Curraghmore, through woods of varied
description, and of the most luxuriant growth.
The entrance of this avenue, which is called the
" Gravel Walk," may be found by turning up a
narrow lane on the left hand side of the road
immediately before coming to the stream of Kilbunny, it passes at the rear of the house of Coolfin, (in which the rector of the parish usually re-
sides,) across the road from Portlaw to Kilmacthomas, and at a short distance behind the village
of Portlaw, (after passing which, it'crosses a second road,) comes in contact with the river Clodagh on its south bank—passes over the precipice
which looks down on the salmon leap, and shortly
after enters the Deer Park by a box turnstile.
Immediately on entering into the Deer Park, a
small wooden bridge presents itself, by which the
river may be crossed to the grand avenue which
runs along the opposite bank of the river. The
Gravel Walk still continues its course along the
south bank, and terminates at an antique stone

bridge, called Bullen's bridge, at a short distance beyond the house, which lies about three hundred yards from the opposite bank of the river.

At the first or entrance gate of Curraghmore, a handsome school-house has lately been built by the direction of the Marchioness of Waterford, for the purpose of educating the children of the surrounding peasantry; the grounds which lie between it and the Clodagh have been laid out in the most tasteful manner. At a short distance from the first gate, but not to be observed from the road, the Clodagh presents an interesting appearance, forming a considerable water-fall, called the Salmon Leap, where the salmon may be observed, at the time of their periodical ascent, making the most persevering efforts to surmount this obstacle, and they are frequently found above three miles higher up than this point. On passing the second gate, the road continues for nearly half a mile parallel to the course of the river, the hills on either side being covered with oaks of the noblest growth.

On approaching within a quarter of a mile of the house, the road turns from the river; but here a small door presents itself on the river's edge, which opens to the pleasure-grounds that lie between the house and the Clodagh, and a gravel walk is continued along the bank, nearly to the western extremity of the demesne, beyond the gardens, which are·situated on the river side. The front approach to the house lies through two magnificent ranges of offices, inclosing an oblong court-yard of extraordinary dimensions, terminated by the ancient castle front, on the parapet of which is the representation of a stag, larger than life, this is the crest of the Beresford family. The castle, which now forms the front, was the ancient residence of the Poer family. At the rear of this castle, a splendid and commodious mansion has been erected by the grandfather of the present proprietor, the castle being converted to the purposes of a magnificent hall, and the upper part of it thrown into one grand apartment, called the castle-room.

The rear of the new house commands a view, in which the grand and beautiful are united in an unusual manner. In the fore-ground, at the extremity of the lawn, is presented a large sheet of water, formed by the extensive embankment of a small stream which runs into the Clodagh, ornamented by fine trees, while the distance is closed in by the stupendous mountains of Monevollagh, which present the most rugged and uncouth precipices. The view in this direction is particularly brilliant and splendid in the evening, when the setting sun illuminates the craggy ridge of the mountain, and sinks its base in almost impenetrable shade.

Passing from the low grounds, the parish church

of Clonegam may be observed at a considerable distance, on the side of a hill. The church, a beautiful little building, was re-edified by the late Marquess of Waterford, in the year 1794 : the wood-work is of beautifully carved Irish oak ; the windows, seven in number, are all of stained glass; the west window is particularly fine, re-presenting, in its various compartments, some of the most remarkable passages of scripture history. In the churchyard is the burial-place of the noble family of Curraghmore, surrounded by rows of beech trees, whose tops uniting produce a gloomy shade, in perfect accordance with the solemn na-ture of the place. Higher up above the church, on the summit of the hill of Clonegam, stands a round tower, built by the late Marquess of Wa-terford, and dedicated to the memory of his eldest son, who was killed at the age of thirteen, almost at the gate of Curraghmore, while in the act of leaping his horse over the paling which joins the entrance. According to the original plan, this tower was to have been raised to the height of one hundred and twenty feet, but has been left in an unfinished state, at about seventy feet elevation. It can be ascended by a winding flight of steps in the inside, and the view from its summit is per-haps the most extensive that can be had from any similar elevation in the kingdom. On the south, at the direct distance of about seven miles, appears the sea, near the watering-place of Bonmahon.

T 2

On the west, the county of Tipperary is widely presented to the view : on the north, at the distance of a mile, runs the Suir, which can be observed for a course of fifteen or twenty miles, separating the counties of Kilkenny and Tipperary from that of Waterford, and winding through that fertile tract of country, which has been called the " golden vale of the south." In the distance, further to the north, appear the mountains of the county of Carlow; while on the north-east and east, arise the mountains of the county of Wexford, which divide that county from the counties of Carlow and Wicklow.

In the direction due east from this tower, it was the intention of the late marquess to have erected an artificial ruin in imitation of those places of religious worship, which are generally observed in the neighbourhood of the ancient round towers in this country; and for this purpose, the stone window which belonged to the west end of the old cathedral of Waterford was transported to this spot, where it has since lain buried in the furze and heath. On returning from the tower by the church and farm-yard, you again come upon the road which passes through the demesne in the direction of Carrick, and shortly after arrive at the last gate.

The entire demesne contained within the walls is considered above 2,500 acres, of which 1,200 are under timber; to this the present proprietor has

added some very extensive farms which lay contiguous to the wall, the greatest part of which he
has planted, so that the whole estate may perhaps
now be estimated at 4,000 acres, of which at least
2,000 are under trees. The character of Curraghmore is grandeur, not that arising from the costly
or laborious exertions of man, but rather the magnificence of nature. The beauty of the situation
consists in its lofty hills, rich vales, and almost
impenetrable woods, which deceive the eye and
give the idea of boundless forests. The variety
of the scenery is calculated to please in the highest
degree, and to gratify every taste; from the lofty
mountain to the quiet and sequestered walk on
the bank of the river, every gradation of rural
beauty may be enjoyed.

About half a mile distant from the last gate, on
an eminence which commands a splendid view of
the Earl of Bessborough's improvements in the
county of Kilkenny, and on the left hand side of
the road, stands a stone of considerable magnitude, raised at least eight feet above the level of
the ground. There are various traditions among
the country people with regard to the causes of
elevation of this stone, and the agents who were
employed in the work, but all of them too absurd
to deserve notice here. Certain marks on one side
of it, have by some been imagined to make part
of an inscription, now almost entirely defaced; by
others they are said to be the marks left by the

fingers of those gigantic beings who amused themselves in the removal and erection of this stone.
At the distance of about forty yards, within the
hedge, on the side of the road, there was discovered, in the year 1810, the entrance into a subterranean chamber eight feet square, and at the
further extremity of this, a passage between two
and three feet square, which led into a second
apartment of the same dimensions as the former,
and from thence into a third. The first discoverers
not being gifted with much taste for subterranean
research, preferred the more expeditious way of
prosecuting their inquiries by digging in the field
above, and having thus loosened the stone arch
which formed the ceiling, the entire of the roof
of the third apartment fell in, and thus put a stop
to any further discovery. It has been supposed,
that the large stone before mentioned, was intended as a mark by which the entrance into
these subterranean chambers might be readily
found, and that the apartments themselves were
used as hiding-places during the various persecutions, disturbances and civil wars, which have for
centuries afflicted this unhappy country.

After leaving Curraghmore, the country adjoining the Suir is sterile and hilly, until you approach
the flat alluvial soil in the vicinity of Carrick.
In an extent of some miles, there is little to excite attention, except the contrast between the
opposite sides of the river; the view of the county

of Kilkenny, which is rich and beautiful, must entirely occupy the mind.

In Carrickbeg, formerly called Carrick-mac-Griffin, and Little Carig, being part of the suburbs of the town of Carrick on Suir, are the ruins of a monastery for Minorites founded in the year 1336, by James, Earl of Ormond.

The list of the inmates of this building is only worthy of notice as containing the name of John Clyn, author of a celebrated chronicle yet extant. Friar John Clyn was translated from the Franciscan Friary of Kilkenny to this monastery, of which he was appointed the first warden: he died of the plague, in 1349.

The founder, Earl James, assigned ten acres of land to the friars, on which, by the aid of charitable donations, they built a church, a dormitory and cloisters. The last prior was William Cormoke, who surrendered the monastery on the 7th of April, 1540, at which time the property consisted of a church and steeple, a chapter-house, dormitory, hall, three chambers, a kitchen, a stable, and about 150 acres of land. This friary and twenty acres of land in the town of Carrick, together with the friary of Athassel in the county of Tipperary, were granted to Thomas, Earl of Ormond. Of the original buildings, the church and steeple alone remain, the latter in almost perfect preservation. The church is of considerable

extent, extremely irregular in appearance, combining the Gothic with a peculiar kind of architecture, which is seldom described.   The principal
entrance is beneath a magnificent and neatly cut
arch, springing from consoles decorated with
flowery carving in the interior, and on the outside with representations of human heads.

The entrance is between the western extremity
of the building, and the centre of the north-wall,
and at a corresponding distance between the
centre and the eastern extremity, a tower or
steeple is raised to a very considerable height.

The steeple is a square building, projecting considerably beyond the wall on which it is erected :
the foundation of the steeple consists of a single
stone, on which the lower part, resembling an inverted cone, rests, and supports the entire weight
of the superstructure.   A beautiful spiral flight of
steps built in the wall conducts to the top of the
steeple.   The interior of the church has been
used as a cemetery, originally for the inmates of
the monastery only, but in later times for the
neighbouring families.   The burial-place of the
friars, which is at the left hand of the altar, is
distinguished by an ornamented fretwork, something like a canopy, which is inserted in the
wall.   A rudely carved figure in high relief
points out the place of interment of one of the
Friars, whom we are justified by nothing more
than our wishes, in calling Friar John Clyn.—

Inserted in the wall, opposite the tower, is a tablet on which are the arms of the Ormond family, and the words—In te, Domine, speravi—Petrus Butler. A monument bearing date 1621 is almost totally illegible

Another monument, much of the inscription on which is legible, except the date, belonged to an individual of the Coolnamuck family who built the castle, the ruins of which are still preserved on the property of his descendant.

As on all the ancient tombs, the inscription, in large Roman capitals, goes round the edge.

GIRALDUS WALE DE CUILMUCK——NOBILIS
CATERINA COMLFORD.

Within a short distance of the ruins of the monastery, a very handsome Roman Catholic chapel has been recently erected. The grand entrance is exceedingly neat; the facing and the arches of the windows and doors are of cut stone.

The figure of a saint is erected in front on the top of the building: at the other extremity, a steeple, a very imperfect imitation of that attached to the monastery, gives an air of splendour to the chapel, and were it not that the ornamental part is too showy, the entire work displays considerable taste and ingenuity in the architect. There is something singular in the position of this chapel, which, contrary to all ancient precedent, stands north and south, completely at right angles with the monastery.

In all places of worship in this country, the direction, allowing for the variation of the compass, is invariably east and west, and a reference to this rule frequently serves to point out the part of old buildings which was appropriated to religious uses, and which it would, otherwise, be difficult to discover.

Nothing can exceed the beauty of the country on the county Waterford side of the Suir between Carrick and Clonmell. The road passes close to the river and at the foot of a lofty range of hills, planted with flourishing trees, or clothed to the summit with the most luxuriant vegetation. The oak seems to thrive here remarkably well; even on the sides of the hill where the rock is near the surface, they are strong and vigorous: at Coolnamuck there are some very fine trees. The ruins of a castle built by Giraldus Wale, whose tomb is shewn in the ancient monastery of Carrick-beg, add considerably to the natural beauties of the demesne of Coolnamuck, and are preserved by the respectable descendant of the ancient proprietor, with perhaps a too cautious fidelity.

At Churchtown, within a part of the ancient place of worship,—which, with a degree of taste not usually observable in modern ecclesiastical buildings, has been preserved, and adjoins the new parish church,—there are two very singular monuments. They stood originally in the interior, and from the great space which they occupy, must have been highly valued by those who afforded such an undue portion for the accommodation of the dead. Though now some years exposed to the weather, the letters, with one or two exceptions, are sharp and well defined. The inscription on the former is, for the most part, written in the large Roman capital; there are, however, some unusual variations in the formation of some of the letters:

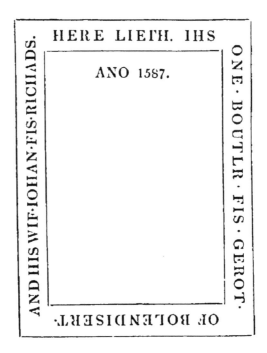

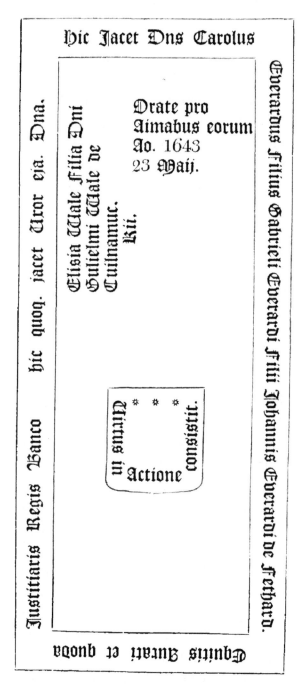

In Sir William Petty's time, the Everards had an ancient castle in this neighbourhood, the site of which is not known.

Within a short distance of Churchtown glebe, a woollen manufactory has been recently established; this and another establishment nearer to Carrick are, unfortunately for the country, the only remains of the former trade which at one time flourished here, and which was forced to yield to the distractions of Ireland, but more particularly to the jealousy of the English manufacturers. There are several persons employed by this manufactory, who work at their own homes, thus combining the quiet and innocence of rural life with the wealth and enjoyments of commerce. Turning from the direct road to Clonmell, and having ascended a steep hill, the ancient castle of Ballyclough is seen frowning over the valley. Nothing is known of its former owners or of the particular purpose for which it was erected, save that it was the work of persons by no means destitute of skill, and who lived in contemplation of wars and tumults. The building was rudely but regularly fortified, being defended by a moat and ditch, which are still discernible, and having all the accessible parts of the hill on which it is erected perfectly commanded by loop-holes and embrasures, which still remain. A circular staircase, in tolerable preservation, conducts to the watch-tower, from which there is an extensive view of a wild and uninteresting country. Returning to the charm and variety of the direct road to Clonmell along the bank of the Suir, the majestic woods of landscape, the property of John Congreve, Esq., and of Gurteen, belonging to Edmund Power, Esq. are seen skirting the way on the left for many miles. On the right, there is a considerable space of low land adjoining the river, which affords a beautiful contrast to the thickly-planted hills which rise abruptly above it.

A deep ravine, now almost concealed by its luxuriant timber, possesses singular beauty, and, were there occasional openings in the trees, could not be passed unnoticed. There is here, in a large bed of gravelly sand, the first indication of the occurrence of lime-stone; in many places in this county these two formations are found in immediate contact. At Gurteen, a magnificent mansion was projected by Mr. Power, but nothing has been completed except the stables, which are of great extent, and exhibit a castellated appearance. A cromlech, or Druids' altar, stands on the demesne; it consists of five irregularly placed upright stones which support a sixth of somewhat larger size, but wanting the flatness and peculiar position of some of the more perfect of these works. On the property of the Earl of Glengall adjoining Gurteen, a prodigious ravine, excavated by winter torrents, discovers the material of the range of hills, which is red sandstone, alternating with a beautiful white siliceous sandstone; and in some places the rock is of a soft slaty nature, readily decomposing by the action of air and water, and forming a yellow ochreous earth, sufficiently pure to be used in manufactures. This earth occurs in large quantities, and may be easily procured. Nearly opposite the ravine are the ruins of the castle of Darinlar, thickly clothed with ivy, and exhibiting indubitable proofs of age. This was a regularly fortified residence, commanding, perhaps, a ford across the river which it immediately adjoins. The tower, which alone remains, was protected by four circular castles, that projected beyond the curtain, and effectually commanded the approach.

The whole superstructure is raised on arches, probably in consequence of the foundation being defective; several vaults are still in perfect repair, and are a source of constant uneasiness to the superstitious peasantry. At the bounds of this barony, near Clonmell, is Tickencore, an ancient residence belonging to Sir William Osborne, near which is a bridge across the Suir: there is also another bridge at the distance of about two miles. Having arrived at Tickencore, all the beautiful parts of Middlethird have been passed over; the interior, including the commons of Clonmell, which are supposed to contain about 5,103 acres, is a wild and uninteresting district, and presents little worthy of observation. It seems probable that this part of the barony, though now less improved than the tract adjoining the river, was, in remote times, the seat of an extended population. The number of monasteries and castles, the ruins of which are still discernible, lead to the belief that civilization had made some advances here even at a distant period. At Rathgormuck the church occupied a large space of ground, and there are near it traces of former improvements. The west wall · of the church is still standing, and exhibits some remains of its Saxon architecture, which appears to have been afterwards, in some degree, replaced by Gothic arches, clumsily affixed to the exterior of the doors and windows. At the distance of about two miles from Rathgormuck, and in the direction of Clonea, is the castle of Feddens, a square building, forming the lower part of a large structure, contrived with all the massive rudeness of a distant period, but not retaining any traces of warlike design. Tradition tells us, that Feddens was formerly the residence of a fraternity of priests, who had, besides the castle, several houses around it. Independent of the good taste of the proprietor, the ancient building and an adjacent Danish rath are indebted for their continuance to the superstitious scruples of the peasantry, who, whatever was the object of builders of former days, are always unwilling to meddle with their labours.

While digging the adjoining lands, the workmen discovered a copper pot, about two years since. At Bolhendesart and at Mothil, in the neighbourhood of Carrickbeg, there were two famous religious houses; of the former nothing is known further than that it was built, probably in the sixth century, by St. Maidoc of Ferns; the latter was also constructed at the same time, or even an earlier period, for we find that in the sixth century St. Coan succeeded St. Brogan, who was the founder of the abbey, and the first abbot. The abbey of Mothil was established for canons regular of St. Augustin, though some assert that it belonged to the Cistertians. The abbots were long engaged in disputes about their property, and in one case which occurred in 1296, the Abbot Adam was nonsuited, he having sued by the name of Abbot of *Morthull.*

Edward Power, the last abbot, surrendered the abbey, 7th of April, 31 King Henry VIII. (1540) being then seised of the same, also of the church, steeple and cemetery, hall, five chambers, dormitory, kitchen, granary, two stables, an orchard and other closes containing six acres, all within the precincts of the abbey, together with lands in Mothil, Killemaspicke, Kilberny and Grange Morlery, exceeding 700 acres, and also the rectories of Rathgormuck, Moynelargy and Ballylaneen, all which were appropriated to this abbey. In two years afterwards, all these possessions were granted to —— Butler and Peter Power, at the annual rent of £6 : 4s. 0d. Irish money. The ruins of this ancient abbey cover a large extent; the west and south wall of what was probably the church are still standing. In the latter, a beautiful Saxon arch, about twelve feet high, opens into a small square chamber: part of the ancient arch has been recently filled up, leaving a narrow entrance, to which an iron gate has been attached. Several modern sculptured stones have been inserted in the ancient work, intended to represent some parts of scripture history. These stones are all together six in number; two of them containing historical representations, and four having figures of the Apostles, three on each. The carving is very rude, but perfectly distinct.

In the small building which appears to have been reserved for the interment of particular families, two of the sculptured stones are inserted in the wall, opposite the entrance, under a piece of ornamental work. Around a flat tomb-stone in this place is the following inscription, in large Roman capitals:

HIC JACET GVALTERUS POWER GENEROSUS ORIUND°
EXANTIO ...... FAMILIA JOHANNIS GULIELMI ET
UXOR EJUS CATERINA PHELAN QUI SUIS SUMPTIBUS
CONSTRUXERUNT HOC MONUMENTUM.

QUORUM   16 JUNII,
ANIMAB   1628.
PROPITII.
TUR DEUS.

In the same place is a monument to the memory of Mrs. Jane Wall, relict of James Wall, of Clonea Castle, 1821. In the ruins of the larger building, an iron railing incloses the burial-place of the Powers, of Gurteen. In the inclosure is a very ancient tomb.

A tomb-stone, narrowing to the foot, which was a form used in very distant times, may be observed near this: the characters are quite illegible. The church of Mothil is a neat modern building, simply ornamented with a tower, instead of the incongruous and mis-shaped steeples with which such structures are usually disfigured.

At the distance of about a mile from Mothil, and in the vicinity of one of the mountains of Cummeragh, are the village and castle of Clonea. The castle is one of the most perfect specimens of the ancient fortified residence, and exhibits clearly all the minute arrangements of such dwellings. The principal building is quadrangular and of great height, divided into several stories, which are approached by a flight of stairs within the walls. The watch tower commands a magnificent prospect.

Outside, and within a few feet of the castle, a strong wall, with circular towers at the angles, inclosed a square piece of ground: this was the first defence, and beyond it were a ditch and moat, a portcullis and fortified keep; a series of defences, which, before the use of artillery, must have been

I 2

Clodagh River

inexpugnable.   Only two of the circular towers
can be distinctly traced; but there can be no
room to doubt, that the ancient arrangement of
the several buildings was as described.   The little
river Clodagh, which flows close to the site of the
castle, and some judicious plantations, give interest to the scene.   A species of muscle is found
in the Clodagh, in which pearls are frequently
discovered: some of these are exceedingly beautiful; they are of a pale blue colour, not regularly shaped, and are considered but of little
value.

muscle producing fine pearls

DECIES WITHOUT DRUM.*

Drum mountain

The two baronies of Decies are distinguished by
the relative situation which they bear to the Drum
mountain.   Decies without Drum is the largest
barony in the county, and contains the towns of
Dungarvan and Kilmacthomas.

In the parish of Rosmeer, a narrow strip of land
which separates the two divisions of Upperthird,
are situated Kilmacthomas and Newtown.   At the
latter place it was intended to build a town, probably as being on the confines of three baronies;
streets were marked out and paved, and a few
houses erected, all of which have long since gone
to ruin, except one.

* This barony is divided into thirteen parishes—Rosmeer, Fews,
Stradbally, Kilrossinta, Kilgobonet, Clonea, Dungarvan, Colligan,
Seskinan, Modelligo, White Church, Kilrush, Affane

Clonea Parish

Kilmacthomas, situated on the road leading from Waterford to Dungarvan and Cork, is built on a steep and dangerous hill, at the foot of which flows the river Mahon. It would appear that this little river was formerly subject to greater floods than have been observed here for many years. In 1649, Cromwell having raised the siege of Waterford, and passing through Kilmacthomas on his way to Dungarvan, the Mahon had risen to such a height, that an entire day was consumed in sending the foot across the river. There is now a handsome stone bridge here. At this place was an ancient castle, which belonged to the Le Poer family, in whose descendants the principal property in the neighbourhood is still vested.

On the sea coast, at the distance of six miles from Kilmacthomas, is the village of Stradbally, consisting of one long and irregularly built street.

The church, which is a modern building, stands on the site of the old church: near it are the ruins of an abbey of Augustinian Friars, the last of whom, called the White Friar, is still the hero of many legendary tales. At Ballyvoney, the traces of an extensive building are still discernible: the length was an hundred and fifty feet, the breadth ninety feet. An open well in front of the building communicated, by a subterraneous passage of two hundred feet, with another well within the walls The water which supplied these wells was brought through an aqueduct, extending nearly half a mile. This building was supposed to have been one of the Knights Templars' houses, of which establishments this county only contained four, the sites of which are all known. There are two Roman Catholic chapels in this parish. The lower orders are of a peaceable and industrious character; the same remark applies to the inhabitants along the coast, from the Suir to Dungarvan; and generally, wherever there is food and employment, the peasantry appear both industrious and contented.

In proof of the improving condition of the people in this parish, it may be noticed that the schools are numerously attended. The late Pierce Barron, of Faha, Esq. bequeathed £30 per annum as an encouragement to education in this place. Adjoining the village of Stradbally, and immediately contiguous to the sea, is Woodhouse, the seat of Robert Umacke, Esq. It is mentioned in Smith's history of Waterford, that, in the year 1742, an ancestor of the present proprietor obtained a premium for having planted 152,640 trees; and it is added, " were they properly taken care of, they would in time make a noble plantation." Notwithstanding their proximity to the sea, these trees have flourished in a remarkable manner, and now demonstrate the practicability of growing timber in almost any situation, provided the requisite care and expense be afforded. Woodhouse was

anciently called Torc-Raith : it was the residence
of part of the sept of the Geraldines, and the scene
of much valorous contention.

The ruins of many castles are still discernible
in this and the neighbouring parishes. At Temple Bric, a vast rock in the sea, distant about forty
yards from the shore, there are traces of an ancient
building, supposed to have been the residence of
O Bric, the chief of the southern Decies. A species of hawk, remarkable for great strength and
courage, frequented this rock, and is occasionally
seen there at the present time.

About two miles to the south-west of Stradbally are the ruins of a castle, called, in Irish, the
house of fortification: it is situated on a very steep
cliff, which overhangs the sea, and was defended
on the land side by a deep trench, over which was
a draw-bridge. This castle was built by the Fitzgeralds, and was inhabited at no very remote period. A little beyond this, near the river Dally-
gan, there stood for many years a representation
of a human figure, rudely cut out of a rock ; it was
considered by the country people as the image of
a saint, and was presented by travellers with a
green branch, a leaf, or flower, and a heap of these
always lay before it. It was afterwards removed,
and cast into the sea. There are in this parish the
relics of Druidical works, if we may judge from
their appearance. At Drumlohan is an inclosure
of an oval form, 182 feet in length and 133 feet in

its greatest breadth : in the centre is a large stone, around which some of smaller size are raised. A subterranean circular chamber, thirty feet in diameter, and roofed with flags which met in a point at top, was discovered some years ago near Woodhouse, and is also supposed to be of Druidic origin. Whilst enumerating the wonders of this neighbourhood, Clough-lowrish, or the speaking stone, must not be omitted. This is an enormous rock or mountain mass, which seems to have rolled down from the adjoining hill, and is now firmly fixed in the centre of a stream, near the road from Waterford to Dungarvan. The stone is split in a remarkable manner, the fissure dividing the mass into two nearly equal parts. There is a tradition that some person, as he passed this rock, expressed a wish that it might speak and divide into two parts, if the declaration which he was making were not true: the story goes, that the stone did split and also speak, and the appellant was consequently convicted of falsehood. The rock is a very coarse pudding-stone, and might have been induced to convict the perjurer, by the influence of frost upon water, which can easily percolate the mass : whether the sound emitted on the occasion was an articulate one, it is not so easy to determine.

In the parish of Kilgobonet, which extends to the mountain of Cummeragh, are the ruins of a church, situated on a hill. This parish derives its name, as well as its consequence, (if it possesses any,) from a saint called Gobnata, who, in the sixth century, was abbess of a nunnery in the county of Cork: the patron day is the 11th of February.

From the parish of Clonea the land inclines as you approach the sea, exhibiting a large tract of alluvial soil, highly cultivated and fertile.

An extensive and enlivening view appears from the summit of Cushcam; beneath is seen the castle of Clonea, the ruins of a church, and a spacious strand, further on, the improvements of Cloncoskoran, and, in the distance, the town of Dungarvan, with its abbeys and towers, which seem as if rising out of the sea.

The town of Dungarvan is supposed to have been built in the seventh century: it was anciently called Achad-Garvan, from St Garvan, who founded here an abbey of canons of St. Augustine.

Without depending too much upon the traditional antiquity of this place, there are many authentic records to assure us that Dungarvan was a considerable town, so early as the reign of Edward the Fourth (1463). In this year, Dungarvan was incorporated by an Act of Parliament still preserved, which recites that " the seignory of Dungarvan was the most great and ancient honor belonging to the king in Ireland." All the privileges which the citizens enjoyed under this act were renewed to them by James the First, as a reward for their fidelity to the crown, during the rebellion in the reign of Queen Elizabeth. The

charter was again renewed in 1659, at which time
the borough of Dungarvan possessed property valued at £203 per annum. The corporation of Dungarvan has long since gone into disuse. It seems
probable, that the conflicting interests of the corporation and of the proprietor of the manor, not
being equally balanced, the divided powers of the
former merged in the more steady influence of
the latter.

The manor of Dungarvan is now the property
of his Grace the Duke of Devonshire. King John
built the castle, and probably it was the same
prince who fortified the town, inclosing it with a
wall, having towers and bastions. The castle and
fortifications having fallen into decay, they were
repaired in 1463 by Thomas, Earl of Desmond, to
whom the customs of the town were delivered, to
be appropriated to that purpose. The walls and
towers are now for the most part removed, except
where they have been joined to modern buildings.
The ruins of the castle and fortifications are still
to be seen. This place of defence, situated within
the entrance of the harbour of Dungarvan, consisted of a castle, placed in the interior of an oblong fort, which was regularly fortified and mounted with cannon, and was protected by circular
towers at the angles. The external defence is
approached by a narrow passage between two
battlemented walls, at the extremity of which is
the entrance or keep, a narrow tower-like build-

ing, flanked on each side by circular castles. The
gateway, which is very narrow, opens into a small
quadrangular space, from which there are recesses
opening into the massy walls—probably intended
to protect those who were stationed at the entrance, and who were thus enabled to annoy the
assailants. The interior building, or castle, was
elevated some few feet above the external fortifications, and was in itself capable of resisting an
attack, even after the loss of the outworks.

There was a well within the inclosure, but it is
now filled up, the water being brackish.

The site of the castle is the property of the
Duke of Devonshire, and is now rented by government, who have erected here a miserable
barrack for the garrison of the town. The barrack, a modern building, planted as it is in the
centre of an ancient and venerable fortification,
looks singularly mean and inappropriate: the soldiers too, with their modern dresses and modern
implements of war, do not harmonize with the
appearances around them, and give the idea of
being intruders on the property of the heroes of
distant times.

The town of Dungarvan is well situated, it
stands to the west of the harbour, an arm of the
sea, which extends inland for some distance, and
is navigable for vessels of considerable tonnage.
According to a map of the town, as it appeared
about the middle of the last century, the streets

and buildings were of the most wretched description, and they continued in the same state until
a very few years since. Crowded with miserable
houses, irregular in appearance, without any or
at all events an inefficient police, Dungarvan deserved the reproachful epithets which travellers
universally bestowed upon it. There were no regular market-places, no public water-works. the
court-house, where the sessions are occasionally
held, was considered unsafe for the purposes for
which it was originally intended: there was no
bridge, and consequently no way of passing from
the town to the Waterford side of the river, except
by a ferry boat, or, as was generally the case with
the lower classes, by fording the stream at low
water. This custom, particularly as practised by
females, gave rise to ridiculous and indelicate
jests, which served to impress upon travellers an
unfavourable opinion of the inhabitants of the town.
In addition to all this, the population were without employment, the fishery neglected, and the
prisons were a disgrace to a civilized country.

Such was Dungarvan, when the present proprietor of the manor, his Grace the Duke of Devonshire, directed his attention to its improvement.
The first great work effected was the erection of
a magnificent bridge across the river, at a little
distance above the town, where it should not interfere with the approach of the shipping. The
river, or rather arm of the sea, is crossed by a

recent to 1834

bridge and causeway which were executed at
the sole expense of the present Duke, in 1815.
The bridge is a single arch of seventy-five feet,
a most beautiful specimen of architecture; the
massive stones of which it was built, were all
brought from England. The causeway is three
hundred and fifty yards in length and must have
been a work of enormous labour. A neat square
and a handsome street connect the town with
the bridge and serve to make an opening to the
? penetralia of the place. Reservoirs of water
conveniently situated, and (what were hitherto
unknown in Dungarvan) market-places for the
sale of fish and meat, are among the improvements already effected. Here, as in all places
where his property extends, the Duke of Devonshire has largely contributed to the establishment of Fever Hospitals, Dispensaries, Poor
Schools and other public charities. The fisheries
of the southern coast of Ireland, whether considered as a source of national wealth, as a nursery
for seamen, as affording employment to a super-
abundant population, and at the same time yield-
ing an ample supply of nutricious food, present
to the enlightened statesman a wide field for the
exercise of political sagacity. The Nymph bank,
as far as has been ascertained, stretches along the
whole of the southern coast, at the distance of
about seven leagues from its eastern part at Dungarvan, to a distance of from fourteen to twenty

leagues from its western part at Cape Clear and the Mizen-head. This bank is supposed to afford an inexhaustible supply of cod, ling, &c. and might be made to add a great accession of wealth to the country, were a few of the harbours improved by piers, and capital afforded to the fishermen to enable them to equip their vessels. From the poverty of the owners, the boats are not in general in the sea-worthy condition in which they ought to be. The heavy expenses even of repairs frequently compel the fisherman to risk his life with cordage and sails which are almost unfit for use, and until the establishment of the bounty, which in some degree operated as a donation of capital, many boats were altogether laid up, their owners being unable to repair them.

Since the tonnage bounty has been in operation, the number of boats and men employed in the fishery of Dungarvan has increased progressively. In the last year 163 boats and about 1100 men have been engaged, and have procured for the country upwards of one thousand tons of excellent fish. The wives and children of the fishermen are also employed in cleaning and salting the fish, so that at a moderate calculation, it may be computed that 5000 individuals depend for their support on this branch of national industry. The sum granted in bounties during the last year, was £2,647.

The fostering care of government has already

produced many beneficial results; it has infused
a spirit of life and vigour into the minds of the
people, and it has called into action a portion of
capital which would otherwise have lain dormant.
Still the fishery of Dungarvan is in its infancy,
and will for some time longer require encouragement and support. The principles of free trade
are not generally applicable in this country and
least of all in the present instance, where nothing
can be done without capital and where capital
does not exist.

All the public and private measures adopted
for their benefit have tended to give new life to
the inhabitants, and it is not too much to say,
that Dungarvan is now a handsome and certainly
an improving town. Previous to the Union this
borough sent two Representatives to parliament :
householders who have a freehold of five pounds
per annum, are entitled to vote for the member
for the borough, and have the further privilege of
voting for the members for the county. There
are no traces of the abbey founded by St. Garvan, nor are there any public buildings which deserve particular attention. Some of the towers
which protected the gates, and the angles of the
wall, still remain. The church, a modern building, commands a fine view of the harbour. A
Roman Catholic chapel was commenced here a
few years since, but the extent of the proposed
building being much too great for the numbers

and wealth of the persons concerned in its erection, the plan has not succeeded. The new chapel, if completed, would be much larger than the great chapel at Waterford, which is generally considered one of the most spacious buildings in the empire; and, in addition to its size, its splendid and costly design opposes impediments to its erection.

There are a number of public schools in Dungarvan, all well attended. Of Roman Catholic children alone there are no less than 777 at different schools.

At the abbey side, and in view of the town, are the ruins of a castle and abbey. Nothing can be discovered relative to the castle further than its having been the property of the M'Graths: it is a lofty square building and was probably intended to protect the abbey. The abbey has been more fortunate in its annals. In the thirteenth century, there was established here, a monastery of the order of Eremites of St Augustin, commonly called Austin Friars, under the protection of the Earl of Desmond. It is said that the M'Graths, one of whom is buried here, were the founders of this house, and that the property attached to the abbey was given by them and by the O'Briens of Cummeragh. There is still much to admire in the ruins of this ancient abbey: the wall and tower, with the entrances and windows, are still perfect, and give a clear idea of the beauty of the building, in its former condition. The original structure comprised a number of apartments or cells for the members of the order, and a place of worship, a narrow edifice, from the centre of which arises a light Gothic tower, sixty feet in height and still in good preservation. The arch which supports the tower springs from the side walls, and is constructed with great elegance and lightness.

The timber used in turning the arches is still to be seen, and though exposed to the air for nearly six hundred years, is not yet entirely decayed. The entrance at the western extremity is through a small Gothic doorway, which opens into the exterior or nave of the church; the arched way beneath the tower forming a communication with the chancel. A large window at the east end, having a rather modern appearance, admits a fine view of the ocean. Immediately beneath a low window adjoining the eastern extremity of the church, there is a very ancient tombstone, around which may be traced the following inscription, in large letters,

DONALD M'GRATH, 1400.

On the foundation of the ancient cells, a Roman Catholic chapel has been lately erected, and is now become a part of the abbey: the interest and sanctity of the ancient building are thus appropriated to the worshippers of the existing gene-

X

ration, while the burying-ground is to remove every remaining distinction between the present and the past. The chapel bell is erected on the summit of the tower.

Over the entrance of the modern building is a rude stone on which is cut a Griffin, and three escallop shells: this formerly stood above the door of the abbey. The walls and entrance to the burying-ground are preserved in good and neat order, and betoken that the present owners contemplate the place with the respect it merits. In the parish of Modelligo, adjoining the parish of Colligan, there are the ruins of many ancient buildings, the principal of which were the property of the M'Graths, who had large estates in this part of the county. The castle of Sledy was built in 1628, by Philip M'Grath. The castle of Knockmoan, in the parish of White-church, is one of the most picturesque buildings in this neighbourhood, and would be esteemed an invaluable object by the admirer of wars and sieges. It is situated on a tall insulated rock commanding an extensive prospect, and perfectly secured by a deep morass which incloses it on every side. This castle is supposed to have been built by a female, whose tomb was long shewn here, but there being no inscription or record of any kind to confirm the idea, the matter is still involved in obscurity.

Sir Richard Osborne was besieged in this place

in the rebellion of 1641: it was afterwards taken by Cromwell's soldiers, and probably it was by them reduced to the ruinous state in which it now appears. Dromana, in the parish of Affane, is one of the most magnificent demesnes in Ireland, and when we consider its historical associations, or its natural beauties, is deserving of some particular notice. The Lords of Decies, the ancient proprietors of Dromana, derived their descent from James, the seventh Earl of Desmond. In 1561, a descendant of this nobleman was created Baron of Dromany and Viscount Desses, and dying without issue, his possessions, but not his titles, descended to his brother Sir James Fitzgerald, who removed from Cappagh to Dromana, where he died in December, 1581.

It was a son of this Lord of Decies who received Sir Walter Raleigh, when he retired from active life to improve his estates in Ireland. It is said that Raleigh first introduced the potatoe, and a fine species of cherry which he brought from the Canary Islands. According to the very interesting account of Raleigh in " Researches in the South of Ireland," it appears that the potatoe was first planted in Youghal: the cherry was domesticated in the neighbourhood of Dromana, where it has continued to flourish to the present time, and is still in high estimation. The value of the cherry is still undisputed; the other importation may be considered as an advantage or a curse to the

country, according to the different theories of
political economists. Sir Walter Raleigh had
considerable estates in this part of Ireland, and
sought, with that zeal for which he was remarkable, to introduce improvements which he had
learned in his intercourse with foreign countries.
In proof of the generous hospitality of the Irish
to the distinguished stranger, it may be mentioned, that the Lord of Decies presented him
with New Affane for a breakfast.

Dromana, now the property of John Villiers
Stewart, a descendant of the original proprietor,
is rather calculated to excite admiration from the
consideration of its antiquity as a residence, and
from the extent of the demesne, than from any thing
remarkable in the house, which is for the most
part a modern building, the greatest portion of the
ancient castle having been destroyed by fire.
To view Dromana to the greatest advantage, it
should be approached by crossing the Blackwater, which runs between it and Lismore. A
cot guided by a female, no mean rival of the
Lady of the Lake, is stationed near Dromana, and
offers a pleasant and picturesque mode of conveyance to the demesne.

The mansion appears suspended over the river,
the land shelving rapidly, in some places perpen-
dicularly, to the water's edge. The view from
this point is grand and striking: the banks of the
Blackwater, thickly clothed with flourishing

trees, which seem to support the projecting windows of the castle, the hanging gardens and the beautiful windings of the stream compose a landscape which it is impossible to behold without admiration.

The gardens, which cover a considerable space of sloping ground, command a fine view of Cappoquin and the adjoining country. A sweet chestnut tree, near the entrance, measures fifteen feet in circumference.

The demesne is of great extent and magnificent in all its parts; the plantations have been arranged with judgment, and with particular attention to the grouping of the different trees. A sad proof of the disturbances of the times is seen in a barrack erected at a short distance from the house, in which were quartered an officer and twenty-one men.

There are here very favourable circumstances for the geological inquirer who wishes to observe the relative position of the rocks in this district.

The land is of considerable elevation at a short distance from the Blackwater, and shelves rapidly, and in some places very abruptly, to the river.

The soil is remarkably fertile, evidently favourable to the growth of trees, many of which are of unusual dimensions. There is no appearance of sterility even when you ascend the neighbouring hill, which is clothed with rich verdure to the summit.

Where the house is built, and contiguous to the river, the rock is clay-slate, large masses of which are exposed. The summit of the hill, which bounds the demesne, is a fine white sandstone resembling Portland stone. In a large and deep hollow in the demesne, there is a white clay resembling white powdered sugar, which, it is said, was employed successfully in the manufacture of glass: traces of copper ore are discernible in the rocks near the river, and at no great distance lead has also been found. At the opposite side of the river, and within a few feet of the surface, the substratum is micaceous red sandstone. The junction of the limestone and slate may be observed on the demesne of Tourin, the seat of Richard Musgrave, Esq. The view from the ancient castle which forms a part of this gentleman's residence exhibits the mineralogical divisions as well as the picturesque beauties of the surrounding country. It has always been supposed that a large tract of country in this neighbourhood abounds with mineral productions. At Kilkeamy, near Mountain Castle, on the lands of Mr. Chearnley, there is a fine lead mine; the ore, in a powdered state, has been taken up with a shovel in considerable quantities, and used by potters for glazing. The ore is close to the surface, and is visible to the most careless observer. From the place where the lead appears, there is a deep ravine, affording the greatest facility to carry off the water, if the mine were worked. In this barony, lime occurs in great abundance; it is found resting on clay-slate, sand-stone, and in some few places it is topped by a coarse gravel of a siliceous nature.

The limestone enters into this county at the western boundary, and, extending towards the east and south, terminates near Clonea, within a few miles of Dungarvan. Wakefield is incorrect in saying that there is no lime in this county east of the Blackwater: lime is found in abundance at Lismore, at Saltibridge, and at Dungarvan, at the north, south, east, and west of the river. The workmen employed to sink for water in the lime-stone at the glebe of the Rev. Mr. Dickson, near Dungarvan, discovered, at the depth of thirty-six feet, large quantities of living frogs: the rock appeared to be a solid mass, without any passage through which the animals could be supposed to have entered.

There are some remarkable caves in the lime-stone district, as is generally the case where this rock prevails. At Shandon is one of considerable extent, and another at Colligan. In the parish of Whitechurch are two immense caverns, situated near each other; one of them, called Oon-a-glour, is of great size, and is divided into two chambers. In the inner one may be seen a small stream, which sinks under ground at Ballinacourty, and after passing through this cave, is seen again

above ground at Knockane, after performing a
subterraneous course of nearly a mile in length.
The other cavern, called Oon-na-mort, is likewise
divided into many chambers, and has been occupied more than once as a place of religious retirement.   These, and several other caves which are
found in the calcareous rocks, are probably natural formations, produced by the action of water
upon the accidental fissures.   In the caves at
Rinagonah and in the Cummeragh mountains,
there are some faint traces of human workmanship; the rock out of which they are excavated is
clay-slate.   In this barony marble is found in
several places.   Near Kilcrump, in the parish of
Whitechurch, there is a black marble without any
mixture of white; and at Ballinacourty there is
a grey marble, some specimens of which are very
beautiful.   At this latter place there are indications of copper.   White hard crystals, which do
not effervesce in acids, are found in yellow clay
here.

DECIES WITHIN DRUM.*

This barony, the south-western division of the
county, is bounded by the sea, by the river Blackwater, and by a range of hills called the Drum,
which separates the two parts of Decies.   It does

* Contains the following parishes —Rinagonah, Ardmore, Kinsalebeg, Aglish, and part of Kilmolash

not appear at what time, or for what reasons, Decies was divided into two baronies; but it is probable, that the great extent of this portion of the county, and the natural boundary which presented itself in the Drum mountain, suggested the division which took place after 1654, at which period Decies is described as one barony. The Drum mountain comprises a large tract of land, much of it already cultivated, and all capable of considerable improvement. The summit is table-land, extending about twelve miles in length and from four to five miles in breadth, and contains nearly 25,000 acres; and all this vast space, though perhaps not unclaimed, is confessedly not the acknowledged property of any individual.—There are several opinions respecting the ancient allocation of this property: it is supposed by some that it belonged to the proprietors of the surrounding estates, who enjoyed this land in common; others imagine that, in consequence of its little value, it was entirely neglected at the time of distribution; while a favourite notion among the common people is, that it was reserved by Queen Anne for the relief of the poor of Ireland.

Parcels of this land have, from time to time, been added to the adjacent property; but a more important appropriation has been made by strangers, beggars, and outcasts from other places, who have built huts or hovels, cultivated a small portion of ground, and thus recurring to original principles, are now the undisputed and indisputable lords of the soil, freeholders by the most ancient, if not the best of all titles, the law of nature.

The improvement and final settlement of this tract of country is a matter well worthy the serious attention of the government. The numerous population who now reside on and near this mountain are peaceable and industrious, and though far removed from the terrors of the law, unstained by any portion of that crime which, strange to say, generally pervades the richest and most cultivated districts. The tenants of this wild heath, though suspicious of strangers, and impatient of opposition or encroachment, are kind and hospitable in their manners, and zealous in proffering their services to those who visit them, when perfectly convinced that their object is not to strip them of their rights. Still it would be absurd to imagine, that the almost total freedom from restraint which exists here may not, on some future occasion, generate disturbance; and equally unreasonable would it be to expect that smuggling, and other illicit practices, should not prevail on a wild and unprotected coast. The interests of the poor people who have settled on this mountain, should be scrupulously regarded; while, at the same time, means should be employed to bring them and their possessions within the range and the protection of the laws To effect these desirable objects, it would be sufficient, to remove anxiety and suspicion, by confirming the rights of the present occupiers, and by such a distribution of direct and cross-roads as would render every part of the district completely accessible. The improvement of this common must be a national work; the expenditure which would be required is beyond the means of individuals, and the place is too remotely situated to be an object of great importance to the county. It is true, that the landed proprietors who have properties near the mountain, would derive great benefit from increased facilities of communication; but this should be an additional inducement to undertake the task, if it could be made to appear that the advantages likely to accrue from it would not be entirely local.

The barony of Decies within Drum is, as it were, cut off from the rest of the county, and is only accessible by a circuitous route, or by attempting the mountain-passes, which are impracticable for a loaded carriage. At this time the produce of the land can only be conveyed to the adjoining markets, by sending it coastwise in boats, or by the agency of miserable horses, who carry it on their backs over the almost impassable footways. It would seem that the passage of this Alpine district was not considered so difficult in former times as it is at the present day, when smooth and level roads have introduced the use of wheel carriages. The intercourse between the monasteries and other religious houses at Ardmore, Clashmore, and Dungarvan, could not have been conveniently kept up, except by the mountain-roads, which were the direct modes of communication between those places; and though it may appear strange to us, that the reverend travellers should expose themselves on this mountain to a motion so unsuitable to their age and habits, yet we can have no reason to question the fact, when we are reminded, that this road, though not an easy, was yet a royal, one, and was the line in which King John and his courtiers travelled, when business or pleasure induced them to cross this part of the county. In the parish of Aglish, at a short distance from Clashmore, are the ruins of an ancient square building, called Clough, which, it is said, King John used as a resting-place in his journies between Cork and Waterford. Clough was a regular fortification, and consisted of a high wall defended by towers at the angles: the entrance, which was protected by a drawbridge, was on the south side; the exterior wall inclosed about half an acre. Amongst the numerous ancient edifices, the remains of which are still discernible in this neighbourhood, may be mentioned the abbey of Clashmore, which was founded by Cuanchear, at the command of Mochoemore of Lethmore, who had raised Cuanchear from the dead that Saint died 13th of March, A.D 655.

The northern face of the mountain bears ample testimony to the correctness of the remark, that slate districts are favourable to cultivation.— Wherever there is an open space, the plough has been brought into operation, and universally with successful results. Almost the entire extent of coast from Dungarvan to Youghal is abrupt and precipitous, or what is termed iron-bound. The danger to navigation is perhaps equally great in those places where the land declines to the sea, as at Ardmore.

The country between the mountain and the sea is naturally fertile; and notwithstanding the disadvantages under which it labours, the soil is tolerably well cultivated. The village of Ardmore is situated on the sea-coast, at the west of the bay or harbour of the same name: it commands a fine view of the ocean, and enjoys a magnificent beach of great extent and smoothness. The parish of Ardmore was anciently a place of some consequence, the favourite retreat of St. Declan, the friend and companion of St. Patrick. According to tradition, Ardmore was an episcopal see, established in the fifth century by St. Declan, whose fame and sanctity are still venerated here.

St. Declan was born in this county, and was of the family of the Desii: he travelled for education to Rome, and resided there for some years; he was afterwards ordained by the Pope, and returned to his own country about the year 402, at

which time he founded an abbey and was made
Bishop of Ardmore; he lived to a great age; and
his successor, St. Ultan, was alive in the year
550. A stone, a holy well, and a dormitory in
the churchyard still bear the name of St. Declan.
" St. Declan's stone" is on the beach; it is a
large rock, resting on two others which elevate it
a little above the ground. On the 24th of July,
the festival of the saint, numbers of the lowest
class do penance on their bare knees around the
stone, and some, with great pain and difficulty,
creep under it, in expectation of thereby curing
or preventing, what it is much more likely to
create, rheumatic affections of the back. In the
churchyard is the " dormitory of St. Declan," a
small low building, held in great veneration by
the people in the neighbourhood, who frequently
visit it in order to procure some of the earth,
which is supposed to cover the relics of the saint.
This edifice, which is extremely plain in appearance, was repaired and roofed about a century
ago, at the expense of Bishop Milles. " St.
Declan's Well" is near the ruins of the church, at
some little distance from the village.

The principal object of interest at Ardmore is
the round tower, that opprobrium of antiquaries
about which so many conflicting opinions have
been advanced, and concerning which nothing
has been satisfactorily proved, except the almost
total ignorance which exists touching the origin
and object of these buildings. The arguments of

Drawn & Etched by W.H.Brooke.

ROUND TOWER, ARDMORE.

all the modern writers on the round tower of Ireland being more calculated to overturn the hypotheses of others, than to support the conjectures which they have themselves advanced, it becomes necessary to abandon all idea of determining what these edifices were, and to rest satisfied with knowing what they were not. They were not intended as places of security to which, in case of sudden alarm, the clergy might retire with their vestments, plate, and valuables, for they are too contracted to serve this purpose, and it is plain, that persons pent up in so narrow a cell must soon be starved into a surrender. They were not erected for watch-towers, for many of them are in low situations, and, in some instances, two or more of them are found very near together, which circumstances completely destroy this notion. They were not fire-towers dedicated to the worship of Baal or the Sun, for their construction does not seem adapted to hold a fire perpetually burning on the summit. They were not penitentiary towers, in imitation of the columns of Simeon the Stylite and his disciples; there are several points of disagreement between them. The miserable occupant of the column was exposed to public view, subjected to the inclemency of the weather, and must have endured almost inconceivable misery. The tenant of the tower was too securely and comfortably lodged, to be considered as undergoing a rigid penance or mortification. Besides, such solid and elabo-

late structures were far beyond these assigned
purposes, and instead of one, they could easily
have accommodated a dozen anchorites. That
they were not intended as belfries is easily proved,
by shewing that they were anterior to the use of
bells in churches, and for the edification of those
who can resist this argument, it may be added,
that several churches which were erected close to
the towers had steeples or belfries of their own. To
enable me to lay some slight claim to the enviable
title of an antiquary, I shall offer, as a conjecture,
that the round towers had some connection with
the superstition which prevailed here at the period of the introduction of Christianity into Ireland,
and that its early propagators endeavoured to
avail themselves of the prejudices of the people,
by erecting their places of worship in the vicinity
of the ancient religious monuments. That the
Christian missionaries attempted to advance their
cause in this manner, appears from the interesting
fact, that many of the very ancient churches were
erected near the Druidic altars, where the people
were accustomed to assemble for the purpose of
religious worship. A striking instance of this
association is given in the account of the altar in
the churchyard near Sugar-loaf Hill in the
barony Gaultier. Having done with conjectures,
it will be some relief to add a few facts.—
The round towers were not built by the Danes,
but were long anterior to their settlement in this
country, and they were subsequently used

as belfries, for which purpose they were well adapted.

The round tower of Ardmore is a beautiful building, composed of cut stones accurately fitted and cemented: it is about ninety feet high, tapering from the base, where the diameter is fifteen feet, to the roof, which consists of a few feet of stone-work meeting in a point. This tower differs from some others in having bands or breaks in the exterior wall, and not exactly tapering from top to bottom: it is divided into four stories, having a window in each, and the entrance is about sixteen feet from the ground. The church, which was built near the round tower, and which anciently derived a degree of sanctity from it, is now almost entirely gone to decay; a part of the chancel only being kept in repair and used for divine worship.

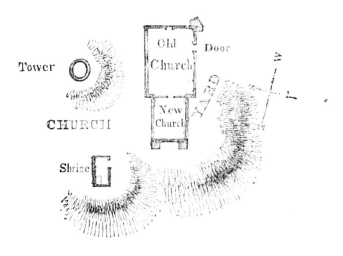

The church was a magnificent building, highly decorated with carved work, and still exhibits in its ruins evident traces of former splendour. A fine Saxon arch, which divided the chancel from the nave, still remains, and denotes the order of the architecture as well as the antiquity of the building. On the exterior of the walls, there are some well carved figures cut in free-stone, which, with a good imagination and some knowledge of the ancient scriptures, may be made to exhibit an epitome of the history of the Old Testament.— Very accurate representations of these figures are annexed.

The ruins of another church are to be seen on the projecting headland, which forms the western termination of the bay. This beautifully situated building, which combines a romantic site with other interesting associations, is in a most ruinous condition, having few traces of ornament or peculiar architecture to illustrate its early history. It is one of those structures which the common people love, probably because it has nothing to recommend it to strangers, and because its very worthlessness has preserved it entirely to themselves: it is remote from any public road or thoroughfare, and seldom visited except by those whom a secret instinct attaches to the place. Still, though fallen and in ruins, this temple is not deserted by the class of persons for whose use it was originally intended: a few fragments of broken arches give note of former magnificence,

To face p. 330.

while vessels intended for religious uses, a clear stream, and a well, reputed holy, draw together the descendants of the ancient worshippers, and excite in their minds melancholy and painful feelings while they meditate on what they consider the faded glory of their country.

The part of the barony which is in the vicinity of Youghal, is much improved, and were there a bridge across the Blackwater at this place, great advantages might be anticipated from an increased facility of communication with the county of Cork. Several plans and estimates have been prepared, and it is more than probable that this important public work will be speedily accomplished.

The river Bricky, which flows along the northern side of the Drum mountain, bounds the limestone formation which extends from Lismore to Dungarvan. The mountain is principally composed of clay-slate, over which red sand-stone and white sand-stone occur. Vast fissures made by winter-torrents, in several places, shew that the beds of sand-stone are of considerable depth, lying in rather irregular masses, and only partially assuming a stratified appearance. Near the summit of the mountain, the white sand-stone partakes of a slaty structure, and when split exhibits the appearance of leaves and fern branches, probably occasioned by the presence of a small portion of iron. Conglomerate is seen scattered about in large irregular fragments, but is no where found in situ. Between the mountain and the sea, limestone again occurs, probably a portion of the formation before-mentioned, and only separated from it by the elevation of the land. The limestone extends into the sea. The junction of the limestone with the slate was originally marked by a small stream, which has since been diverted from its course. Mineral veins, containing lead, iron, and copper ore, were formerly worked in this barony, and are said to have been very productive. Iron mines were opened in several places: at Minehead, so called from the adjacent works, and at Ardmore, very valuable metal was procured, which was afterwards converted into steel, and was highly esteemed. It appears from a note in the first Earl of Cork's diary, that his iron mines at Ardmore were let, in 1636, at 50*l.* per annum. Copper and lead mines were also worked at Ardmore, and from the fragments which are still found, it is supposed that the ores are very rich.

COSHMORE AND COSHBRIDE *

The barony of Coshmore and Coshbride, the most western division, has been called the garden of the county; and if cultivation and picturesque scenery can entitle it to this distinction, the name is not improperly applied.

* Contains six parishes—Lismore, Mocollop, Tallow, Kilwatermoy, Kilcockan, and Temple Michael. In 1654, this barony was divided into five parishes.

The navigable river Blackwater, anciently called Avonmore and Broadwater, and famous in the time of Ptolemy, who calls it Daurona and Necham, takes a winding course through this barony, and contributes to the beauty of the country, as well as to the convenience of its inhabitants. The Blackwater rises in the county of Kerry, and, after a course of about forty miles, enters this county at its western boundary. The course of the river from this place is due east, until it reaches the town of Cappoquin, from whence it proceeds in a southern direction until it meets the sea at the harbour of Youghal.

The Blackwater is navigable for vessels of considerable tonnage as far as the bridge of Cappoquin, and might, without much difficulty, admit ships to a greater distance. A canal was cut at the expense of the late Duke of Devonshire to facilitate the communication with Lismore, but the navigation is every day becoming more difficult, which may be attributed to the checks given to the current by the erection of bridges, and also to the greater extension of the bed of the stream. On the banks of the Blackwater, and to the southward of that river, the land is fertile, and the face of the country highly improved; but to the northward, there is a range of lofty hills which bounds this barony, and separates it from the county of Tipperary.

The place of greatest consequence here is Lismore, formerly ranked amongst the most flourishing cities in Ireland, the seat of science and learning, the birth-place of Congreve, Boyle, and the ingenious Henry Ecles, and the school from which, it is believed, Alfred derived the knowledge which has since immortalized his name. In the year 636 Lismore was a bishop's see, and had a famous school of philosophy established by St. Carthagh, who, in the holy days of Easter, was driven out of Rathenin in the county of West-meath, and took sanctuary here. An old writer thus describes this place: " Lessmor is a famous and holy city, half of which is an asylum, into which no woman dares enter; but it is full of cells and holy monasteries; and religious men in great numbers abide there: and thither holy men flock together from all parts of Ireland; and not only from Ireland, but also from England and Britain, being desirous to remove from thence to Christ." The school of Lismore continued in high repute for many years, and was visited by " prodigious numbers both from the neighbouring and remote countries." Many of the bishops of this see were men remarkable for religious austerity, as well as for learning and sanctity, and it was through their influence that the rigid discipline of the monastic orders was observed. The rules of the abbey of regular canons founded by St. Carthagh were particularly severe. When any of the monks returned from a mission, it was the custom to kneel down before the abbot, and in that humble posture relate the events which had occurred: all kinds of severities were practised here, and their food was restricted to vegetables which they cultivated with their own hands. Subsequent to the arrival of Henry II. the bishops were usually nominated by the Crown, and generally through the influence of the Pope; though, on some occasions, on the death of the bishop, the king granted a license to the Dean and Chapter to elect a successor to the see. The Bishops of Waterford and Lismore had continual quarrels and jealousies, and, as opportunity offered, plundered the property of the rival sees, until at length these disputes were terminated by the junction of the two bishoprics, which were consolidated by what is called a real union, in 363, by Pope Urban V. which union was confirmed by King Edward III. on the 7th of October of that year.

There were many, some say twenty, churches in Lismore, of which the ruins of seven were discernible a few years since; but all the ancient buildings of this ungallant city are now entirely removed, except the cathedral and the castle. The Cathedral, erected by St. Carthagh in 636, is situated on high ground in the immediate vicinity of the Blackwater; it is shaped like a cross, the grand entrance looking towards the south. There is reason to think that the cathedral of Lismore escaped the destructive fires and plunderings which the city experienced after the time of St. Carthagh, as it appears that on every calamitous occasion, the bishops used every exer-

tion to preserve the church; and particularly in
the year 1173, when Raymond and Earl Richard
wasted and plundered the Decies, the plunderers
extorted a large sum of money from the prelate
who then governed the see, to prevent the cathedral from being burned. However, shortly after,
an accidental fire wholly consumed Lismore, and
involved almost all the churches in the ruin.

The cathedral was again repaired, and plundered, at various times; and, at length, in the
rebellion of Munster, was almost totally demolished by Edmund Fitzgibbon, called the White
Knight, in which state it continued until it was
re-edified in 1633, at the expense of the Earl of
Cork. The cathedral of Lismore was originally
constructed in the Saxon style; the windows
were narrow, terminated with circular arches,
each surmounted with a small window in shape
like a circle. These round windows were also
over the entrance, and at the extremities of the
transepts. This style of architecture, which was
generally used in our very ancient buildings, and
which is, of itself, strongly indicative of antiquity,
has, with singularly bad taste, been replaced by
the florid Gothic, which, though beautiful, does
not harmonize with the general appearance of the
place. The alterations and repairs which were
commenced about ten years since, have as yet
only advanced to the completion of one transept
and the exterior entrance, giving a most incon-

gruous appearance to the building, part of it
being in the Saxon, and part in the Gothic style.
Divine service is performed in the place newly
fitted up, which, taken by itself, is a beautiful
little church.   Over the entrance, and beneath a
pure Saxon arch, a handsome organ has been
erected : the windows are of stained glass, richly
and exquisitely executed, the work of a native
artist, George M'Alister of Dublin, who devoted
his youth and talents to discover the lost art of
painting on glass, and who died at an early age,
after having made himself master of the secret.
The pulpit and the seats for the chapter are of
black oak, neatly carved.   The walls of the interior of the building are faced with a beautiful
sandstone, quite equal in beauty to Portland
stone, and apparently much more durable.

Only one ancient monument has escaped the
ravages of time : it is a highly-ornamented tomb,
which was originally raised above the ground, but
is now laid flat, and surrounded by the side
stones.   The date, 1548, is legible; but the inscription, which runs round the stone, can be only
very partially deciphered :

𝕵𝖔𝖍𝖊𝖘 𝕸'𝕲𝖗𝖆𝖙𝖍 . . . . . . uror . . . . . . 𝕶𝖆𝖙𝖍𝖊𝖗𝖎𝖓𝖆
    𝕿𝖍𝖔𝖗𝖓𝖊.   1548.

On the side stones are figures of the Apostles
in high relief. the upper stone is splendidly decorated and divided into compartments, in which

various characters and devices are represented.
The most intelligible are, a heart pierced with
swords—beneath, the words *Ave Maria*—a figure
of our Saviour, with the motto *Ecce Homo*—and a
character dressed in bishop's robes offering up
the host. This tomb is in the unfinished transept.

The castle of Lismore, which was erected on
the site of an ancient abbey, was built by King
John in the year 1185. It was afterwards taken
by the Irish, and was for many years the episcopal residence, until Miler Magrath, Archbishop
of Cashel and Bishop of this see, granted it, together with the manor of Lismore, to Sir Walter
Raleigh, from whom this and other property was
purchased by Sir Richard Boyle, afterwards Earl
of Cork. The annals of the castle are so intimately interwoven with the history of this remarkable personage, it will be necessary to dwell a
little on his character and the principal events of
his life. Amongst the manuscripts at Lismore
Castle, is the diary of this extraordinary man, in
which he kept a regular journal of almost every
occurrence in which he was concerned. The particulars of his arrival in Ireland are well known:
they are related in his journal with a minuteness
which is quite characteristic, and with a conscious
feeling of the powers which could construct a
noble fortune with the most trifling means. His
talents and industry soon procured him wealth

and honours, and raised him to situations of the greatest importance in the administration of the affairs of Ireland. To compensate his otherwise good fortune, it may be remarked, that he passed his life in a continued warfare, at one time assailed by the partizans of government, and nearly at the same moment engaged in regular war with the acknowledged rebels of the country.

A few extracts from the voluminous manuscripts preserved at Lismore Castle will best illustrate the character of the Earl of Cork, and the times in which he lived.

" 1643, May 28. This Sunday morning about two o'clock, 200 rebels, with a party of horse, (in revenge that my son Francis, with the forces of Lismore, had, the Friday evening before, taken, plundered, and burned the town of Clogheen, and brought Luke Everard and another of that name, with one Mr. Englys, the freeholder of Rochestown, prisoners home with him,) for want of good works, they secretly, before it was day, entered the town of Lismore, burnt most of the thatched houses and cabbins in the town, to the outgate of my castle. Took Brian Cavenagh the portrieve, Garrett Fitz Eustace Roch, my servant John O'Donovan, and two soldiers away with them prisoners: burnt my alms-houses, killed Morice Roche and old Pollard, being two of my almsmen, and about sixty of my Irish tenants, men, women, and children, and hurt many more, as Peter Baker and his wife.

" 1643, June 3.   Sir Charles Vavasour with his
regiment of foot, and my son Francis with the
troop of horse, gained with baterry the strong
castle of Cloghlagh in Condon's country, and put
all the rebels therein to the sword; for which
good achievment God make us all thankful.

" 1643, July 10.   This day the rebel Lieutenant
General Purcell, commanding again in chief, in
revenge of his former defeat received at Cappoquin, reinforced his army to 7,000 foot and 900
horse, with three pieces of ordnance, and drew
again near to Cappoquin, and there continued
four days, wasting and spoiling the country round
about, but attempted nothing of any consequence.
And when the 22d at night, that the Lord Viscount Muskric came to the Irish army with some
addition of new forces, they removed from Cappoquin in the night, before my castle of Lismore,
and on Sunday morning the 23d July, 1643, they
began their battery from the church to the east
of Lismore-house, and made a breach into my
own house, which Captain Broadripp and my
warders, being about 150, repaired stronger with
earth than it was before, and shot there till the
Thursday the 27th, and never durst attempt to
enter the breach, my ordnance and musket-shot
from my castle did so apply them. Then they removed their battery to the south-west of my castle,
and continued beating against my orchard-wall,
but never adventured into my orchard, my shot from

my turrets did so continually beat and clear the curteyn of the wall. The 28th of July, God sent my two sons, Dungarvan and Broghill, to land at Youghal, out of England, and the 29th they rode to the Lord of Inchiquin's, who with the army were drawn to Tallagh, and staid there in expectation of Colonel Peyn, with his regiment from Tymolay, who failed to join, but Inchiquin, Dungarvan and Broghill, and Sir John Powlett, the Saturday in the evening, (upon some other directions brought over by Dungarvan from his Majesty,) he made a treaty that evening with Muskrie and others, and the Sunday the 30th, they agreed upon a cessation for six days. Monday night, when they could not enter my house, they removed their siege and withdrew the ordnance and army . . . . two or three barrels of powder . . . two or three pieces of ordnance of twenty-three pounds, and killed but one of my side, God be praised.

"1643, August 10. Brian Cavenagh, Portrieve of Lismore, having been taken prisoner at the burning of my town, was enlarged by exchange of another prisoner of theirs, but returning home pillaged and stripped, I gave him a doublet, breeches, and stockings, and a new coat made for my own wearing, garnished down before with silver buttons and gold fringe work, that I had never worn.

Regno Eliz. Regin et Jacobi primi Regis.
Copie of a Particular of part of the first Earl of Corke's
Comonwealth's Workes, performed by him for the
service of the Crown and good of the Commonwealth
and of the province of Munster wherein he resided.

Imprimis, The Earl of Corke hath re-edified the great decayed church of Youghal, wherein the townsmen in time of rebellion kept their cows, and hath erected a new chappel therein, and made it one of the fairest churches in Ireland.

He hath also new built the College-house of Youghal, and added five turrets thereunto, and raised platforms of earth fit to plant any ordnance upon, which may command the town and harbour.

He hath formed a faire free school there, and built convenient lodgings for the schoolmaster and usher, and erected there an almshouse for old decayed soldiers, which are filled, and hath given of his own lands in perpetuity of the clear yearly value of fourscore pounds a year for their maintenance.

He hath built four incorporate and market-towns, which before were waste places without any habitations, and planted them all with English inhabitants of the religion, viz. Tallaugh, in which he hath built a new church and chancel, a sessions-house, a market-house, and a strong prison. 2. Lismore, wherein he hath re-edified the demolished chancel of the cathedral church. 3. Cloghnikilty, wherein he hath built a fair new church, and made a plantation all of English Protestants.

Bandonbridge, which twenty years past was a great many woods, he hath now made an English towne there, and hath built two fair new churches two sessions-houses, two market-houses, and a strong prison in the same, and compasses the town round about with a strong wall of lime and stone, it being of a far greater length, strength, and circuit than the city of Corke is, and hath fortified the town wall with six turrets and three strong large castles, and furnished them with ordnance, and fully inhabited it all with English Protestants and tradesmen, to the great strength and comfort of all the western parts of Munster, all these four new corporations send two burgesses apiece to Parliament, all Protestants.

He hath built and erected thirteen new castles in and upon the streights of his seigniories and English plantations, viz. one at Ballinetry, one at Corneveagh, one at the Parke, one at Inchiquin, one at Ballyknock, one at Agharnin, one at Shane, one at Ballyduff, one at Corbegh, one at Ballygarron, one at Ballyin, one at Cappoquin, one at Innesheane, besides the three castles at Lismore, and the great strengths there and at Youghal, all of his buildings, which are large and fit for garrisons, to command and secure all those parts of the country.

He hath built four stately bridges, viz. two

bridges over the great river of the Bride, one at Tallough, the other at Connotry, and two other bridges over the river Blackwater, whereof one at Fermoy, the other at Cappoquin. The workmanship of which bridges, besides all the materials, cost him between eleven and twelve hundred pounds, and by building those bridges he hath lost the rent of his several ferries, which is eight and thirty pounds per annum, for ever.

He is able (as the Lord Deputy hath seen mustered before him) out of his new plantations about Tallough, to bring into the field, for his Majesty's service and defence of those parts of the country, one thousand foot and one hundred horse, and at and about his plantations about Bandonbridge eight hundred foot and sixty horse well armed, all English, and of the religion, with able captains and officers of his own tenants to command them.

He payeth every week in the year two hundred pounds for wages to workmen, and there is maintained by the money that goes out of his purse to labourers four thousand people, young and old, on his lands and plantations, to the great benefit of the commonwealth.

Upon the Lords of the Council in England, letters, he lent in ready money, for his Majesty's use, to clear the great necessities of the fleet soldiers which arrived in Munster, one thousand pounds, and when the forts at Corke and Water-

LISMORE CASTLE.

Drawn & Etched by W.H.Bartlett

Published by John Murray 1837

Sir Walter Raleigh

ford, last year before they were defensible, were at a stand for want of money, he lent other five hundred pounds, wherewith they were again undertaken and made tenable.

" Lastly, he never had acre of land, pension, ward, entertainment, or other matter of benefit, given him from the late King or Queen, or from the state in Ireland, neither ever was a suitor for any such benefit or gift."

The castle of Lismore is one of the most magnificent of the ancient Irish residences, and is seen to great advantage from being built on a very elevated situation on the verge of a hill, the river Blackwater running close to the foundation. The circular towers which flank the northern front are partly concealed by trees, which seem to grow out of the river, and which throw into shade large intervals of the rocky base of the building ; these remarkable objects, combined with the abrupt position of the castle which is seen hanging over the dark and rapid stream, compose a romantic and striking picture which has scarcely ever been adequately represented. The first door-way is called the riding-house, from its being originally built to accommodate two horsemen who mounted guard, and for whose reception there were two spaces which are still visible under the archway. The riding-house is the entrance into a long avenue shaded by magnificent

trees, and flanked with high stone walls, this leads
to another doorway, the keep or grand entrance
into the square of the castle.   Over the gate are
the arms of the first Earl of Cork, with the motto
" God's providence is our inheritance."   The
castle and its precincts were regularly fortified,
and covered a large space of ground, the bounds
of which may still be traced by the existing walls
and towers.   It is highly interesting to examine
the various parts of the defences so minutely and
vividly represented in the first Earl of Cork's
diary.   " My orchard," and " my garden," and
" the turrets, which did so continually beat and
clear the curteyn of the wall," all are religiously
preserved, and have been recently brought into
view and cleared of the obstructions which time
and neglect had accumulated about them.

The great square of the castle has rather an
unfinished appearance, and, from the introduction of modern doors and windows, offends against
all the rules of uniformity and architectural con-
sistency.   The sombre appearance of the buildings around the square is admirably contrasted
with the interior of the castle.   The rooms are
fitted up with all the convenience of modern improvement, the doors are of Irish oak of great
thickness and beauty; and the windows, composed
of large squares of glass, each pane opening on
hinges, combine accommodation with harmony of
appearance.   The drawing-rooms are ornamented

with tapestry, and contain some good oil paintings. One of the towers is still retained in its rude and dilapidated state, serving as a contrast to the modern adornments, as well as showing the great ingenuity and taste which have been displayed in combining the luxuries of the present day with the romantic beauties of so ancient a building.

An anecdote which is told of James II., who is said to have visited the castle and dined in the great room, has given one of the windows the name of King James's window. It is said, that on looking out of this window, the agitated monarch was so struck at perceiving the vast height at which he stood and the rapid river running beneath him, that he started back with evident dismay. To look unexpectedly upon the river immediately under the apartment, is indeed a startling prospect, and might naturally excite surprise from the great depth of the rear of the building compared with the level ground at the entrance. From King James's window, and more particularly from the flat roof of the castle, the view is magnificent and beautiful. The eye embraces a vast extent of country, and receives the impression of a splendid picture, realizing all the vivid colouring, and all the variety and contrast, which the imagination of a painter only can conceive.

Directly in front is the mountain of Knockmeledown, towering above the range of lofty hills

which stretch away to the eastward · a thickly
planted ravine, with rude projecting masses of
rock appearing through the foliage, serves to
guide the eye from the mountain to the level
ground, and connects the wildness of nature with
the cultivation and improvements of man.   On
the right is Cappoquin, with its church spire
rising above the houses and its light bridge
crossing the Blackwater.   The rich vale through
which the river flows is thickly planted and ornamented with several handsome residences.   To
the left of Lismore there is much natural and picturesque beauty of situation, as well as many
highly improved demesnes.   amongst others is
Balleen, a delightful place belonging to Dean
Scott.   It is a relief to the mind to wander through
the garden ground of this charming spot; it is
true we miss the grandeur, antiquity and magnificence of Lismore Castle, but the neatness, taste
and simplicity exhibited here are worth them all.
The view of the surrounding country has a noble
termination in the lofty hills seen indistinctly in
the distance, exhibiting a dark and irregular outline, and by the contrast adding to the richness of
the scenery nearer to the spectator.

    The mountain of Knockmeledown, in form re-
sembling a sugar loaf, is situated about four miles
to the north of Lismore, and separates the north-
western extremity of this county from the county
of Tipperary.   As you approach the mountain,

the height of which is about 2,700 feet, the ascent appears most easy on the western side; the northern face is nearly perpendicular: half way up the mountain, a slate quarry has been opened. From the summit the view is magnificent, extending in every direction as far as the eye can reach. To the north, the Rock of Cashel and the cathedral are distinctly visible. to the south, the ocean, the harbours of Dungarvan and Youghal, and a great extent of sea-coast may also be observed. About the middle of the last century, there were red deer on this mountain, but they have been long since driven away. The plant called London-pride grows here. The summit of this mountain is remarkable as being the burial-place of the ingenious Henry Eeles, who published many papers on electricity. In his principal work, which appeared in the form of Letters from Lismore, and was printed in Dublin in 1771, he claims the credit of discovering the identity of electricity and lightning. According to his own directions, Henry Eeles was buried on the highest part of Knockmeledown, with his horse and dog.

Lismore, once a celebrated city, became afterwards a neglected and miserable village, consisting of a few hovels, and without any trace of its former magnificence, except what might be gathered from the ruins of the castle and the church. It continued in this state for many years, and is thus represented about the middle of the last century. Since that time, the Duke of Devonshire has expended large sums in improving and beautifying the town and precincts of Lismore, and, by the greatest liberality to his tenantry, has entirely removed all the grounds of complaint taken notice of by Wakefield and other writers. The bridge, which was built at the sole expense of the late Duke of Devonshire, in 1775, is one hundred feet in the span of the arch. The present Duke has erected a most convenient sessions-house and gaol, a commodious inn and offices, and contributes largely to all the charitable institutions. There are six alms-houses at Lismore founded by the first Earl of Cork, for decayed Protestant soldiers, with an annual stipend for each. There are also extensive poor schools, one for boys and another for girls, built and supported by the Duke of Devonshire, but placed under the inspection of the Hibernian School Society, who add a donation to the master and mistress. The classical school at Lismore, originally endowed by the first Lord Cork, has been much enlarged and improved by the present Duke. A new school-room has been built; and an extensive play-ground and garden inclosed, with a ball-court, &c. have been added. The establishment is now under the management of the Rev. Mr. Stokes. The Duke of Devonshire, who occasionally visits this country, has an able representative in Colonel Curry, whose residence is the castle of Lismore. To have a few such absentees and so represented would be extremely fortunate for Ireland.

Lismore is now a thriving town, and, if we may judge from the spirit of building which prevails, and from the many new streets now in progress, the trade and wealth of the inhabitants are evidently increasing.

Under the castle there is a very extensive salmon fishery, where, during the season, great abundance of fish is taken daily and exported, packed in ice, to Liverpool and other distant places. Any fish taken in the inclosures, above the number required, are driven into a space divided off, where they may be had at a short notice; and, in addition to this, there are two or three wooden boxes, from which they may be taken without the delay of a minute. Eight hundred fish are sometimes taken at one time. The road between Lismore and Cappoquin, on the northern bank of the Blackwater, runs along the base of a range of hills which skirts the river. This neighbourhood is highly improved, and, for romantic scenery, may bear a comparison with the most celebrated places Throughout the whole way, the road is overarched with the finest timber trees, giving the appearance of a riding through a magnificent demesne. At various

places there are deep ravines crossing the range
of hills: one of these, called the valley of Glen-
ribbon, which separates the properties of the
Duke of Devonshire and Mr. Chearnley, is thickly
planted on the right, and, winding between the
hills, runs up a considerable distance from the
road; the view from the elevation which terminates this valley will amply repay the labour of
ascending it. A very excellent slate quarry has
been worked here for thirteen years, giving constant employment to nine men.

The slate is of good quality, splitting easily
into large and smooth planes, almost equal in size
and appearance to ton slates. There are other
quarries of the same material in the vicinity; one
of these, opposite to the bridge of Lismore, has
been worked for a great length of time. The
supply of slates does not exceed the demand,
which, from the contiguity of water-carriage, may
be supposed to be considerable. The bed of
roof-slate, which is not of any great thickness,
rests upon a coarse clay slate: above the roof-
slate is a rock of a siliceous nature; higher up is
a bed of conglomerate, consisting of imbedded
siliceous particles, and above these is sandstone,
varying from a fine building material resembling
Portland stone, to a coarse soft rock, having the
appearance of indurated sand. On the summit
of the hills is a bed of fine sand, which, at Mr.
Chearnley's and at Lismore, is of great extent.

At the latter place, immediately opposite the
bridge, a bank of sand is exposed, many hundred
feet in height, and so steep and inaccessible that
great flocks of swallows have taken possession of
the higher parts, in which to build their nests
securely.   The river may be considered the
boundary of the preceding formations, although
the limestone which occurs at the other side is
found at some depth at Saltibridge, and probably
under the sand opposite Lismore.   The component
parts of the hills in this part of the county, though
varying in some slight particulars, may generally
be classed according to the preceding imperfect
description : in some places, the siliceous slate is
wanting, and in others the sandstone is red, but
the general character of the different formations
is nearly similar to those already mentioned.
There is something extremely curious in the
detached masses of sand which occur here and in
some other parts of the county, and which are
generally found resting on limestone.   The round
hill near Lismore is a singular instance of these
formations.   The rocks in this district are rich
in mineral productions, iron, copper and lead
ores are of frequent occurrence, and have, at
remote periods, engaged the attention of the proprietors of the soil.   The great obstacle to the
progress of mining pursuits in this county, and
which has either discouraged or impeded such
undertakings, has been a want of fuel, this want

and a deficiency of capital have long rendered the vast mineral treasures of the county totally unavailable. Lead ore is found at the bridge of Lismore; and iron in many places, particularly at Araglin, at Saltibridge and at Ballinatray, where mines were formerly worked by the Earl of Cork.

About two miles from Lismore is the village of Cappoquin, situated on the northern bank of the Blackwater, where the course of the river describes a right angle, in its progress to the sea. There is a wooden bridge here, which is shortly to be replaced by a stone one.

Cappoquin possesses nothing worthy of particular notice, except a new church, ornamented with a neat spire, and a Roman Catholic chapel, which stands immediately contiguous to it.— It is in contemplation, when the new bridge is completed, to open a line of road on the bank of the river, leading directly to Youghal. At Kilbree may still be seen some remains of an ancient castle built by King John : it was situated on an eminence which commands the river, and might in former times have been a place of strength.

Contiguous to this place is the Deer Park of Lismore, formerly entirely inclosed by high walls, and still partially surrounded by the ruins of its former greatness. A vein of iron ore, running from east to west, passes through this extensive tract, and may be traced by the eye, on account of the sterility occasioned by the proximity of the mineral.

Of New Affane, associated as it is with the recollection of Sir Walter Raleigh, it would be satisfactory to be able to give some detailed information : that it was his property, presented to him by one of the ancient proprietors of Dromana, we have unquestionable authority for asserting; whether it continued in his possession, and partook of the improvement which his cultivated taste was so well qualified to bestow upon it, we have not sufficient grounds to enable us to determine.

Amongst the traditional wonders of this part of the county, it may not be amiss to mention, without demanding a too implicit credence to the minuter circumstances connected with the narrative, two remarkable works of which the traces are still discernible. The first is a large double trench, called, in Irish, Rian Bo Padriuc, or the trench of St. Patrick's Cow. This road or trench commences eastward of Knockmeledown, passes through the Deer Park of Lismore, and, crossing the Blackwater near Tourin, where the remains of laborious workmanship may still be seen, proceeds in a direct line to Ardmore.— There is an unfortunate discrepancy in the traditions concerning this curious trench; some asserting that it was the work of St. Patrick's cow, on her way to Ardmore, in search of her calf which had been stolen, while others are more inclined to believe that the cow had been carried away by thieves to Ardmore, and that her labours commenced there, on her return to her master at Cashel. Without hastily concluding, that " the one story is as probable as the other," as Doctor Smith has ventured to do, it will be satisfactory to hear his ingenious conjecture, which is, " that these ridges were no other than the remains of an ancient highway drawn from Cashel to Ardmore, between which two places there was probably in the time of St Patrick, and his contemporary, St. Declan, a frequent communication, and that this road was made by the direction of these Saints, in imitation of the Roman highways, which they must have often met with in their travels."

The other traditional wonder alluded to is also a trench, which extends along the sides of the mountains from Cappoquin into the county of Cork, and which, according to the conjecture of Doctor Smith, was a boundary or fence made to preserve the cattle against wolves.

At the western extremity of this barony is the town of Tallow, formerly a place of some consequence : it was erected into a borough by charter, bearing date 10th James 1., by which the liberties of the borough were to embrace a circuit of a mile and a half round the church. This town returned two members to the Irish Parliament, and was for many years remarkable for the elec-

tioneering contests which occurred here. Since
the union, when it ceased to return representatives, its trade and industry have constantly de-
clined.

The appearance of Tallow has very little to recommend it. The church is a handsome modern
building, and there are a few good private houses;
but the public buildings, as the market and sessions house, and the gaol, are in a state of extreme
dilapidation. The gaol consists of two apartments, each twenty feet by fifteen : it is a manor
gaol, though frequently used as a place of confinement for persons committed by the magistrates of the county. There is no day room, no
classification, employment or instruction. On
some occasions, prisoners committed by the county
magistrates are confined here for many weeks.
The manor of Tallow is the property of the Duke
of Devonshire, by whom the Seneschal of the town
is appointed.

The seneschal has very rarely occasion to commit to prison, and if those confined in Tallow gaol
were only those who come within his jurisdiction,
the infrequency of commitments, and their limited
duration, would preclude the unpleasant consequences which may now be naturally expected.
It is when considered as a county prison, that the
gaol of Tallow requires investigation and reform. It
is understood to be the wish of the Duke of Devonshire to erect commodious places of confinement

in this town, and also in Dungarvan, if his grace's enlarged views are met with a corresponding liberality on the part of the gentlemen of the county.

In this neighbourhood, perhaps as being the boundary of the county, there were many fortified castles and houses of defence, chiefly the property of the Earls of Desmond. Amongst these, the castle of Strancally holds a distinguished rank, as well on account of its extent and picturesque appearance, as in consequence of the traditional tales recorded of it. The castle of Strancally is situated on a high rock on the bank of the Blackwater, which is here of considerable breadth. The castle enjoyed a bold and commanding situation, was fortified, and in every respect a place of strength. From the foundation on which it stood, an extensive subterranean cave, with a passage communicating with the river, was cut through the solid rock, and thus provided, the worthy Lords of Desmond were no contemptible imitators of the ancient giants. It was the custom of these gentle lords to invite their wealthy and distinguished neighbours to partake of the festivities of Strancally; and having thus gotten them into their power, the victims were carried through the rocky passage into the dungeon, where they were suffered to perish, and from thence, through an opening which is still visible, their corpses were cast into the river: thus disposed of, their fortunes became an easy prey. These practices continued for a long time, until at length, one, more fortunate than his fellow-prisoners, escaped the final doom, and gave information of the facts to government. The castle and cave were immediately ordered to be demolished by gunpowder. The plate of Strancally Castle in Grose's Antiquities of Ireland, admirably displays the effect of the explosion . the cave is entirely laid open, and one half of the walls of the castle removed, thereby exposing to view the entire arrangement of the interior of the building. The scenery on the banks of the Blackwater, which may be seen most advantageously by descending the river in a boat, is extremely picturesque, and will afford much enjoyment to those who have leisure to inspect it minutely.

After passing Strancally, the principal objects to be noticed are Molana, Temple-Michael and Rhincrew. Molana, formerly an island, but now united to the mainland, was the site of an Abbey, belonging to regular canons of St. Augustine, which was established in the sixth century by St. Molanside, who was also the first abbot. On the suppression Queen Elizabeth granted this abbey and its possessions to Sir Walter Raleigh, by whom it was assigned to the Earl of Cork.

GLANAHEIRY.*

This barony is of very limited extent, containing only about 16,531 acres, a great proportion of which is mountain and uncultivated land.

The Suir, even here a considerable river, separates this barony from the county of Tipperary. From near Clonmel to the junction of the Suir and Nier the country is extremely beautiful; and at that part where the demesne of Kilmanehin is separated only by the river from the Earl Donoughmore's seat, Knocklofty, in the county of Tipperary, nothing can exceed the richness and variety of the scenery.

Limestone is found near Kilmanehin, and again at one or two places at the extreme boundary of the county in this direction. The beds are of small extent, and are entirely detached from one another. After leaving Bally M'Kee, where the Suir first enters the county of Waterford, the face of the country still retains the wild and uncultivated appearance which it probably exhibited when it was the boundary between two hostile districts. Four of the castles, which marked out and protected the limits of the adjoining counties, are still visible: two of them, Castle Conagh, and Castlereagh, are in the county of Waterford: Castle Clonagh and Newcastle are in the county

---

* Contains the commons of Clonmel and the parish of Kilronan In the year 1654 this barony contained two parishes

Sketch to illustrate the proposed Embankment of the Back Strand Tramore.

TRAMORE

LORD DONERAILE'S Estate.

A.

Isthmus of Tramore.

Fresh Water Streams.

G. F. LANE'S Estate.

TRAMORE BAY.

BACK STRAND

OF

TRAMORE

Dry at low Water.

Sand Hills.

Bishop's land.

Low and Marshy.

1

3

2

Kilmacleague Glebe.

RINESHARK HARBOUR.

KILMACLEAGUE PILL.

CROBALLY PILL.

Bishops land.

Kilmacleague Glebe.

EARL FORTESCUE.

The Estate of

Summerville.

Bishops land.

of Tipperary. Castle Conagh is built on a high limestone rock, on the bank of the river Nier. The castle is a square building, and was protected by two round towers at the side next the river. A narrow valley, called the glen of Rossmore, through which the boundary line runs, is commanded by Castle Clonagh. The former castle, which is square, the form usually adopted by the English, proves that this district was within the pale, while, from the circular shape of Castle Clonagh, it may be conjectured that it was the work of more ancient settlers.

As a conclusion to the topographical description of this county, and as tending to confirm a suggestion which has been thrown out in another part of this work, the following observations and suggestions are offered by a gentleman * who is perfectly conversant with the subject on which he treats, and whose remarks will be found highly deserving the attention of all speculating men :—

ON THE PRACTICABILITY OF BANKING IN THE BACK
STRAND OF TRAMORE.

The general richness and luxuriant verdure of ground embanked from the sea, is so universally known, that very few observations are necessary to press its value and importance on general con-

* William Hughes, Esq

A A

sideration.   Some of the most valuable lands in
England have been inclosed from the ocean, particularly Romney Marsh in Kent, which adjoins
the Channel, and contains upwards of 24,000
acres.   Such is the fertility of its pastures, that
they afford to London a considerable weekly
supply of two very much-relished necessaries of
life—beef and mutton.   In many parts of Ireland
there are large tracts of ground which might be
easily converted into excellent land by embankment, and which would not only liberally remu-
nerate the proprietors for the expense, but by
providing employment for the poor, enable them
to earn their subsistence by their own industry;
the most substantial benefit that could be conferred on the redundant population of the country.

Among those tracts, the back strand of Tramore, in this county, affords, from its situation
and extent, a variety of inducements to embankment.   Several maps have been made of this
strand, which, including the Channel, contains
about 1,000 acres.   On an examination of these
maps, some difference appears in the acreage,
which has been occasioned in all probability by
the want of accurate information as to the precise
boundaries· 1,050 acres is the highest, and 979
the lowest, return of its extent.   When it is of
such magnitude, the difference of a few acres is
immaterial.

A very considerable part of this strand is a

deep, rich composition of fat earths, mixed with dead animal and vegetable substances, which have been accumulating for ages, by the flowing of the tides. It has been repeatedly drawn and laid out as manure on the neighbouring farms. A small part of the strand is sandy, with a slight intermixture of gravel, but the entire would become productive after its embankment. It contains within itself the means of immediate improvement: such is the quality of the soil, that (although the tendency of salt-water to extinguish vegetation is well known) the surfaces of particular parts, which are rarely covered at times of high spring tides, become green in the interval between those tides, and bear testimony to its amazing fertility. Part of this strand, containing about forty-five acres, heretofore banked in, before it was neglected and almost destroyed by breaches in the banks and by the overflowing of the tides, produced herbage far superior to any found in the neighbourhood, and remarkable for its fattening qualities: no reasonable doubt can therefore be entertained, but that the ground when embanked would be most valuable. Before the depression of all agricultural produce, ground of such a description was seldom let at less than 5*l*. an acre, and frequently at a much higher rate. If, therefore, we estimate that the strand, on an average, when properly drained and divided, would bring but half that rent, namely 2*l*. 10*s*. an acre, the income of 1,000 acres, at that rate, would be £2,500 per annum, and would, probably, sell for £50,000, for, as an act of parliament would be necessary for its embankment, the title would be most unexceptionable. The above rent may be considered very moderate, particularly when it is recollected that, from the number of streams running into the strand, fresh water could be introduced into every part of it.

From the annexed sketch, which presents a tolerably accurate view of its situation, it appears that there are three places where embankments may be advantageously made. No. 1, direct from the sand-hills, across the channel to Earl Fortescue's estate; No. 2, from the sand-hills to the projecting point of land adjoining Crobally Pill; and No. 3, from the sand-hills to the glebe of Kilmacleague. The first and the last appear to be most worthy of consideration.

The first line of embankment (direct across the channel) although attended with difficulties which the last is free from, particularly in the facility of letting off the back-waters, would be productive of some advantages that could not result from the latter. By stopping up the channel, the danger arising to vessels getting into Tramore Bay would be considerably lessened. When the tide is coming in, with the wind from S.S.E. to S.W., it rushes from all quarters of the bay towards this channel · the rapidity of the current is of course increased by the narrowness of the entrance, and the great indraught of water must operate against vessels extricating themselves from the bay. This indraught would cease on the embankment being made, and it is not only probable, but almost certain, that, in time, the tides not having a passage into the channel, would throw up against the embankment vast quantities of sand, and ultimately render it secure beyond the possibility of accident; for such is the natural tendency of water on meeting with obstacles which it cannot conquer. It is well known, particularly in America, that currents have not unfrequently created small islands, by encountering in their passage trees, or even their branches firmly fixed, and depositing small quantities of sand or mud against them, which by constant accumulations have become at length excellent land. The course of the Ganges has been, it is said, repeatedly changed in this manner, in short, it is an admitted fact, that all floods, from the muddiness of their streams, leave on the verges of their quickest currents, a sandy or muddy settlement, and a very trifling impediment stopping that sand or mud in the course of the current, which would otherwise flow with it, and that sand or mud forming a barrier to the next parcel, ground is thus ultimately created

If the bank is made from the sand-hills to the glebe at Kilmacleague, the following advantages will attend it. The harbour of Rhineshark will remain open as usual for fishing-boats to take

shelter in: the streams and floods which at particular seasons rush with great violence into the
pills, would, by means of sluices, have their passage as heretofore open to the sea: the tides
would run not *against*, but *by the side* of the bank,
and never could have the same effect as if the
bank directly *fronted* them: should the tide rush
in with the greatest violence at the mouth of the
channel, yet as the two pills run off in a contrary
direction from the proposed bank, the tide would
of course oblique to that side where the passages
were open, so that it would neither have a *direct*,
or even a strong *lateral* operation on it: the bank
would require much less solid work than if it ran
across the channel; would be less liable to accidents during its construction, and (a most material
consideration) the foundation could be constantly
examined, and repaired instantly if any accident
occurred.   These are a few of the reasons which
appear favourable to the embankment from the
glebe to the sand-hills.

With respect to the manner of making the
embankment, plans and estimates should be procured from experienced engineers conversant with
works of such a description, and such plans should
be well-digested and perfectly understood by all
parties previous to the commencement of the
work. One point in particular should be strongly
inculcated, namely, that although all unnecessary
expense should be carefully avoided, that ill-
judged and too-prevalent economy which, to save

a trifle not worth recollecting, would hazard substantial security, should be equally shunned.

In making any embankment or fence against water, the first and great object of attention should be to make a firm and secure foundation; in fact, unless this great essential is obtained, there can be no security. Wherever there is to be a great pressure of water against a bank, all possible precautionary measures should be adopted for the security of the foundation. Most of the accidents which have hitherto occurred in embankments have been occasioned by neglecting this grand point. Wherever water meets with any encouragement, or can fasten on any conductor in a dam, such as a piece of timber running across it, it will work and insinuate itself with wonderful perseverance, until it at length conquers every impediment: if, on the contrary, it once meets with firm opposition, it will increase that opposition by depositing, as before-mentioned, the sand and mud which it is prevented carrying forward.

It may not be irrelevant to state, as a reason for observing such particular caution in the foundation, that the pressure of all fluids against banks, the sides of containing vessels, &c is as the square of their depth, that is, if the pressure be one pound against the uppermost inch, it will be four pounds against two inches deep, &c. &c.: that the water undermost is pressed by all the rest, and must of course operate more powerfully at the bottom than at the top, is ascertained by a very simple experiment,—a pipe fixed under the most surfaces of water will discharge the most water; if it is fixed four times as deep below the surface of the water, as another of the same diameter, it will discharge twice as much in the same time, and so in proportion.

The foregoing is stated, as persons may be concerned in the embankment, not previously aware of the necessity of making such a foundation as would resist any pressure that could possibly affect it   It is also to be recollected that not only the mere pressure of the water is to be resisted, but likewise the force with which it may rush against the bank, and, when the wind blows strong from S. S. E. to S. W., there is generally a great rolling sea into Tramore Bay, which increases the force and rapidity of the current into the harbour of Rhineshark.   With respect to the construction of the embankment and its probable expense, the writer of these observations must refer to persons whose profession and practical experience qualify them to enter into the necessary details: he certainly has viewed and examined several embankments, and so far has endeavoured to acquire such information as might justify the hints suggested in this article:—to this extent only his pretensions are limited.

As he is not aware of any intelligent treatise or exclusive publication on embankments, it occurs to him that the best mode of construction is to be collected from an accurate knowledge of the situa-

tion of the ground to be embanked—the probable
operation of the tides on it—the different methods
heretofore pursued in embanking ground in particular situations—to observe in what respect the
ground in question differs from ground heretofore
taken in, and from a due consideration of all circumstances, to arrange such a plan of embankment as may be likely to combine duration with
general utility. The latter term is here introduced, because there can be no doubt but that a
good road made on the top of the embankment
and along the isthmus of Tramore to the town of
Tramore, thus connecting by the sea-side the
baronies of Gaultier and Middlethird, would be
of essential benefit to that part of the county.
Wherever the line of embankment is to run,
(if on examination the ground on which it is to be
raised should appear to be soft and insecure,) it
might be well to drive a row of piles dovetailed
into each other, after the manner of sliding black-
lead pencils formerly so much in use, by which
means it would be impossible for water to pene-
trate through or under them, if driven to a proper
depth, as they would thus form one complete
shut, and, if made of fir, the dovetailing would
swell and grow close. These piles are to be made
long or short according to circumstances, while
the method of dovetailing keeps each pile in its
proper groove while it is driving. This plan
appears to have been originally the invention of a
Captain Parry, who, about a hundred years ago,

successfully introduced it, in making an embankment on the river Thames, near Daggenham.   All
the lands in the immediate neighbourhood of this
place had been completely inundated by a breach
in the banks, made by a tremendous tide; and
various efforts were made by different engineers
to stop up this breach, which was 400 feet wide
and 18 feet deep at low water; but they were all
ineffectual, in consequence, as it was clearly demonstrated at the time, of their being unacquainted
with a proper method of securing the foundation.
Captain Parry, however, was at length employed
by the land-owners, and, after struggling with
considerable difficulties, from the jealousy of those
who had previously failed in the undertaking and
from other causes, at length secured the foundation by driving the dovetailed piles before mentioned, and raising a bank on each side of them
42 feet in height, which completely protected the
adjacent country from future inundations.

When the foundation is effectually secured and
the embankment proceeded in, a sufficient slope
should be presented to the sea, which is indis-
pensably requisite in all works of this kind: the
force of the water is then destroyed, as, from not
meeting with direct opposition, it will smoothly
glide up the inclined plane.

Those who know that the power of any inclined
plane is as its length is to its height, namely, that
a cylinder will be rolled up an inclined road of
twenty yards in length and but one yard perpen-

dicular height with one twentieth part of the
force that would be necessary to lift it perpen-
dicularly that yard, may readily estimate its effect
and utility. In all cases of currents it is far better
to bend than to break them, they should be subdued by stratagem and not by force.

The quantity of ground taken in from the sea
at various periods in different countries, and the
great tracts of valuable alluvial soil obtained by
judicious embankment, almost exceed credibility.
In England, exclusive of Romney Marsh before
mentioned, there are millions of acres brought
into cultivation in this way and by draining, which
are particularly productive. Vermuyden, a
Fleming, and a colonel of horse under Cromwell,
was celebrated for his skill in works of this description. Holland furnishes a remarkable example of what persevering industry may do in
this respect; it is literally stolen from the sea,
and only preserved from what Cobbett would call
the *grab* of its original proprietor by immense
embankments The Dutch appoint respectable
persons for the sole purpose of inspecting and
taking care of these embankments; and it has
been said, that formerly a neglect of this important duty was viewed in so criminal a light that
the punishment of death was inflicted on the of-
fender and a stake driven through his body, in
the breach occasioned by his inattention Persons
sailing into Dutch ports may see cattle grazing
and corn growing considerably below the level of

the sea. A number of lakes in that country have been, in consequence of the great increase of its inhabitants, drained from time to time. One in particular called the Beemster, containing 1800 acres, was, in former days, when steam-engines were unknown, made dry by the working of windmills, and is considered as the richest ground in the country. In Flanders immense tracts of land have been banked in and drained, and the fertility of the ground is proverbial. In Italy, along the river Po, there are extensive embankments, which preserve the adjoining country from inundation. The Romans frequently employed their soldiers in draining marshes and making embankments, particularly the Pompeian marshes. According to Dugdale, the Pomptine fens were laid dry by Cornelius Cethegus, and such was the richness of the soil that twenty-three towns were said to have been built in it.

The great fertility occasioned by muddy streams is in no part of the world more gratefully felt and acknowledged than in Egypt, where drains are cut for the express purpose of letting the Nile water the country and leave its fat mud on the earth. Of such consequence is this to the inhabitants, that unless the Nile rises to a particular height, famine is the consequence. The Egyptians, from experience, have framed the following calculations on this subject: twelve cubits only in height occasion famine; thirteen hunger, fourteen bring mirth; fifteen security, and sixteen plenty. The richness of that part of Egypt called the Delta (from its somewhat re-sembling in form the Greek letter of that name) is to be exclusively attributed to the mud of the Nile waters. The late celebrated and Rev. Sir Henry Bate Dudley, Bart. who resided at Brad-well Lodge in Essex, about twenty-five years ago made a very interesting communication to the London Society for the encouragement of Arts, Manufactures and Commerce, of a method of gaining land from the sea, and for which the gold medal was adjudged to him by the society. Sir Henry had, about eleven years before, made another embankment, for which he also received a gold medal from the society; but he found that he had not given it a sufficient declension in front for an easy ascent and descent of the waves His second embankment particularly deserves to be noticed, as the exposed situation of the ground, according to the description of it, rendered it more difficult to be embanked than the back strand of Tramore. It directly fronted the sea, and ex-tended nearly one mile in length, and with the returning bank, inclosed between two and three hundred acres. The whole of the embankment was composed of earth alone: it was begun on a base of thirty-two feet, raised to the height of seven feet, leaving a plain of five feet on the top. The first embankment having nearly given way at the foundation, on a great tide running against it, owing to the erection of new earth on the sur-

face, Sir Henry, to guard against similar danger
in the present one, had a trench six feet wide, and
about two feet deep, cut along the centre of the
line of embankment, and this trench, by admitting the new earth into, as it were, an incorpora-
tive adhesion with the soil of the base, rendered a
separation, after it was well rammed down, almost
impossible. The entire work was completed in
seven months by twelve men experienced in such
undertakings. Sluices were fixed at each end of
the embankment for letting off the land waters, and
the ground was afterwards divided, and from drains
made, and the introduction of small intersecting rills
of fresh water, the entire became excellent land;
not less than 800 Southdown sheep, and from sixty
to eighty horses, were constantly grazed on it. As
it was the general opinion of the county, that
ground thus taken from the sea would not grow
corn for a number of years, Sir Henry, in some
short time after the inclosure, dug part and sowed
it with horse-beans and oats, and had a good return. He, in the following year, sowed the same
spot with wheat, and it yielded a choice crop.
On the sea being shut out, the part inclosed
became coated with grasses of good quality,
different clovers, trefoil, &c. from whence Sir
Henry concluded, contrary to the general opinion,
that the natural operation of the sun and air upon
particular soils will produce grasses without their
being artificially sown.

It is a certain fact respecting that part of the back strand of Tramore, marked A in the sketch, which, many years ago, had been and continued for some time banked in by the late Bartholomew Rivers, Esq. that in about three weeks or a month after it was inclosed, a most intolerable smell proceeded from it, occasioned, as it afterwards appeared on examination, from the putrifaction of small fish, &c. deprived of their food and support by the shutting out of the tides. This piece of ground contained about seventy acres, but the bank (the remains of which are still visible) was badly executed ; the foundation was not carefully attended to, and no sufficient precaution taken to guard against high tides, or to let them off by proper sluices, when they flowed over or broke through the bank ,—the result was, the destruction of the work

It must be satisfactory to those who may wish to forward and encourage the embankment at Tramore, to be informed, that in every instance which has come to the writer's knowledge where a work of such a description has been well and carefully executed, considerable profit, far exceeding an adequate return for the money expended, has been uniformly made.

It appears from a statement in Mr. Tighe's Statistical Survey of the County of Kilkenny, that the late Mr. Devereux of Ringville, in that county, made a considerable addition to his property by embanking between eighty and ninety acres, adjoining the river Barrow. The ground, which was covered every tide and of no value, became after the embankment worth four pounds an acre. The embankment is about an English mile in length, and Mr. Tighe says, " probably cost him in all about £2000, which was the same thing as purchasing a fee-simple of £4 for £25. Supposing that only eight acres were reclaimed, had it cost £4000 it would still be cheap, and shews what *great profit* may be made by such improvements. In the reclaimed ground, potatoes were first planted *without manure*, and gave a great crop: barley * succeeded and did not answer, the soil not being suited to it, but grass seeds sown with it grew well, and immediately supported sixty cattle the whole year both with grass and hay: great part is now grazed, and throws up thick and strong herbage." Here is a striking instance in our immediate neighbourhood of the amazing profit resulting from judicious embankment, and no person can view the more favourable situation of Tramore strand for embankment without a well grounded expectation of a similar result.

As to its practicability there cannot be any doubt; the only difference of opinion that can reasonably exist is as to the expense being re-

---

* Qu Will our fastidious English neighbours call this a bull?

mumerated by the return. At all events, it must
be perfectly clear that the object is well worth
the inquiry. According to a sensible article
which appeared some months since in a Waterford paper, the estimate for taking in the back
strand by stopping up the harbour of Rhineshark
was but £19,834. This estimate was made by
Mr. Musgrave an engineer, who is engaged in the
superintendence of the Waterford bridge, and who
offered to guarantee that the expense, under his
management, should not exceed that sum. If
Mr. Musgrave is correct in this estimate, the return must be most lucrative, for the value of the
ground, in any point of view, would, it is conceived, sanction an expenditure to a much greater
amount in embanking and reclaiming it On the
formation of a company for this very desirable
work, a committee of the subscribers, as is usual
in such cases, should be appointed to consider
and report fully on all points connected with the
undertaking. Debentures of £50 each, it is suggested would afford a ready investment for capital, and enable many to become members of the
company, whom a larger sum would exclude
from it

THE PEASANTRY.

ON THE CONDITION OF THE PEASANTRY OF THE
COUNTY OF WATERFORD

———

IT is difficult except by a detailed description
to give to those unacquainted with Ireland, an
adequate idea of the state of the lower orders.
There is something anomalous in their condition :
it is not enough to say that they are less improved
than the people of England, it is not sufficiently
explanatory to observe, that they are many years
behind them in the progress of civilization. General assertions such as these are often question-
able, and in the present case they are only partially true. they are true as far as regards the
practice of agriculture, and what may be called
the comforts and decencies of life, but they are
not correct if applied to the understandings of the
people and to the degree of their practical information

The Irish peasant is seen in the worst possible
point of view, he labours under all the disadvantages of a foreigner, he generally speaks and
always thinks in Irish · our prejudices too are
against him, he has earned a bad name and it
attaches to him incessantly. It might be sup-

posed, that a flattering description would be given of this class of persons, and in such a manner, generally speaking, it would be right to represent them generous, hospitable, high minded: this is perhaps the natural character, but it is not the character which circumstances have now impressed upon them.

The Irish peasant is shrewd and suspicious in an extreme degree; he looks on all as his enemies; he dreads his superiors—" et dona ferentes," his mind has lost its energy and elasticity; his heart is hardened against every man, because he is persuaded that every man's heart is steeled against him; he is insensible to hope, and therefore it is that so much, perhaps all, of his enjoyments are of a negative kind, arising rather from the absence of evil than from any positive good; such gratifications as are derived from the use of spirituous liquors But though depraved and degraded, and very low in the scale of humanity, he is not without intelligence · it is not too much to say, that the mind of the lower orders in Ireland is as acute and as much enlightened as that of the same class, under similar circumstances, in any other country.

The Farmers and Cottiers,—I speak of them indiscriminately, for they compose only one class —are perfectly aware of their degraded state; they can understand and value the superior civilization of their English neighbours, but they are

accustomed to consider it hopeless to endeavour
to emulate it—they look on it as on something
infinitely beyond their reach; they are taught
to account themselves an inferior caste, and have
no expectation, scarcely any desire, of improving
their condition.   The great misfortune of Ireland
appears to arise from the state of degradation
in which the peasantry exist, compared with
the intelligence and knowledge which they possess : their minds have been enlightened, while
their enjoyments are every day becoming less, or
in other words, their physical condition has not
kept pace with their moral improvement.   In
proof of this, it may be observed, that two hundred years ago, wages were almost as high as at
present, while articles of consumption were infinitely lower.   In 1631, labourers' wages were
sixpence per day, and at the same period a sheep
could be purchased for a shilling.

The peasantry of Ireland have been so often
represented in the glowing colours of romance, it
is to be feared that the sober language of truth
and reality will be received with reluctance.   The
mind is at all times unwilling to give assent to
disagreeable truths, it gladly turns from such subjects, and is disposed to reject them on the con-
solatory supposition that they originate in falsehood or misapprehension.   Accounts of Ireland
have been not only vague, but incorrect.   The
friends and the enemies of the country have both

transgressed the bounds of soberness: if the one
has described it as the favoured region of heaven,
the isle of Saints, and the land where no poisonous reptile can exist, the other has more than cancelled the unqualified approbation, by admitting
that there is nothing poisonous in Ireland, " except the men and women."

Until of very late years, the people of England
knew nothing of the Irish peasantry. It may appear paradoxical, but it is nevertheless true, that
the slaves on the coast of Africa were more
attended to than the miserable freemen of this
country. The people of England were taught
to consider the Irish as savages, despising the
comforts and decencies of civilized life, and only
happy when engaged in massacre and rapine —
Every thing that could degrade the national character was eagerly published; all their natural
and acquired vices, their errors of temperament,
and the ferocious acts which have so frequently
disgraced them, were anxiously brought into view,
while nothing or next to nothing was said of the
particular circumstances which, though they could
not excuse, might in some degree account for
them.

A few words will be sufficient to give an idea
of the misery in which the peasantry exist: it
is not intended to describe their situation when
visited by famine or disease, it will be sufficient
to pourtray their every-day life, the mode of living

inherited from their fathers, and the same which
they expect will be the lot of their children. It
has been already observed, that no considerable
distinction is perceptible in the condition of all
those personally engaged in the cultivation of the
soil. The holder of land, varying from ten to
fifty acres, may be more plentifully and more
constantly supplied with food than the cottier
whom he employs; he may exhibit a more respectable appearance at a funeral or at his place
of worship, but this difference does not sufficiently
distinguish them, to enable us to arrange them
in two classes; comparing their general habits,
we shall find them in their enjoyments, their con-
veniences and manner of living, very nearly resembling each other. The privations and wretchedness of the Irish peasantry have been depicted
even to loathing, and yet the picture has not been
overcharged. In their habitations, furniture, diet,
clothing, in the education and in the provision
for their children, they are not superior to the
Russian boor. Comparing their physical condition
with that of the same class in other countries,
and taking into account the relative intelligence
of the parties, it may be safely asserted that the
lowest class in Ireland is the most miserable in
the world. Nothing can appear more disgusting
or more repugnant to every idea of neatness, than
the interior of an Irish cabin There is no exag-
geration in the multiplied statements on this head·

their hovels are, literally speaking, shared with their pigs and poultry, and, as it has been well remarked, when the intruder is occasionally repulsed, the perseverance of the animals attests the frequency of their visits. The food of the peasantry is universally potatoes and skimmed milk, and in the many cases where a cow is not kept, salt becomes a substitute for milk during a considerable portion of the year. Throughout extensive tracts of country, animal food is never tasted, even by the better class of farmers, except perhaps at a festival or a wedding.

The condition of the females has fortunately engaged the attention of those who can best appreciate what their sex and condition require, and who will learn with regret that their strength and constitution yield at an early age to the destructive and unsuitable employments imposed upon them. The clothing of the peasantry is that in which they are least deficient : I mean the out of door dress, for the furniture of their beds is but too often a very small addition to their ordinary apparel. In the article of clothing, the condition of the peasantry has been improved. It is in the recollection of persons still living that the dress of farmers who brought their goods to market at Waterford formerly consisted of a loose great coat tied round the body with a band of hay, without shoes or stockings, shirt or hat.

It would be tedious to dwell on this part of the

subject; a deficiency of food and clothing implies a want of the other necessaries of life. When these habitual privations are rendered more acute by a year of scarcity, and when they are attended, as they generally are, with mental anxiety, the intensity of suffering may be estimated by the inevitable result, disease, assuming a slow but a fatal character, and already well known by the name of typhus fever, the consequence and the remedy of the vices and improvidence of man.

For the origin of this misery and degradation, we are to look into circumstances over which the peasant has no controul. It is not choice which makes him abstain from animal food; he does not prefer, from choice, the association with filthy animals, if he endures the nastiness of a crowded, dark, and smoky hovel, it is because its imperfect construction, and the want of clothes and fuel enforce him to recur to such expedients to procure the necessary temperature. in a word, necessity is the cause of the peasant's wretchedness, and the consequence of his wretchedness is indolence and filth, and ultimately discontent and insurrection.

The cultivators of the soil in England and in this country are differently estimated In England the third part of the produce of a farm is usually allotted to the occupier, here, the entire produce, deducting tithe and taxes and the potatoes and milk consumed, are exacted by the landlord. Supposing that the occupier's portion is, in both cases, barely a subsistence, the portion appropriated in England exceeds that in this country as much as the mode of living of the English farmer exceeds that of the Irish.

It is said that an Irish farm, if properly cultivated, might produce much more than it now does, leaving the landlord the same rent, and giving to the occupier a more suitable remuneration. This cannot be denied. But where is the skill and capital and energy, without which this increased production cannot be effected? Procure for the Irish peasant these requisites, and then the rents now exacted will not be exorbitant; but until this can be accomplished, let the portion allotted to him be more commensurate with his reasonable wants. Rent should be the surplus of the nett produce after deducting the taxes and a fair remuneration to the occupier.

A great source of the misery of Ireland is the food of the lowest class. I do not mean to adopt all the reasonings of some who have written on this subject, but it cannot be denied that the simplicity and cheapness of the food consumed, affords to the avaricious landlord a mean of estimating the minimum of produce which must be deducted for the use of the occupant, or when the proprietor is excusable, enables the farmer to carry competition to the greatest length. When we attempt to discover the source to which we are to look for an explanation of the misery and degradation of the Irish peasantry, it is too much the custom to fasten upon some one particular circumstance as the origin from which the entire evil results

The misery of this country is by some attributed to tithes, by others to want of employment, to want of education, to the absence of landed proprietors · these are among the most prominent topics brought forward by those who have written on the state of Ireland. There is no doubt that much is attributable to these causes, and that were the evils connected with them amended, the general condition of the country would be improved. But they should be altered alotgether, not in detail it would not be sufficient to lessen the number of evils, the consequence would be that the mischief would be only concentrated amongst those which remained A greater extension of education would more clearly open the eyes of the people to the misery of their situation : the improvement likely to result from greater intercourse with their superiors would be more than compensated by discovering their wants without enabling them to satisfy them.

It is not unusual to hear it stated that tithes are the sole cause of the misery of Ireland, and that were tithes abolished, the country would be happy Tithes as they are now collected, perhaps in any shape, are vexatious, but they are

not the only evil of which the peasant has to com-
plain; nay more, if they were not combined with
excessive rents, their pressure would be scarcely
perceptible. The weight of tithe as it now presses
upon the Irish agriculturist may be estimated in
this way: the rent is the nett produce of the land,
after deducting a miserable allowance to the occupier; tithe is afterwards to be taken from this
already scanty portion.

Were tithe abolished without recurring to the
other evils of the system, the boon would be given
to the landlord and not to the occupier: it is well
known that when land is tithe free, or when the
landlord is proprietor of the tithes, the difference
of rent exacted from the tenant far exceeds what
he usually pays when the property is vested in
the Church. It is the opinion of some eminent
writers on political economy, that the weight of
tithe falls upon the consumer. I do not presume
to question the truth of this observation on general principles, but in the present state of agriculture the opinion does not appear well founded.
The value of agricultural produce is not now regulated by the usual relation of supply and demand: the average annual supply exceeds the
demand, and therefore the value is a fixed quantity, and can only affect those immediately interested in the land, or, in other words, a given
amount is to be divided between the landlord,
the parson, and the occupier. Now if the tenant's

share be a bare subsistence, and therefore a fixed quantity, it will follow that the value of agricultural produce rests between the landlord and the clergy, and that what is taken from one becomes the property of the other. Another consideration is also to be attended to: the landlord and the clergy conceive (how justly it matters not) that their remuneration is inadequate. In this state of things, if the landlord alone abate his demand, he only enables the clergyman to obtain more in lieu of tithe: again, if the clergyman alone abate his tithe, he only gives the landlord a power to exact more rent.

Reduction, to be effectual, must be mutual: let the landlords and the clergy unite in reducing their demands, and then the sum of their abatements will go to relieve the occupier.

These observations respecting excessive demands are, of course, merely general; there are many and splendid instances of liberality and fairness amongst the land-owners of this county, and independent of my feeble testimony, the comparative moderation of rents may be demonstrated by a reference to the more peaceable condition of the people, as compared with the inhabitants of some of the other counties.

At the same time it must not be concealed that a trifling additional pressure, or a few wanton acts of cruelty, would soon excite the spirit which, though not in immediate action, is yet in full vi-

gour, and which only requires an inconsiderable
movement to cause it to burst forth with destructive fury.

It is one of the misfortunes of the present state
of things that there is little apparent or immediate
encouragement to induce landed proprietors to
alter the system. In the many cases where a
more liberal mode of acting has been pursued, it
has been met with ingratitude on the part of those
whose benefit was sought: moderate rents have
produced a relaxation of exertion, and kindness
has been returned with fraud. Together with a
steady and improved system, it will require much
time and an invincible patience to teach the peasantry that their interests and those of their
landlords are inseparably united; it will require
all the incitements of hope, the force of example,
and some of the fruits of their labours to convince
them that their happiness depends upon their
own exertions

But tithes and excessive rents are not the only
evils: independent of these considerations we
have, in a vast unemployed population, an unfail-
ing source of misery and crime

It is not pretended that our population is excessive; though great, it is still unquestionably
beneath the means of subsistence · it is not excessive as it regards subsistence, but it is excessive as it respects employment   Ireland is abundantly competent to support its population · the

evil is, that a great proportion must be supported
as paupers. If amongst the many circumstances
which oppress this country, one alone should be
attended to, that one is the useless or unemployed
population. Turn where you will, the same evil
recurs. Does a benevolent landlord wish to improve the condition of those beneath him? The
multitudes residing on some farms preclude the
possibility of doing this, except by giving up all
rent, and there are cases where even this sacrifice
would not be sufficient.

The Irish peasant is particularly anxious to
" enlarge himself," and will take any quantity of
ground, although unable to cultivate it, representing that he has " good help," has a grown up son
who would get a wife and fortune, if he could
give him a bit of ground and a cabin. For the
money received by this sort of traffic, he gives
half of what is over and under ground, meaning
by the latter, the corn and potatoes growing, and
then portions off his daughters, and thus the
wheel goes round.

The subdivision of farms (a system beneath
the influence of which population soon becomes
excessive) has been carried to such an extent
that the produce is barely sufficient to support
the occupiers. Do we expect that the value of
land will find its own level? Our unemployed
millions forbid us to look for this desirable event·
they will offer the value and more than the value;

they will require a bare subsistence, they will
threaten and terrify and murder to procure a resting place, and thus the evil goes on increasing,
carrying within itself the seeds of future mischief.

Disturbance and discontent have for years existed in Ireland. Whence do they arise? They
cannot be attributed solely to the misconduct of
the government, for there have been so many different rulers, and so many different plans of go-
verning, it were impossible that some of them
would not remove the evils, if they were really
derivable from this source.

The historical sketch with which this volume is
commenced abundantly shews the wrongs and
the sufferings of Ireland, and exhibits a black ca-
talogue of unjust acts, which makes England still
her debtor. This hateful system, which parcelled
a great country among ten strangers, and taught
that all who loved her were "degenerate" or
"rebels," can only be said to have terminated
since the commencement of the last reign: it was
productive of many evils; it excited cruelty and
oppression in one country, and it infused rancour
and prejudice into the other. The former may
be observed in the arbitrary change of Irish names
and fashions; the latter is ludicrously exhibited
in the unaccountable reluctance with which a
family of the county of Waterford assumed the
name of Condon, in place of Mac Majoke. The
injustice and misgovernment of England in former
times may have produced many evils and were

perhaps the remote cause of the existing misery of Ireland. But how can the present misgovernment of the country, even admitting its existence, be connected with the prevailing disturbances; how can the disorders of the peasantry be connected with the errors of their rulers?

Besides if the governments of Ireland were in fault, why have the disturbances been partial?—why have they been confined to particular districts and to particular classes? Above all, why have they prevailed principally amongst those whose connection with the executive is least observable? The same reasoning applies in a great degree to the opinion that religious differences are the cause of insurrection and disturbance: this opinion must also be unfounded, the argument drawn from it would prove too much. If discontent, arising from religious disabilities, were the source of the insurrectionary acts, then the same spirit should pervade every part of Ireland, and the same consequences follow from it. Religious distinctions are more observable in towns and cities, while disturbance is confined to the country, and is most prevalent where there is a similarity of religious feeling, and no political disabilities are felt It would be a mockery to the Irish peasant to condole with him upon his political degradation, or to demand his gratitude for the gift of the elective franchise. The source of discontent must be sought elsewhere

The exciting causes of the insurrectionary spirit which has so long harassed Ireland are to be traced to the misery of her peasantry, to their wretched and precarious subsistence, to their miserable hovels, to the privations they endure, to the abject state of dependence in which they exist, and above all, to the rapacity and oppression which they frequently endure.

When the condition of the peasantry is brought fully under our observation, it is a matter of surprize how they can exist in such circumstances. —We are amazed how they can endure such misery, but are not prepared to think that insurrection is the necessary consequence.

Extreme suffering will break through all bounds; a wretch with a family around him, famishing in a hovel, or, what is still more dreaded, turned upon society without a home to receive, or even hope to comfort him, is prepared to violate all restraint and justice and order; the iron grasp of the law is mercy to him. How gladly would he change conditions with the slave in the West Indies, or with the convicts in a prison-ship, except indeed that he had rather die at home! It is a fact of every day occurrence, that the prisoners in our gaols are unwilling to return to their miserable homes, and that it becomes necessary to compel them to the enjoyment of liberty and wretchedness.

The strong arm of the law can do much; it may

force men to endure great misery, but it has its limits; it can only chain down the body, the mind is still free, it may compel men to suffer, but it cannot make them contented. We seek too much when we expect that the Roman Catholic clergy should, in every case, repress the outrages and check the bad passions of the people We are unreasonable, when we seek a remedy for varied and complicated evils in the unsupported influence of religious teachers. I know that many of the Roman Catholic priesthood are anxiously and incessantly engaged in promoting peace and harmony, order and regularity, amongst their people. I have witnessed their zealous and indefatigable labours, and am convinced that their authority is exerted perhaps beyond its limits. But how little is to be expected from preaching patience to misery, how little sway can religion maintain over men inflamed with the spirit of demons!

Let us, from a consideration of the nature of the disturbances, endeavour to trace their origin. On referring to the accounts of the various tumultuous assemblages, which under the names of Steel Boys, Oak Boys, White Boys, &c., have served to fill up the modern history of Ireland, we find that they all have had the same origin and the same object. The inclosing of a common, heavy fines on leases, compulsory work on roads, actual or fancied oppression, more or less endurable, has called the bad spirit into action, and, when excited, the object has invariably been to lower the rent of lands, to check competition by discouraging the proposals of strangers, to abolish tithes, and, in some shape or other, to acquire what the Irish peasant has never had, a reasonable interest in the property of the soil.

The disturbances spring from some cause connected with the landed interest: to that quarter, and to that only, must the remedy be applied. There is some real or supposed unsoundness in the system, which requires investigation; if the former, it should be brought to light; if the latter, it will vanish before inquiry.

The want of connection between the higher and lower ranks, which is justly considered one of the greatest evils, is of itself sufficient to shew that the peasantry cannot have a common cause with any other party. There are two classes of persons in Ireland who are discontented. One desires political power, the other, more humble, seeks even less than the degraded Roman populace—they only ask for food. What bond of union.—what connecting link can exist between these two classes, except perhaps a real or fancied community of suffering ? The peasantry are now susceptible of every impression; their wants have rendered them easily acted on by a force which otherwise would have no attraction for them. Restore them to a healthy state, and the contagion will be innocuous.

Still, amidst all these gloomy and disheartening appearances, there are some faint indications of more cheering days. Amidst all the depravity of the times, there are not a few redeeming virtues hovering about the Irish peasant which encourage the hope that he may again assume the proud rank in the scale of humanity, which anciently belonged to his character and nation. The hospitality of the country flourishes in all its pristine vigour: the traveller, even the wandering wretched beggar, enters without hesitation and seats himself freely at the fire-side of the most perfect stranger. If, on some occasions, a portion of the frugal meal is not pressed on the superior visitor, it is because they esteem it unworthy his acceptance, and dread even the semblance of presumption.

The recklessness and total absence of selfishness, which are constantly exhibited, are almost incredible. When a prospect of temporary enjoyment is held out, as a hurling-match or a horserace, sports of which he is passionately fond, the Irish peasant has been known to rush from the calamity of a legal process, and to riot in unrestrained pleasure, not knowing whether at his return at midnight he should have a farm to support, or a roof to shelter, him. He is much attached to his devotions, and most regular in his attendance at chapel. The following fact, which occurred in this county, exemplifies his respect for his religion. A farmer, passionately attached to whiskey, (in which he was by no means singular,) always became very turbulent and abusive to his family when he took more of his favourite beverage than agreed with his understanding, an occurrence which not unfrequently happened. His wife and children adopted the following ingenious plan of protecting themselves from his violence and effectually succeeded. As soon as they were aware of his approach to his cabin, which he uniformly announced by screaming and hallooing, they all dropped on their knees as if to pray; he immediately followed their example and soon fell into a sound sleep, he was then instantly caught up and rolled into bed.

The lower orders are susceptible of singular attachment to the persons of their superiors, an attachment partly derived from the custom of fosterage, which in former times connected the different ranks in this country in the same way as Patron and Client united the corresponding classes in ancient Rome.

Those qualities which are now converted into vices, may again be restored to their true tone and healthfulness.

The Irish peasant is already free from selfishness, he is generous by habit and by nature, and kindness may again induce him to be attached and grateful. Much may be done by the wealth and the beneficence of England; her capital may introduce profitable employment; every new source of employment will diminish competition in land; the farmer will be more esteemed; he will be raised in his own estimation; he will partake of the enjoyments of life and thus become contented.

Gloomy as Ireland has been, her day of peace may not be far distant. The united efforts of all ranks and all parties may effect the change, banish misery and strife, and, falsifying the prediction of the historian, render Ireland peaceable and contented " much before doomsday."

APPENDIX.

A List of the MAYORS, BAILIFFS, *and* SHERIFFS *of the* CITY OF WATERFORD, *from the Year* 1377 *to* 1824, *inclusive.*

MAYORS.

1377	William Lumbard	1407	John Walsh
1378	William Lumbard	1408	John Lumbard
1379	William Chapman	1409	Walter Attamen
1380	William Madan	1410	William Power
1381	Philip Spell	1411	John Roberts
1382	Robert Sweetman	1412	John Rocket
1383	Robert Sweetman	1413	Simon Wickins
1384	William Lumbard	1414	John White
1385	William Forstall	1415	Nicholas Holland
1386	Robert Bruce	1416	William Russell
1387	William Lumbard	1417	William Lincolne
1388	William Poer	1418	John Lumbard
1389	William Poer	1419	John Lumbard
1390	Milo Poer	1420	Roger Walsh
1391	Walter Spence	1421	Simon Wickins
1392	William Chapman	1422	Thomas O Kabrane
1393	John Rocket	1423	Gilbert Dyer
1394	Milo Poer	1424	John Eyenas
1395	William Forstall	1425	Thomas O Kabrane
1396	William Attamen	1426	William Lincolne
1397	William Lincolne	1427	Peter Strong
1398	Andrew Archer	1428	Robert Lincolne
1399	John Eyenas	1429	Peter Rice
1400	William Forstall	1430	Walter Attamen
1401	John Lumbard	1431	Peter Strong
1402	John Lumbard	1432	Gilbert Dyer
1403	Nicholas Lumbard	1433	Foulke Commerford
1404	William Poer	1434	Peter Strong
1405	William Poer	1435	Nicholas Gough
1406	Richard Brushbone	1436	John Corr

1437 John White
1438 Nicholas Mulgan
1439 John Rope
1440 Thomas Hull
1441 Nicholas Gough
1442 William Sattadel
1443 Nicholas Mulgan
1444 Nicholas Mulgan
1445 William Corr
1446 William Corr
1447 John Rope
1418 Foulke Commerford
1449 William Lincolne
1450 William White
1451 Richard Walsh
1452 Maurice Wise
1453 Patrick Rope
1454 John Madan
1455 William White
1456 Robert Butler
1457 John Madan
1458 Richard Walsh
1459 William White
1460 Laurence Dobbin
1461 John May
1462 John Sherlock
1463 John Corr
1464 John Corr
1465 Peter Strong
1466 Nicholas Mulgan
1467 John Butler
1468 John Mulgan
1469 James Rice
1470 Nicholas Devereux
1471 James Rice
1472 James Rice
1473 John Corr
1474 John Corr

1475 John Sherlock
1476 Peter Lovet
1477 James Rice
1478 William Lincolne
1479 John Corr
1480 James Sherlock
1481 Maurice Wise
1482 John Butler
1483 James Rice
1484 James Rice
1485 Richard Strong
1486 James Rice
1487 John Butler
1488 James Rice
1489 Robert Lumbard
1490 William Lumbard
1491 Patrick Rope
1492 William Lumbard
1493 Robert Butler
1494 Henry Fagan
1495 *John Madan
1510 John Madan
1511 John Butler
1512 Nicholas Madan
1513 John Madan
1514 James Butler
1515 Nicholas Madan
1516 John Madan
1517 Patrick Rope
1518 Nicholas Madan
1519 James Sherlock
1520 John Morgan
1521 Richard Walsh, who was
     the last that governed
     the city of Waterford
     without Bailiffs or She-
     riffs

MAYORS

BAILIFFS.

1522 Peter Walsh	. .	Henry Walsh, Pat Lumbard
1523 Nicholas Wise	.	Nich Morgan, Wil Lincolne
1524 Nicholas Madan	.	Nicholas Strong, John Lumbard
1525 James Sherlock	. .	James White, Tho Lumbard
1526 John Morgan	.	Wm Lincolne, John Lumbard
1527 Nicholas Wise	.	Rob Sherlock, Peter Sherlock

* From the year 1195 to 1509, no charter.

MAYORS	BAILIFFS.
1528 Patrick Walsh . .	Nich Walsh, James Devereux
1529 James Sherlock	John Sherlock, Tho. Lumbard
1530 John Morgan	Wm Lincolne, Edw Sherlock
1531 Nicholas Wise .	James Wise, Tho Sherlock
1532 Patrick Walsh .	Rob Strong, Jas Walsh
1533 William Wise	Jas Sherlock, Peter Dobbyn
1534 James Sherlock	Jas Walsh, James Sherlock
1535 William Lincolne	Peter Dobbyn, Tho Lumbard
1536 John Morgan .	Tho Woodlock, David Bayley
1537 Thomas Lumbard .	John Butler, Nich Madan
1538 Edward Sherlock .	John Butler, Edw Sherlock
1539 James Walsh .	James Sherlock, David Bayley
1540 William Wise	James Woodlock, Nich Lee
1541 Peter Dobbyn	Rob Strong, Rob Walsh
1542 James White .	Nich Lee, Tho Grant
1543 William Lincolne	Rob Walsh, Will Morgan
1544 Edward Sherlock . .	Maurice Wise, Henry Walsh
1545 Thomas Lumbard . .	Nich Lee, David Bayley
1546 Peter Dobbyn .	Tho Grant, Wm Lumbard
1547 James Walsh .	Tho Wise, Wm Wise
1548 James Madan . .	Maurice Wise, Nich Lee
1549 Thomas Sherlock .	Jas Woodlock, Jas Grant
1550 Walter Coltie . . .	Tho Wise, John Sherlock
1551 David Walsh	Jas Woodlock, Jas Walsh
1552 Peter Dobbyn .	Peter Strong, John Wise
1553 James Dobbyn	John Neal, Peter Walsh
1554 Maurice Wise .	Peter Aylward, John Sherlock
1555 Robert Walsh	John Wise, Paul Lumbard
1556 Henry Walsh .	Peter Walsh, John Walsh
1557 Peter Dobbyn .	John Neal, Jas Grant
1558 Maurice Wise .	Jas. Lumbard, Phil Commerford
1559 John Sherlock . .	Nich Lumbard, Rich Lacket
1560 Peter Strong .	James Lumbard, Jas Grant
1561 John Wise	James Walsh, Paul Lumbard
1562 James Walsh .	John Walsh, Pat. Dobbyn
1563 Henry Wise .	Nich Lumbard, Jas Madan
1564 Peter Walsh .	Jas Butler, James Sherlock
1565 John Neal . . .	John Madan, Peter Sherlock
1566 Peter Aylward . .	Geo Wise, Nich Lumbard
1567 Patrick Dobbyn	Jas Lumbard, Phil Commerford
1568 Nich Lumbard	Jas Sherlock, John Sherlock
1569 Peter Walsh .	Jas Butler, John Lumbard
1570 Phil Commerford	Peter Sherlock, Nich Commerford
1571 George Wise	Tho Wise, Jas Lincolne
1572 John Madan .	Rich Strong, Pat Commerford
1573 John Madan .	Rich Strong, Pat. Commerford
1574 James Walsh	Rob Walsh, Pat Commerford

MAYORS	SHERIFFS
1575 James Butler .	Rich Strong, Nich Lee
1576 Peter Sherlock .	Edw Walsh, John Leonard
1577 Peter Aylward .	Jas Lumbard, Pat. Commerford
1578 Sir Pat Walsh . .	Rob Walsh, Tho Wise
1579 Pat. Dobbyn .	John Leonard, Nich Commerford
1580 James Sherlock .	Nich Lee, Alex Briver
1581 Richard Strong . . .	Nich Commerford, Ed Commerford
1582 Nicholas Lee . .	Rob Walsh, Balthaz Woodlock
1583 James Madan . .	Nich. Wise, John Lynch
1584 John Leonard .	John Walsh, Pat Morgan
1585 Nicholas Commerford	Alex Briver, Nich Walsh
1586 James Wise .	Pat Morgan, John Tew
1587 Alex. Briver .	Wm Lumbard, Pat Lumbard
1588 Rich Strong . .	John Walsh, John Tew
1589 Patrick Dobbyn .	Wm Lincolne, Paul Sherlock
1590 James Sherlock	Nich Wise, James Madan
1591 John Leonard .	Balthaz Woodlock, Tho White
1592 Nicholas Aylward .	Nich Wise, Paul Strong
1593 Patrick Morgan .	Tho Wise, Geo Commerford
1594 Paul Sherlock . . .	Rich Madan, Geo Commerford
1595 James White .	Rich Madan, Geo Commerford
1596 Tho Wadding .	Rob Walsh, John Lumbard
1597 Paul Strong	Tho Wise, Tho Walsh
1598 Tho. White .	Jas Lumbard, John Commerford
1599 Rich Madan .	Jas. Sherlock, Wm Barrow
1600 Sir Edward Gough	Geo Sherlock, T Knaresborough
1601 Rob Walsh	Nich Madan, Walter Sherlock
1602 Rob Walsh .	David Walsh, Mich Browne
1603 James Lumbard	Tho White, John Sherlock
1604 Rich Madan	Tho White, Paul Strong
1605 Tho Wise	Nich Wise, Paul Sherlock
1606 John Sherlock . .	Tho Dobbyn, Jas Walsh
1607 Tho. Strong .	Rob Strong, Rob Walsh
1608 Stephen Leonard .	Walter Sherlock, Nich White
1609 Stephen Leonard	Walt Sherlock, Nich White
1610 James Levett	Jas Briver, Alex Leonard
1611 Richard Wadding	Rich Butler, Wm Lincolne
1612 Michael Browne	Pat White, John Skiddy
1613 Rob Walsh . .	Jas Walsh, Nich Wise
1614 Walter Sherlock	Jasper Woodlock, Pat Meyler
1615 Nicholas White	Jas Lumbard, Jas. Lumbard
1616 John Joy	Zabulon Berrick, Wm Philips

MAYORS	SHERIFFS
1617*Alexander Briver	. John Murphy, Tho Burgess
1626 James Woodlock	. Rob. Leonard, Matt. Grant
1627 Sir Peter Aylward	Barth Lincolne, Wm Lincolne
1628 John Sherlock	Paul Sherlock, John Levett
1629 Will Dobbyn .	John Fagan, Wm Cleere
1630 Rob Wise	. Tho White, Jas Lumbard
1631 James Walsh . .	Tho Maine, Pat White
1632 Sir Tho Sherlock . .	Nich Browne, And Wise
1633 Sir Tho Gough .	Christ Sherlock, Nich Strong
1634 Rich Strong . .	Math Grant, Rich. Nicholas
1635 John Skiddy .	Wm Lincolne, Garret Lincolne
1636 Rich Butler .	Fra Briver, Rich. Fitz Nicholas
1637 James White . .	John Levett, Rich Fitz Nicholas
1638 Nich. Wise .	John Bluet, Girke Morgan
1639 Rob Lumbard .	Luke White, John Fitzgerald
1640 Mathew Grant	Matt Porter, Henry White
1641 Francis Briver .	John Power, Wm Woodlock
1642 Tho White .	. Wm English, Tho Walsh
1643 Redmond Gerald .	Mich Sherlock, And White
1644 Luke White .	. Nich Jones, Laur White
1645 Garret Lincolne .	Peter Morgan, John Lincolne
1646 Paul Wadding	Edw Geraldine, John Walsh
1647 John Bluet	Francis Butler, Martin Gall
1648 Sir John Walsh	And Morgan, Bar Sherlock
1649 John Levett .	Nich Geraldine, Jas Lynham
1650 John Aylward	Math Everard, Rich. Fitzgerald

(From 1650 to 1656 the city was governed by Commissioners appointed by Oliver Cromwell)

1656 Geo Cawdron .	Tho Coote, Edw Smart
1657 Tho Watts .	Wm Cooper, Tho Wallis
1658 Andrew Rickard .	Henry Seagar, John Morris
1659 John Houghton	John Gregory, John Bamblet
1660 Sir Tho Dancer	Sam Busmead, Sam Browne
1661 Wm Halsey	Geo Waters, Rich Wilkinson
1662 Wm Bolton .	Chi Timeman, Rob Tunbridge
1663 John Eyeres	Math Johnson, Zach Clayton
1664 Tho Christmas . .	Tho Briscoe, Wm. Dapwell
1665 Geo Deyos .	Tho Prince, Wm Fuller
1666 And Rickard	Rich Barret, Nath Marriot
1667 Tho Exton	Tho Eyres, Will Hurst
1668 John Heavens	Tho Eyres, Edw Stone
1669 John Heavens	Dav Owens, Joseph Osborne
1670 Will Hurst	Franc Knowles, Will Joy
1671 Tho Bolton	Joseph Ivie, Wm Lamb

* From the year 1617 to the year 1626, there was no settled government, the magistrates, for refusing the oath of supremacy, and for nonconformity, were turned out, and sent prisoners to Cork.

MAYORS	SHERIFFS.
1672 Henry Aland . . .	Mich Head, Rob. Seay
1673 Tho Coote . .	Wm Dennis, Rich Watridge
1674 Joseph Ivie .	And Lloyd, Tho Hitchings
1675 Mich. Head .	Nath Marriot, Edw Collins
1676 Henry Seagar . .	Wm Godrick, John Bamblet
1677 Wm Cooper .	Sam Taylor, Franc Barker
1678 Wm. Denis .	Benj Powel, Jos Hopkins
1679 Rich Seay . .	Rich Mabank, Tho Foulks
1680 Zach Clayton . .	Henry Aland, Will Smith
1681 Wm Fuller .	John Snow, Theod. Jones
1682 Rich Mabank . .	Pat Moore, Ben. Marriot
1683 Wm Fuller . .	Jonath Aland, Joseph Bare
1684 Mich Head . . .	Edw Collins, Francis Barker
1685 Wm Godrick . .	David Lloyd, Francis Barker
1686 Wm. Godrick .	Theod Jones, Tho Smith
1687 David Lloyde . .	John Winston, Ben. Lamb
1688 Tho Wise .	Wm Dobbyn, John Aylward
1689 Nich. Porter .	Tho Lee, John Donnaghow

(The city surrendered to King William, July 25, 1690, and the Protestant government restored)

MAYORS	SHERIFFS.
1690 David Lloyde . .	Ben. Bolton, Ben. Lamb
1691 David Lloyde .	Sam Austin, Tho Evans
1692 David Lloyde .	Sam Austin, Tho. Evans
1693 Francis Barker	John Head, John Lamb
1694 Joseph Hopkins . .	Samuel Frith, Charl Hart
1695 Rich Christmas .	Charles Hull, David Lewis
1696 John Mason .	John Lapp, Wm Weekes
1697 Sir John Mason .	John Lapp, Wm Weekes
1698 Will Smith . . .	Wm Jones, Jas Eccles
1699 Tho Smith .	Caleb Wade, Rob Glen
1700 John Head	Charles Bolton, Rich Graves
1701 Theod Jones .	Rich Morris, Edm Feild
1702 Wm Weekes .	Jas M'Carrol, Wm Morgan
1703 John Lamb and John Lapp }	John Francis, Joshua Cockran
1704 Wm Jones	Tho Aikenhead, Rob Backas
1705 David Lewis . .	Joseph Price, Wm Cari
1706 James Eccles .	John Moore, John Morgan
1707 Jas Eccles, afterwards David Lewis }	John Espaignet, Wm. Martin
1708 David Lewis . .	Francis Barker, Ben Morris
1709 Sir John Mason . .	Wm Ecles, Jeremy Gayot
1710 David Lewis . . .	Tho Head, Wm. Ecles
1711 David Lewis	Jas Medlicot, John Morris
1712 John Mason .	Arth Taylor, John Graves
1713 Francis Barker	Arth Taylor, John Graves
1714 Sam Austin . .	Arth. Taylor, John Graves
1715 Tho Christmas	Rob West, John Barker

	MAYORS		SHERIFFS
1716	William Jones	.	Joseph Ivie, William Roche
1717	Thomas Aikenhead		Arthur Taylor, William Roche
1718	Thomas Aikenhead		William Barker, John Barker
1719	Benjamin Morris		John Barker, William Roche
1720	John Moore	.	Wm. Thompson, Simon Newport
1721	Thomas Aikenhead		Jeremiah Gayot, John Barker
1722	John Morris	.	Joseph Price, John Graves
1723	Joseph Ivie	. .	Edward Weekes, Robert Glew
1724	William Alcock	.	Richard Weekes, Wm Weekes
1725	Thomas Christmas		Arthur Taylor, Wm. Martin
1726	Simon Vashon	.	Bev Usher, Edward Harrison
1727	Simon Newport	.	William Eeles, John Barker
1728	Edward Weekes		William Jones, Thomas Roach
1729	Joseph Ivie	.	Stephen Lapp, Samuel Barker
1730	Henry Mason	. .	William Roach, Thomas Roach
1731	Richard Weekes	. .	Alexander Boyde, Wm Alcock
1732	John Moore		Henry Alcock, William Morris
1733	William Barker	.	William Eeles, John Barker
1734	Henry Mason	.	John Barker, Jos Price
1735	William Morgan	.	Peter Vashon, William Morgan
1736	Ambrose Congreve	.	John Barker, William Martin
1737	Samuel Barker	.	Thomas Alcock, Francis Barker
1738	Simon Vashon, jun		William Dobbyn, Corn Bolton
1739	Simon Vashon, jun.		William Price, Francis Barker
1740	Robert West	.	David Lewis, George Backas
1741	Samuel Barker		George Backas, John Portingal
1742	Robert Glen	.	Phineas Barret, Jeffry Paul
1743	Cornelius Bolton		John Morris, Robert West
1744	Beverly Usher	.	Thomas Miles, John Portingal
1745	William Eeles	.	William Paul, John Price
1746	Christmas Paul	. .	George Backas, Hans Wallace
1747	Francis Barker		George Norrington, George Carr
1748	Thomas Christmas and Robert Glen . .		Michael Hobbs, John Boyd
1749	William Paul	.	John Portingall, Geo Wilkinson
1750	William Paul	.	Daniel Ivie, John Lyon
1751	William Paul held over, George Backas .		John Portingall, Thomas Carr
1752	Samuel Barker	.	John Portingall, John Price (21st June, 1753,) George Norrington in the room of Price
1753	William Alcock	. . .	Francis Price, Benjamin Morris
1754	William Morgan		William Hobbs, George Norrington (who died), Geo Lander
1755	Thomas Miles	.	Jas Henry Bennett, Rob Backas
1756	Simon Newport	.	Francis Price, Robert Backas
1757	Henry Alcock	. .	Samuel Newport, William Bates
1758	Thomas West	. .	William Bates, Francis Price
1759	Benjamin Morris	.	William Bates, William Barker

MAYORS.	SHERIFFS.
1760 Michael Hobbs* . . .	William Bates, William Barker
1761 Michael Hobbs held over, Cornelius Bolton .	Jas Henry Reynett, Wm Barker
1762 Thomas Miles . . .	William Bates, William Barker
1763 George Wilkinson	Jas. Henry Reynett, Wm Barker
1764 William Alcock .	William Bates, William Barker
1765 John Lyon . .	William Bates, William Barker
1766 Henry Alcock .	John Lander, William Barker
1767 William Price .	William Bates, William Barker
1768 William Alcock . .	William Bates, William Barker
1769 Bolton Lee . .	William Bates, Thomas Jones
1770 Benjamin Morris	Richard Kearney, William Price
1771 Francis Barker . .	Samuel Morgan, Robert Lyon
1772 William Bates	James Moore, Wm Alcock, jun.
1773 William Hobbs . . '	James Kearney, John Alcock
1774 John Lander	Jas Moore, Adam Rogers, jun
1775 James Henry Reynett '	Richard Kearney, John Alcock
1776 James Henry Reynett	Richard Kearney, John Alcock, held over for want of an election
1777 Henry Alcock, jun	Daniel Ivie, Thomas Alcock
1778 Simon Newport . .	Thomas Price, Samuel King
1779 Samuel Morgan . .	John Usher, Samuel King
1780 William Paul . . .	Thomas Alcock, Samuel King
1781 William Alcock .	William Barrett, James Ramsay
1782 Simon John Newport .	James Ramsay, James Sempill
1783 James Moore . . .	James Ramsay, Thomas Price
1784 William Newport .	Thomas Price, George Boate
1785 John Alcock .	John Burchall, Simon Newport
1786 Samuel King	Thomas Backas, William Roache
1787 Benjamin Morris .	Thomas Backas, William Roache
1788 William Weekes .	William Roache, John Denis
1789 Thomas Alcock	Thomas Backas, Edm Stevenson
1790 James Ramsay	Thomas Sargent, Edm Stevenson
1791 Thomas Price . .	Thomas Backas, Henry Sargent
1792 Sir Simon Newport, Kt	Thomas Backas, Samuel Boyce
1793 Thomas Price .	John Denis, George Cottom
(Thomas Price died in the Mayoralty, 17th November, 1793, and James Moore was elected)	
1794 Edmond Stevenson	George Cottom, Robert Hunt
1795 Benjamin Morris, jun. .	Thomas Backas, Edward Briscoe
1796 Simon Newport . . .	John Burchall, George Cottom
1797 James Sempill	John Burchall, Corn L. Wallace
1798 Samuel Boyce .	John Burchall, William Kearney
1799 James Sempill .	John Burchall, Edw V Briscoe
1800 Samuel King . . .	John Burchall, Edw V. Briscoe

* Michael Hobbs held to the 15th February, 1762, when Cornelius Bolton, Mayor, James Henry Reynett and William Barker, Sheriffs, were sworn into office by virtue of three peremptory mandamuses, which issued out of the Court of King's Bench, and directed to the said Michael Hobbs for that purpose

MAYORS	SHERIFFS.
1801 Samuel Morgan .	John Denis, Edward Weekes
1802 James Henry Reynett .	John Burchall, James Hackett
1803 Henry Alcock .	John Burchall, John Snow
1804 James Henry Reynett	Henry Sargent, James Hackett
1805 James Moore . . .	Henry Sargent, Jas Wallace
1806 Robert Lyon . .	Wm. Murphy, Jas H Reynett
1807 William Alcock	John Denis, James Burkitt
1808 Robert Lyon . . .	Nicholas B Skottowe, M Evelyn
1809 John Burchall . .	Jas H Reynett, Robert Carew
1810 Cornelius Bolton . .	William Kearney, Wm Hassard
1811 John Denis . .	James Burkitt, John Perkins
1812 James Henry Reynett	James Hackett, Wm Hassard
1813 Henry Sargent . .	Sir Nich Skottowe, Wm Johnson
1814 Robert Lyon . . .	James Burkitt, Henry Alcock
	(Henry Alcock resigned and James
	Hackett was elected)
1815 Harry Alcock	James Hackett, Corn. Bolton
1816 Cornelius Bolton .	James Hackett, John Lyon
1817 Samuel Morgan . .	James Hackett, Henry Alcock
1818 Sir John Newport	Henry Alcock, William Weekes
1819 James Hackett	Henry Alcock, Henry H Hunt
1820 Samuel King .	Henry Alcock, William Hobbs
1821 William Murphy	Wm Weekes, Alex M Alcock
1822 Edward Weekes	Wm M Ardagh, Richard Pope
1823 James Hackett . .	Samuel Newport, John Harris
1824 Sir Simon Newport	Sam Newport, Mat. Poole, M.D.

INDEX.

LIST OF THE PLATES.

LONDON:

PRINTED BY C. ROWORTH, BELL YARD,
TEMPLE BAR.

ALBEMARLE-STREET, January, 1825.

Mr. MURRAY

HAS JUST PUBLISHED

THE FOLLOWING WORKS.

1.

" Who Wrote ΕΙΚΩΝ ΒΑΣΙΛΙΚΗ ?" Considered, and Answered, in Two Letters to his Grace the Archbishop of Canterbury. By CHRISTOPHER WORDSWORTH, D D., Master of Trinity College, Cambridge, and Rector of Buxsted with Uckfield, Sussex. 8vo. 10s. 6d.

2.

MEMOIRS of the AFFAIRS of EUROPE, from the Peace of UTRECHT. 4to 2l. 10s.

3

The BOOK of the ROMAN-CATHOLIC CHURCH, in a Series of Letters addressed to ROBERT SOUTHEY, Esq , LLD , on his BOOK of the CHURCH. By CHARLES BUTLER, Esq , of Lincoln's-Inn 8vo. 9s. 6d.

4.

A SKETCH of the MANNERS and CUSTOMS of PORTU-GAL, made during a Residence in Lisbon, in the Years 1821, 22, 23. By MARIANNE BAILLIE. With Plates, 2 vols. small 8vo.

5.

LETTERS from the IRISH HIGHLANDS. fc. 8vo. 10s. 6d.

6.

CORRECTED REPORT of SPEECHES delivered at the Meeting for erecting a Monument to the late JAMES WATT, Esq. 8vo. 4s. 6d.

7.

The BOND, a Dramatic Poem. By Mrs. CHARLES GORE, 8vo. 5s 6d.

8.

ITALY, a Poem, by SAMUEL ROGERS. Fourth Edition. fc. 8vo. 7s. 6d.

9.

The SIEGE of JERUSALEM, a Poem. By CHARLES PEERS Second Edition. 8vo. 12s.

" We were agreeably surprised to find a Poem of real merit. The production of Mr. Peers is indeed poetical, both in its form and its subject. It has all there is in Romance to move us, added to the charm of incontestible history."—*Monthly Review*, Oct. 1824.

10.

TALES of a TRAVELLER. By the Author of the SKETCH BOOK. A NEW EDITION, in 2 vols. post 8vo. 16s.

Also New Editions of

SKETCH BOOK, 2 vols. 8vo. 21s. 2 vols post 8vo. 16s.
BRACEBRIDGE HALL, 2 vols. 8vo. 24s. 2 vols. post 8vo. 16s.
KNICKERBOCKER, 8vo 16s

11.

CHINESE MORAL MAXIMS. With a Free and Verbal Translation, affording Examples of the Grammatical Structure of the Language. Compiled by JOHN FRANCIS DAVIS, F.R S., Member of the Asiatic Society. 8vo. 5s. 6d.

WORKS NEARLY READY FOR PUBLICATION.

I.

GREECE DURING the SUMMER of 1824. 8vo.

II.

A VISIT to GREECE, containing various Facts respecting the Revolution, which have been very lately collected in that Country. By GEORGE WADDINGTON, Esq., Author of Travels in Ethiopia. 8vo.

III.

HISTORY of the late WAR in SPAIN and PORTUGAL. By ROBERT SOUTHEY. VOL. II. 4to.

IV.

A Brief Narrative of an UNSUCCESSFUL ATTEMPT to reach REPULSE BAY through the WELCOME, in His Majesty's Ship GRIPER, in the year 1821. By Capt. LYON, R.N. With a Chart and Five Engravings by FINDEN. 8vo.

V.

A SHORT NARRATIVE of LORD BYRON'S LAST
JOURNEY to GREECE, extracted from the Journal of COUNT PETER
GAMBA, who attended his Lordship on that Expedition. 8vo.

VI.

CONWAY PAPERS, from the Collection of the Marquess of
HERTFORD. 5 vols 8vo.

" But now for the recoveries—think what I have in part recovered! Only
the state papers, private papers, &c &c., of the two Lords Conway, Secretaries
of State. How you will rejoice, and how you will grieve. they seem to have
laid up every scrap of paper they ever had, from the middle of Queen Elizabeth's reign to the middle of Charles the Second's. By the accounts of the
family, there were whole rooms full, all which, during the absence of the last,
and the minority of the present, Lord, were, by the ignorance of the steward,
consigned to the oven, and to the uses of the house What remained, except
one box that was kept till almost rotten in a cupboard, were thrown loose into
the lumber-room, where, spread on the pavement, they supported old marbles,
and screens, and boxes. From them I have dragged all I could, and have
literally, taking altogether, brought away a chest near five feet long, three
wide, and two deep, brim full Half are bills, another part rotten, another
gnawed by rats, yet I have already found enough to repay my trouble and
curiosity—not enough to satisfy it. I will only tell you of three letters of the
great Strafford, and three long ones of news of Mr. Gerrard, Master of the
Charter-house, all six written on paper edged with green, like modern French
paper There are hand writings of every body, all their seals perfect, and
the ribands with which they tied their letters. The original proclamation of
Charles the First, signed by the privy council, a letter to King James from
his son-in-law of Bohemia, with his seal, and many, very many, letters of ne-
gotiation from the Earl of Bristol, in Spain, Sir Dudley Carleton, Lord Chi-
chester, and Sir Thomas Roe. What say you, will here not be food for the
press?"—LORD ORFORD's *Letters to George Montagu.*

VII.

TRAVELS in SOUTH AMERICA, during the years 1819,
20, and 21. By ALEXANDER CALDCLEUGH, Esq. With Maps and
Engravings. 2 vols. 8vo.

VIII.

The PLAYS of SHIRLEY, now first collected and chronologically arranged, and the Text carefully collated and restored. With occasional Notes, and a Biographical and Critical Essay. By WILLIAM GIF-
FORD. 6 vols. 8vo, uniform with MASSINGER and BEN JONSON

Five volumes are already printed.

IX.

The PLAYS of FORD, chronologically arranged, and the
Text carefully collated and restored. With occasional Notes, and a Biographical and Critical Essay. By WILLIAM GIFFORD. 2 vols 8vo., uniform
with MASSINGER and BEN JONSON.

X.

FAIRY LEGENDS and TRADITIONS of the South of Ireland. With Wood Engravings. fc. 8vo.

XI.

On the PRESENT STATE of the LAW of ENGLAND, By JOHN MILLER, Esq , of Lincoln's-Inn. 8vo.

XII.

A HANDBOOK, or, Concise DICTIONARY of the TERMS in ARTS and SCIENCES Small 8vo.

XIII.

APPENDIX to CAPTAIN PARRY'S SECOND VOYAGE of DISCOVERY, containing the Natural History, &c. 4to.

XIV.

PROGRESSIVE GEOGRAPHY for CHILDREN. By the Author of " Stories from the History of England " Part I., 12mo. half-bd.

XV.

The CENTURY of INVENTIONS of the MARQUIS of WORCESTER from the Original MSS., with Historical and Explanatory Notes, and a Biographical Memoir. By CHARLES F. PARTINGTON, of the London Institution. With Explanatory Wood Engravings. 12mo.

" A practical mathematician, who has quickness to seize a hint, and sagacity to apply it, might avail himself greatly of these scantlings. It is extremely probable that Savary took from the Marquis the hint of the Steam Engine, for raising water with a power made by fire, which invention alone would entitle the author to immortality "—*Grang Biog. Hist.* vol. v. p 278.

" Here it may not be amiss to recommend to the attention of every Mechanic, the little work entitled a *Century of Inventions*, by the Marquis of Worcester, which, on account of the seeming improbability of discovering many things mentioned therein, has been too much neglected ; but when it is considered that some of the contrivances, apparently not the least abstruse, have, by close application, been found to answer all the Marquis says of them, and that the first hint of that most powerful machine, the steam-engine, is given in that work, it is unnecessary to enlarge on the utility of it."—*Trans of the Society of Arts*, vol iii. p. 6.

XVI.

NOTES to assist the MEMORY in various SCIENCES. Small 8vo.

XVII.

DIALOGUES on VARIOUS SUBJECTS. By ROBERT SOUTHEY, LL.D. With Engravings. 8vo.

XVIII.

SYDNEY PAPERS, consisting of an unpublished JOURNAL of the EARL of LEICESTER, and original Letters of Algernon Sydney. Edited by R. W. BLENCOWE, M.A. 8vo.

XIX.

A LATIN GRAMMAR. By I J G SCHELLER. Translated from the German, with an Appendix and Notes. By GEORGE WALKER, M.A., late Fellow of Trinity College, Cambridge, and Head Master of the Grammar School, Leeds. 2 vols. 8vo.

XX.

EXCERPTA ARISTOPHANICA. By THOMAS MIT-CHELL, A.M., Late Fellow of Sidney Sussex College Cambridge. In one vol. 8vo.

XXI.

VOYAGE of DISCOVERY in the INTERIOR of AFRICA, from its WESTERN COAST to the RIVER NIGER, in 1818, 19, 20, and 21. With an Account of the Proceedings of the Expedition under the command of the late Major Peddie and Captain Campbell By Brevet-Major GRAY, of the late Royal African Corps, and StaffsSurgeon DOCHARD. *Undertaken and published by order of the Right Hon.* EARL BATHURST. With a Map and Engravings 8vo.

XXII.

FOUR VOYAGES of DISCOVERY, undertaken to complete the Survey of the Western Coast of NEW HOLLAND, within the Tropics, between the years 1817 and 1822. *Undertaken by order of His Majesty's Secretary of State for the Colonies,* in H. M. Surveying Vessels, MERMAID and BATHURST. By PHILIP PARKER KING, R.N., Commander of the Expedition. With Maps, Charts, Views of Interesting Scenery, &c. 2 vols. 8vo.

XXIII.

TRAVELS in the HEDJAZ. By the late JOHN LEWIS BURCKHARDT. With Plates, 4to.

WORKS NEARLY READY FOR PUBLICATION.

XXIV.

FAUST, a Drama, by Goethe, with other Translations from the German. By LORD FRANCIS LEVESON GOWER. Second Edition, 2 vols. fc. 8vo.

XXV.

PROCEEDINGS of the EXPEDITION *despatched by His Majesty's Government*, to explore the Northern Coast of Africa, in 1821 and 22; comprehending an Account of the SYRTIS and CYRENAICA; of the ancient Cities composing the PENTAPOLIS, and other various existing Remains. By Captain F. W. BEECHEY, R. N., and H. W. BEECHEY, Esq. With Plates, Maps, &c. 4to.

XXVI.

GEOGRAPHICAL MEMOIRS on NEW SOUTH WALES, containing an Account of the Surveyor-General's late Expedition to two New Ports, the Discovery of Moreton Bay River, with the Adventures for Seven Months there, of Two Shipwreck'd Men, a Route from Bathurst to Liverpool Plains, together with other Papers on the Aborigines, the Geography, the Geology, the Botany, &c., of New South Wales

The Official Papers published by authority of the EARL BATHURST, to whom the Work is dedicated. Edited by BARON FIELD, Esq, late Judge of the Supreme Court of New South Wales. With a Map. 8vo.

XXVII.

MEMOIRS of PIERRE du TERRAIL, the CHEVALIER de BAYARD, the Knight sans peure et sans reproche. 2 vols. post 8vo.

XXVIII.

The THIRD Volume of the ORLANDO FURIOSO of ARIOSTO. Translated by WILLIAM STEWART ROSE. post 8vo.

XXIX.

TRAVELS through TIMANNEE, KOORANKO, and SOOLIMA COUNTRIES, to the Sources of the ROKELLE and NIGER, in the year 1822. By Capt. A. GORDON LAING. With a Map & Plates. 8vo.

XXX.

APOLOGY to the TRAVELLERS' CLUB; or, Anecdotes of Monkeys. Fc. 8vo.

This Day is Published, with Plates, Wood-Cuts, &c. in Octavo, 7s. 6d.,

THE

QUARTERLY JOURNAL,

No. XXXVI.

CONTENTS.

Printed for JOHN MURRAY, Albemarle-Street.

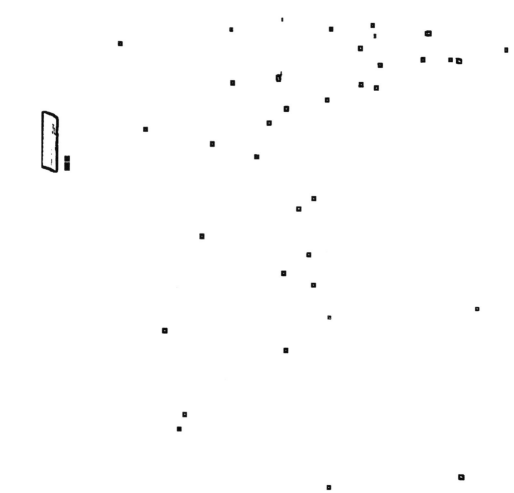

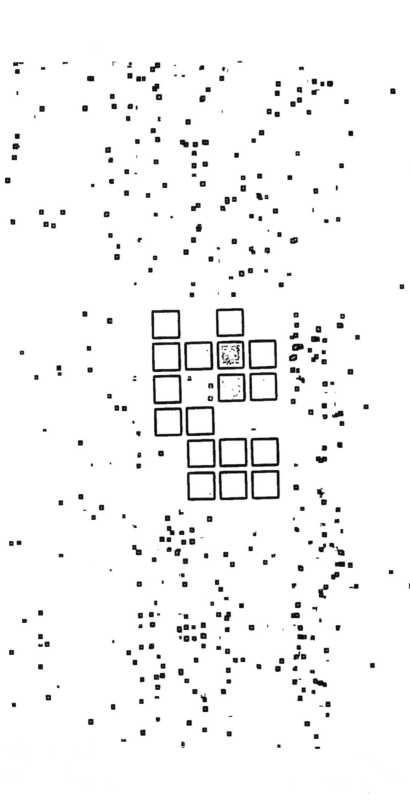

Return address:
Unit 5, Gateway12 Business
Park, Davy Way, Hardwicke,
Gloucester, GL2 2BY, UK

Kathleen Hill
1160 Garden Court Dr
Windsor
Ontario
N8S 2S3
CANADA

Lightning Source UK Ltd.
Milton Keynes UK
UKHW02f1024170918
329041UK00004B/647/P

9 781363 210114